Greek
Political
Reaction to
American
and
NATO
Influences

GREEK POLITICAL REACTION TO AMERICAN AND NATO INFLUENCES

Theodore A. Couloumbis

NEW HAVEN AND LONDON
YALE UNIVERSITY PRESS
1966

Published with assistance from the Louis Stern
Memorial Fund.

To My Mother
Angela Couloumbis

Preface

Although this book deals with Greece's participation in NATO, Greek postwar orientation toward Western Europe and the United States, and Greek foreign policy in general, these topics are not analyzed in all their facets. Analytical emphasis is reserved to the *reaction* of Greek politicians and press to these policies. This work could be characterized as a "reaction analysis," where the assumption is made that the action (or stimulus) is either well known or will be exposed elsewhere. It presents and analyzes effects, rather than defining and analyzing the causes. It should not be viewed, therefore, as a definitive source for all the aspects (political and military) of Greece's participation in NATO and her relations with the West. Its primary purpose is to isolate, contrast, and study the attitudes of the major Greek political movements during a twelve-year period (1952–63). Much of what is cause or action becomes apparent as the narrative unfolds through the exposition and analysis of the effect or reaction.

There are undoubtedly sins of omission or commission in this work. For all these I claim sole responsibility. Much of what is positive, however, is owed to the advice and assistance of others. I am especially thankful to Professor Charles O. Lerche Jr., Dean of the School of International Service of American University who, as chairman of my dissertation committee, guided my work and channeled it into fruitful and organized investigation. Professor Robert S. Jordan of George Washington University read the draft with painstaking thoroughness and offered numerous and welcome suggestions for changes and improvements. Professors Mary E. Bradshaw and Abdul A. Said, both of American University, offered excellent and constructive suggestions which saved me considerable embarrassment once they were incorporated. Professor Stephen G. Xydis of the Mershon Center for Education in National Security read the entire document, and his numerous substantive suggestions and corrections were heeded gladly, thus adding some of the wealth of his experience and good judgment to this volume.

I would be highly neglectful if I did not mention Mr. Stefanos Zotos (Press Attaché at the Greek Embassy in Washington in 1962). My conversations with Mr. Zotos and his keen insight into Greek foreign affairs helped in the formation of some of the basic concepts of this work. My brother, Constantinos A. Couloumbis (currently with Mobil Oil Company in Greece) has probably been the most invaluable contributor to my effort. He has read the manuscript tirelessly at various stages of its development and has made numerous suggestions of substantive content as well as improvements in judgment and style.

If this book is in a readable form today it must be attributed primarily to the fine editorial hand of Ruth L. Davis of the Yale University Press and to the advice that she so kindly imparted throughout the period preceding publication. Then, for a very fine job of what I call "creative proofreading" many thanks should go to Miss Sonya Lee Brockstein and Mr. William F. Ahlstrom, either of whom could easily find a needle in a haystack. Finally, I should mention two of the key contributors who made this work possible, Miss Anna Tompros and Mrs. Denise Kyriacou. They both worked endlessly and diligently to type a multitude of capricious and changing rough drafts and attempted to correct some of my proclivities for error. Their abilities to create order out of chaos are possibly unmatched.

T.A.C.

Washington, D.C.
September 1965

Contents

Introduction

Greece, by virtue of its small size, strategic location and vulnerability, has had to participate in numerous alliances during its recent history. Since its modern national genesis in 1830, Greece has enjoyed the protection of the Great Powers. Conversely, it has been restrained and chastised by those very protectors for seeking national and territorial expansion based on various historical claims. The modern history of Greece illustrates continuous trends of intervention by the Great Powers and competition among them for a controlling voice.[1]

Participation in military alliances is not a revolutionary development in Greek foreign affairs. The nature of NATO, however, as a dynamic alliance organization, lends a unique and unprecedented aura to the relationship existing between Greece and the remainder of the "Atlantic community." NATO has no precedent among peacetime alliances in the extent of integration and complexity of inter-member relationships. To some students of international politics, NATO represents a step away from the "national state system" toward some form of supranationalism.[2] NATO's extensive organiza-

1. For a more detailed treatment see infra, pp. 11–13.
2. The works listed below are cited as examples and by no means exhaust the list of writings touching on this subject: Mary Margaret Ball, NATO and the European Union Movement (London, Stevens & Sons, 1959); Carol E. Baumann, Political Cooperation in NATO (Madison, National Security Studies Group, University of Wisconsin, June 1960); Ben T. Moore, NATO and the Future of Europe (New York, Harper & Bros., 1958); Robert E. Osgood, NATO, The Entangling Alliance (Chicago, The University of Chicago Press, 1961); Morton A. Kaplan, System and Process in International Politics (New York, John Wiley & Sons, 1957), pp. 139–42.

tional machinery for multilateral decision-making, the integrative tendencies of NATO members' military establishments, the confrontation with a common external military—as well as political and ideological—antagonist, the effects and limitations of the nuclear disarmament stalemate—all these factors have promoted, to varying degrees, the uniquely close relationships of the fifteen NATO member nations.

The central question for purposes of this study is related to the political *reaction* in Greece precipitated by membership in NATO and close relations with the United States. No claim will be made of a direct cause and effect relationship between Greece's Western associations and any set of events in the Greek political spectrum.[3] An effort has been made, however, to illustrate and elucidate certain political trends, to attempt to capture the spirit of the times, to test for indications, to judge from impressions, to take the pulse of the politically articulate regarding Greek reaction to its NATO and Western associations.

This subject is vast indeed. Greek participation in NATO is integral to Greece's policy of close postwar association with the United States. These are in fact the two major foreign policies of Greece in the post-World War II era. The political effects of Greek–NATO and Greek–United States relations can be analyzed from at least three levels: (a) effects on Greek national policies, domestic or foreign; (b) effects on interparty struggles and polemics; and (c) effects on the Greek people and their attitudes. The effort to isolate effects has entailed a search of the literature of political speeches and editorial comment of the period under study.

Major emphasis has been placed on pre- and post-election periods. Key speeches of candidates from representative political parties have been studied, and governmental program declarations, together with the reactions in Parliament of occasional opposition parties, have been analyzed for their relationship to Greek participation in NATO. Political reaction on the subject of NATO and Western orientation,

---

3. There is a plethora of factors affecting Greek politics. Some are internal, others external; some clearly identifiable and others imponderable. For our purposes let us dismiss them as *ceteris paribus.*

as manifested during acute national or international crises, has also been subjected to analysis.

The major sources of information used are Greek newspapers. Newspapers representing the three major political movements in Greece were selected as follows: *Kathimerini*[4] and *Vema*[5] (before 1956) for the conservative Right position; *Vema* (after 1956) and *Eleftheria*[6] for the Center position; and *Auge*,[7] the newspaper of EDA[8] (first published in August 1952), as the best indicator of Communist-inspired positions in Greek foreign affairs. Texts of political speeches were used in most cases as published in these newspapers. Editorials were spot-checked primarily to determine whether the press tended, at times, to go beyond the limitations set by the political leaders it supported. The Greek "Congressional Record" has also been an invaluable primary source for comparing political viewpoints as presented to the highest public forum in the Greek nation, either in program discussions or debates on critical foreign policy issues.

I have gained further insight into this topic by conducting interviews with representative political figures in Greece, and have discussed the problem of Greek participation in NATO in a systematic way with the aid of a structured questionnaire.[9] Interviews, for the purposes of this work, have not been of any great research value because the interviewees, being in the midst of vigorous pre-election activity, could not devote any appreciable length of time to a full and searching discussion of matters included in the interview agenda. Secondary sources of information were used within the limitations of the fact that few works have been written to date relating to the political problems of Greece's participation in NATO. Most of the writings deal with military or strategic aspects.

I have tended to oversimplify the Greek political subdivisions and group them in three primary movements: the conservative Right,

4. *Kathimerini* (*Daily*). Published in Athens daily.
5. *Vema* (*Tribune*). Published in Athens daily.
6. *Eleftheria* (*Freedom*). Published in Athens daily.
7. *Auge* (*Dawn*). Published in Athens daily.
8. EDA—Unified Democratic Left. Founded in August 1951, this party filled the vacuum created by the outlawing of the Greek Communist party.
9. See Appendix A, infra.

the liberal Center, and the Communist Left. In reality, the Greek political structure can be characterized as a constitutional democracy with numerous and fragmented personality parties.[10] Political parties most often revolve around powerful and well established personalities. Party platforms and credos reflect the beliefs of their occasional founders rather than party philosophies.

To simplify, I have clustered the beliefs of the various liberal Center parties and presented them as representative of the "Center movement." The conservative Right movement was consolidated in 1951 under the leadership of the late Premier Papagos into one solid party called Greek Synaghermos.[11] With the death of Papagos in 1955, Constantine Karamanlis gained the support of the majority among Synaghermos deputies, and formed a new party called Greek Radical Union (ERE). This party succeeded Synaghermos to power and remained in control until June 1963. ERE has managed to retain the majority of conservative elements united within its ranks, thus preventing the balkanization which had been characteristic of the Center movement.

The Communist party was outlawed in Greece as a result of its post-World War II armed effort to gain control of the country. The vacuum created was filled with the foundation of the Unified Democratic Left (EDA) in August 1951, headed by John Passalides. EDA was, in all but name, representative of the Communist point of view, particularly in the field of foreign policy.

In spite of the simplification of the discussion in terms of Center, Left, and Right movements, I have often had to refer to individual parties and their political activities. Such references are likely to be somewhat confusing to the reader who may not be thoroughly familiar with the Greek political structure. Therefore I have prepared Appendix E, which should be referred to whenever there is a need to establish whether a party or its leader was representative of the Center, Right, or Left movements. Appendix E lists the results of all the Greek elections which have been held since 1952, showing a break-

10. See Gregorios Dafnis, *The Greek Political Parties: 1821–1961* (Athens, Galaxias, 1961), which presents a brief and rather cursory picture of Greek political parties and their evolution.
11. Freely translated, it means "Greek Rally."

down of the parties and the movements of which they were representative.

I have attempted throughout this study to present the positions of the three political movements objectively, and have sought to eliminate bias as completely as was consciously possible. However, it would be presumptuous to claim, in a work of political content and analysis of this type, that complete objectivity has been attained.

The structure and content of this study have been determined to a large extent by the nature of hypotheses and propositions that have been tested for possible verification. Basic among them are those listed below, which should be kept in mind throughout the reading of this book:

1. Greek participation in NATO, as manifested in the 1950s, was a by-product of Greek-American association.

2. The association with the United States and NATO has exerted direct and indirect pressures and influences on Greece. These influences contributed to the strengthening and subsequent stabilization of Greek conservatism.

3. Participation in NATO committed Greece to a policy of cooperation and friendship with Turkey, notwithstanding a number of historical conflicts and political disputes which often strained the relations of the two countries to the point of rupture.

4. NATO participation limited Greece's foreign policy flexibility because of imperatives of cooperation with Western nations and Turkey. These limitations evoked quite a sharp reaction, expressed primarily by Center and Communist parties.

5. There were no supranationalist loyalties created among the Greek public or in large sections of the Greek political world as a result of Greek membership in NATO. NATO membership as such was supported primarily because of its beneficial effects upon Greek national interests: namely, safeguarding the territorial integrity of Greece and preventing the internal reemergence of the threat of communism.

6. The policies of the Conservative movement have best suited the objectives of the United States and NATO. The policies of the Communists (EDA) have supported strictly Soviet objectives. The

Center parties, plagued by internal disunity, have adopted a generally pro-Western policy which wavered considerably when tested by intra-NATO disputes such as the one over Cyprus.

I believe that the narrative which follows has to a large degree supported the validity of these propositions. I invite the reader, however, to form his personal and independent conclusions.

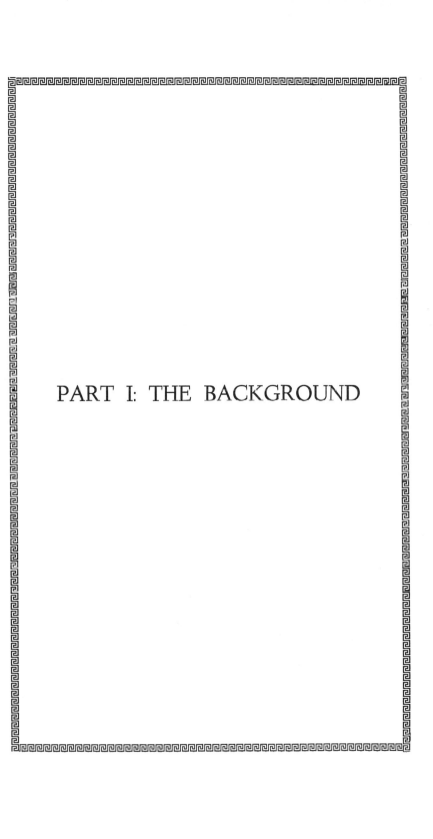

PART I: THE BACKGROUND

Chapter One
Greece:
A Background of Intervention[1]

Paradoxically, the development of superpowers in this "atomic era" has led to a disproportionate strengthening of the independence and freedom of action of smaller nations. The lack of a superpower concert (as had been envisioned in the Charter of the United Nations in the guise of the Security Council), and the resultant conflict of the Eastern and Western "leviathans," have given rise to at least three different brands of small nations who can "talk back" to great powers in a fashion quite disproportionate to their relative possession of force.

One category is the nonaligned (neutralist) nation belonging to neither bloc and being courted by both. In this balanced position, the smaller nation enjoys many of the attentions and courtesies (as well as stratagems and intrigues) that a young and uncommitted debutante faces in an array of furiously competing suitors.

The second category is the Soviet bloc "satellite." Within this bloc a country is subject to many influences and directives emanating from one of the centers of communism (either Moscow or Peking). Yet, when outside the bloc, relying on the forces of the powerful Soviet protective umbrella, it can afford to gaze upon a superpower such as the United States and "spit in her eye." This situation is possible, however, only as long as the "balance of terror" paralyzes the super-

1. This chapter is heavily based on a recent book by Stephen G. Xydis, who presents an outstanding treatment and analysis of events in Greece (1944–47) which led directly to the proclamation of the "Truman Doctrine." See Stephen G. Xydis, *Greece and the Great Powers: 1944–47* (Thessaloniki, Institute of Balkan Studies, 1963). Xydis' book excels in illustrating the perplexing interrelationship of Greek political objectives, in view of the pervasive parameters of Great Power politics in the Eastern Mediterranean.

powers into inaction, and the cold war of ideological incompatibility prevents them from reaching an old-fashioned understanding and dividing the world into mutually acceptable spheres of influence. Within the Soviet bloc the "nucleus–satellite" relationship is constantly feeling the corrosive effects of disintegration, precipitated by national communism, polycentrism or intrabloc balance of power (e.g. the Sino-Soviet dispute), and thawing of the cold war tensions through an increasing range of cooperative contacts between the Eastern and Western superpowers.

In the third category fits the type of small nation "ally" which belongs to one of the intertwined Western bloc alliances such as NATO or SEATO. There is a close relationship existing between the small ally and the leading superpowers of the Western bloc. We in the West would like to think of this relationship as one of "lover and loved." Be that as it may, there are influences and directives emanating from the larger powers and flowing into the smaller ones. The reaction to these influences and directives in a nation such as Greece is the central theme of this work. Perhaps it is in the degree and nature of the reaction which is allowed to emerge and be heard in open Western societies that the major difference between "Eastern satellites" and "small Western allies" lies. But let us continue further with our analogy. These small allies, feeling the powerful, protective strength of their Western leaders[2] and relying on the unprecedented (in peacetime) ties and guarantees of territorial integrity, can afford also to "spit in the eye" of giants such as the Soviet Union or Communist China. The "lover–loved" relationship suffers also from divisive factors which have been increasing in frequency and seriousness in the 1960s. These, as in the case of the Soviet bloc, include nationalism (e.g. the complex Cyprus dispute), polycentrism in the Western bloc (e.g. the United States vs. France), and relaxation of tensions between the United States and the U.S.S.R.

The "interventions, influences, and reactions" affecting Greece during the 1950s can be understood better if viewed within the scope of modern Greek historical experience, especially that of the immediate post-World War II era. Due partly to its geographical location

2. For Greece, the United States and Britain, with France and West Germany closely competing for the number three position.

and to the willingness of its politicians to accept external assistance, Greece has been the recipient of influences, pressures, and directives emanating from the great European powers which were, also, the very guarantors of its independence as a modern nation.

Intervention in the Nineteenth Century

Greece had been under the constant influence and protection of the Great Powers throughout the nineteenth century. A few examples will suffice to illustrate this trend of foreign influence and intervention.[3] In 1832, for example, following the assassination of Count John Capodistrias, the first elected president of the Greek Republic, the protective powers (Great Britain, France, and Russia), in order to avert a civil war, took matters into their hands and resolved the crisis by transforming the Greek state from a republic into a monarchy.[4]

Political parties were born in Greece during the reign of King Otto, who was imported from Bavaria. These parties differed from one another in that they were either pro-French, pro-British, or pro-Russian.[5] This Great Power orientation among Greek political parties, rather than political philosophy or conviction, has been a key variable of the Greek political mentality and has plagued modern Greek history as well as having facilitated the infusion of external interventions, intrigues, and subterfuges. This mentality also explains the great bitterness and disillusionment with which certain Greek statesmen and politicians have viewed the actions of their championed Great Powers whenever these powers have antagonized or attacked Greece, or treated her without fidelity and gratitude.

Intervention during World War I

The pattern of intervention did not change considerably during the twentieth century. The manner in which Greece entered World War I is the best example of how external interventions have determined the outcome of political events in Greece. Doros Alastos, the

3. For greater detail on this subject during nineteenth century Greek history see S. M. Sophocles, A History of Greece (Thessaloniki, Institute for Balkan Studies, 1961). See also John A. Levandis, The Greek Foreign Debt and the Great Powers, 1821–1898 (New York, Columbia University Press, 1944), pp. 88–92, 112–15.

4. Sophocles, p. 343.

5. Ibid., p. 344.

biographer of Eleftherios Venizelos, summed up events in Greece during 1916 in the following characteristic quotation:

> The year was one of a series of limitations for Greece—of the ENTENTE's interference in the internal affairs of a neutral country becoming more flagrant—of German propaganda casting a cloud over Athens—of German and Allied spies competing against each other in sensational discoveries—of agitators touring the countryside and inciting the peasantry against their opponents. Every semblance of freedom was taken away. Anyone in Athens during 1916 might have legitimately wondered who was ruling Greece. The German Embassy owned three quarters of the daily papers. The French Embassy, through its agents, was organizing demonstrations against the government, or attacks upon Allied citizens in order to force the Allies into action. Greek ships were stopped and searched on the high seas. Cargoes were confiscated. There was the fictitious scare of German submarine bases round the Greek coast, deliberately engineered by the French Embassy.[6]

In the 1914–18 era, the Greek political world had been acutely polarized into two opposing and uncompromising camps whose foreign policies were mutually exclusive. On one pole there were the monarchists, gathered around King Constantine I of Greece, who were sympathetic to the Central Powers and Kaiser Wilhelm. The monarchists felt that the Central Powers were assured the victory in the war and they advocated a policy of benevolent neutrality toward them because joining them in war would render Greece, with her vulnerable coastline, an easy target for the Entente which was dominating the Mediterranean Sea.

On the opposite pole were the Greek republicans, dominated by the imposing figure of Eleftherios Venizelos. His belief was that the war was bound to be won by the Entente. As early as 10 August 1914, he had publicly declared that the sympathies of Greece lay on the side of the Entente.[7] Venizelos' policy was based on the deduction

6. Doros Alastos, *Venizelos* (London, P. Lund, Humphries & Co., 1942), p. 166.
7. *The Vindication of Greek National Policy: 1912–17* (London, George Allen and Unwin, 1918), p. 73.

that the best possible stand for Greece would be participation in the war on the side of the Allies; in this way the nation stood to gain the most in terms of postwar territorial adjustments. On the other hand, whether Greece opposed, sided with, or remained neutral vis-à-vis the Central Powers, if they won Greece was bound to emerge weakened territorially.

In this situation of uncompromising differences over domestic as well as foreign policies, the conditions described by Doros Alastos, quoted above, prevailed. The Central Powers—Bulgarians and Germans in this case—occupied a large part of Eastern Greek Macedonia and committed atrocities against the Greek population there. Meanwhile the Entente Powers, primarily France, resorted to naval blockades, economic sanctions, threats and subterfuge, and pronouncements of military law in the area of Eastern Greek Macedonia where Entente troops were operating under the command of General Sarrail.

In September 1916 Eleftherios Venizelos spearheaded a revolution against the King, spurred by the latter's monolithic devotion to a policy of outright friendliness toward the Central Powers at a time when their military edifice was crumbling. Venizelos' forces soon controlled most insular and northern parts of Greece. His government, recognized by the Entente as the de facto government of the territory it controlled, immediately declared war on the Central Powers. The Entente Powers subsequently pressured King Constantine to abdicate in favor of his son Alexander, and Venizelos returned to Athens in June 1917 to lead a united Greece (albeit by external force) in the successful prosecution and conclusion of World War I.

The interwar period found Greece in a costly, unceasing conflict between republicanism and monarchism which succeeded each other in power in the 1920s and 1930s. This era was marred by military coup d'états and great instability. It culminated with the imposition of General Metaxas' dictatorship, established with the assent of King George II on 4 August 1936. Metaxas' regime was dissolved four years later by the attack of Fascist Italy on Greece on 28 October 1940, and the subsequent German attack. Greece effectively resisted the Italian aggression and drove Benito Mussolini's forces back, but following Hitler's reinforcing attack of April–May

1941, Greece, with the exception of Crete (which fell in June 1941), became another Axis-controlled country, occupied by Italian, German, and Bulgarian forces.

The Greek Communist Party: Background

The role of communism in Greece in the period between the two world wars was not at all significant. The Greek Communist party was first established on 16 November 1918.[8] Its original name was Socialist Labor Party of Greece. It applied for admission to the Comintern in April 1920 and was accepted on 21 September of the same year. Its present name, Communist Party of Greece (KKE), was adopted during the third Party Congress (26 November–3 December 1924). At the outset, the party's leaders were members of the intelligentsia who were fascinated by the ideas of the Bolshevik revolution. Members were recruited initially from tobacco worker groups of northern Greece. Following the great influx of refugees from Turkey, as a result of World War I and the subsequent Greco-Turkish war, the Communist party recruited many city inhabitants whose poverty-stricken living conditions made them receptive to the communist materialistic ideology.

The KKE was not a successful political force in Greek interwar politics. The Communists never managed to secure more than ten per cent of the popular vote and they elected deputies to the Greek Parliament only when the election system of proportional representation was used (e.g. in the elections of 1926, 1932, and 1936).[9] It did not find widespread support among the Greek masses, who were suspicious of its apparent subordination to the Comintern, its gradual "Bolshevization," its connection, after 1924, with the Balkan Communist federation movement, and its advocacy of an autonomous status for Macedonia and Thrace.[10] All of these positions were distasteful to the average nationalistic and individualistic Greek voter.

The only time during the interwar period when the Greek Communist party played an important role, quite disproportional to its quantitative strength, was in the aftermath of the 26 January 1936

8. Xydis, pp. 8–9.
9. For specifics, see Gregorios Dafnis, *Greece Between Two Wars: 1923–1940* (Athens, Ikaros, 1950).
10. Cited in Xydis, pp. 8–9.

elections. The fifteen elected Communist deputies, representing 5.76 per cent of the vote, could tip the balance either way. They were in a position to install in power either the Populists (conservative and traditionally royalist) or the Liberals who had approximately an equal number of seats. This situation was used by John Metaxas, a strongly anti-Communist royalist, to mastermind a successful coup d'état on 4 August 1936. This event signaled the suspension of parliamentary democracy in Greece and the simultaneous outlawing of the Greek Communist party.

World War II: The Seeds of Dualism

During World War II, with the ever-growing anti-fascist resistance movement, the seeds of dualism were once more sown in the Greek political climate. This mutually exclusive bipolarity was to be the cause as well as the effect of British (later United States-supplemented) vs. Russian postwar conflicts over Greece. On the one pole was the effective, Communist-controlled, and oddly enough, British-supported resistance movement of the National Liberation Front (EAM). As in the case of Tito's Partisans in Yugoslavia, EAM was more effective against the Germans than its rival resistance groups such as EDES, led by General Napoleon Zervas (loosely the counterpart in Greece of General Draga Mihailovic's Chetniks). As a consequence of its effectiveness, EAM enjoyed the moral and material support and recognition of the British.[11] On the other pole was a government-in-exile under Premier Tsouderos, which was in effect the legal continuation of the Greek state of General John Metaxas and King George II. As the war reached its successful concluding months, the covert Communist domination of EAM became quite overt, as well as vocal, and British hopes for maintaining influence in Greece were pinned on the nationalist, anti-Communist government-in-exile.

Emmanuel J. Tsouderos, the Greek prime minister-in-exile, conducted his foreign policy, to quote the chief chronicler of this period, ". . . in such a way as to promote the realization of his assumption that after the war, Britain would continue playing a preponderant

11. L. S. Stavrianos, *Greece: American Dilemma and Opportunity* (Chicago, Henry Regnery, 1952), see pp. 64–90, 95–98.

paternalistic role in his country just as it had done during most of
the interwar period, as well as on several other occasions in modern
Greek history." [12] The Greek forces-in-exile were under British command throughout World War II. They fought primarily with British
equipment, and were reorganized along British lines. Tsouderos, like
Eleftherios Venizelos, was in principle desirous of having Greece participate in a Balkan federation. He realized, however, that the territorial claims of Greece against Albania and Bulgaria precluded postwar peaceful cooperation with those countries. So he was most eager
to guarantee Greece's territorial integrity through a postwar alliance
with Great Britain. In a letter to Eden written in March 1943,[13] he
described in detail the strategic usefulness of Greece for those wishing
to control the Mediterranean and Yugoslavia, and he offered to provide Britain with Greek bases, access routes, etc., after the war. His
major fear was that Greece would be abandoned after the war by
the great sea powers and would become Communist, as well as lose
large portions of her northern territories to the Bulgarians.

In 1944, with the war tide turning to favor the Western Allies,
the antagonism among the competing successors to the Greek state
became quite acute. Within Greece, EAM established on 12 March
1944 the Political Committee of National Liberation (PEEA), which
was intended to serve as the nucleus around which a postwar Communist-controlled government could evolve.[14] At the same time, the
government-in-exile underwent some serious convulsions. Following
a revolt staged by Greek officers of republican leanings in April 1944,
Premier Tsouderos was replaced by Sophocles Venizelos, and the
government-in-exile was broadened considerably to include representatives of PEEA. On 26 September 1944 the historically important
Caserta agreement was signed, defining the relationship of the Greek
government-in-exile to the British government. The Greek government at that time, headed by George Papandreou, included six cabinet members from EAM–PEEA. The agreement provided that all guerrilla forces in Greece, together with the Greek exiled armed forces,

12. Xydis, p. 5.
13. Ibid., pp. 26–27.
14. Ibid., p. 33.

would be placed under the coalition government which, in turn, was under the military command of the British.[15]

The German occupying forces evacuated Greece in mid-September 1944. The British forces entered, at the request of the coalition government, on the first of October of the same year. Conditions in the country at that time approximated utter chaos. Greece was devastated, starved, without an exchangeable currency, without savings, without public confidence, politically divided into uncompromising camps, the countryside having been dominated by the Communist EAM and ELAS[16] (the military arm of EAM). Following a brief period of liberation festivities, a disagreement over the terms of disarming resistance groups led the Communists to walk out of the government, and precipitated the Communist coup d'état of 3 December 1944. A minor war, which lasted through the early part of January 1945, evolved. This little war involved 60,000 British troops and culminated with a truce (signed on 11 January 1945), and a "peace treaty," concluded at Varkiza on 12 February 1945. The Greek Communists agreed at Varkiza to a cessation of hostilities, admitting that they had miscalculated British determination to prevent a Communist take-over in Greece.[17] Their tactics changed at this time, in favor of awaiting the end of the larger war against the Germans. A German defeat, they were hoping, would free the Soviet Union to provide greater support for the Greek Communist cause.

While the British were busy crushing the Communist bid for take-over in Greece, Stalin displayed a curious, sphinxlike silence, non-interference with the British action in Greece, and general lack of compassion for the efforts of his "comrades" in the small Balkan country. Perhaps unknown at the time to the Greek actors of the December 1944 drama was the famous "percentages agreement" reached in Moscow on 9 October 1944 between Stalin and Churchill. In this agreement, Rumania and Bulgaria were allotted to the Soviet sphere of influence, Greece to the British, and Yugoslavia 50–50. Stalin kept his bargain scrupulously as long as the war against the

15. Ibid., p. 49.
16. ELAS stood for "Greek Popular Liberation Army."
17. Xydis, pp. 60–61.

Germans was still raging.[18] It will possibly remain an academic question as to what would have happened if the Greek coalition government had not invited the British to move their forces into Greece in October 1944. Would the British have stood by and watched the Communists slowly take over? Another question that needs to be answered concerns the reasoning which prompted the Communist representatives to agree to the British troops' entrance into postwar Greece (the Caserta agreement).

Nationalist Postwar Objectives

The postwar objectives of the Greek nationalists can best be summarized in the combined views of Emmanuel Tsouderos[19] and Philip Dragoumis.[20] Tsouderos argued that the best policy for postwar Greece would be a peacetime alliance with Britain and the United States which would guarantee Greece's territorial integrity. He was opposed to an alliance with Turkey, however, because he felt it would entangle Greece in case of a Russo-Turkish war, which was considered quite likely. Tsouderos felt that if Greece were to remain neutral, she would have to exert every effort to conclude nonaggression pacts with her Balkan neighbors and attempt to dispel Soviet suspicions that Greece would become a potential Soviet enemy. Tsouderos was also in favor of a mild and patient policy toward the Greek Communists in an effort to gain even their minimum, reluctant cooperation.

Dragoumis, in a speech before the Constitutional Committee on Foreign Affairs (20 August 1945), brought his views to the fore. He was decidedly anticommunist compared to the cautiously tolerant Tsouderos. Dragoumis outlined in this speech some of the basic guidelines of the early postwar foreign policy of the Greek government.

He felt that Greece should remain on the side of the world's sea powers, which also represented the liberal, democratic ideals of the Western world. He emphasized that the prohibitive expenditures which were required to maintain modern weaponry rendered small

18. Ibid., pp. 54–55.
19. Ibid., pp. 103–04.
20. Ibid., pp. 122–24.

states dependent on great powers and international organizations for protection and defense against aggression.

He argued that a major clash between the United States and the U.S.S.R. was not very likely, thanks to the existence of the atomic bomb; he therefore discounted neutralist arguments to the effect that Greece would be an early victim in a world war if she chose association with either of the two power blocs. Dragoumis believed that Greece's territorial integrity and national claims would be as good as the Western allied support they could muster. He alerted his listeners to the age-old desire of 200 million Slavs to gain access to the Aegean Sea, if necessary, over the dead body of Greece. The only way this could be prevented was through complete reliance on Anglo American material and moral support. Unlike Tsouderos, he mentioned the need for close cooperation with Turkey,[21] and common, coordinated defense in Thrace to prevent the Slavic descent onto the Aegean. He also cautioned against excessive territorial claims against Greece's northern neighbors (recommending that they not exceed a distance 90 miles north of the Aegean shores). Still on the subject of territorial claims he suggested that Britain should cede Cyprus to Greece as a gesture of her friendship and a sign of her gratitude for Greece's sacrifices in the Allied cause throughout World War II.

TERRITORIAL CLAIMS   As the analysis of Tsouderos' and Dragoumis' statements indicates, one of the basic postwar objectives of the Greek governments was the attainment of certain national territorial claims. The key claims were: cession of Northern Epirus by Albania; a readjustment of the Greek-Bulgarian border, to seal Greece's strategic exposure that had enabled Bulgaria to attack Greece three times in the twentieth century; and acquisition of the Dodecanese Islands from Italy. Greek governments pressed these claims very vigorously during the Paris Peace Conference and the various meetings of the Council of Ministers. They were opposed, however, by the U.S.S.R. and to a lesser extent by the United States, and no territorial gains were secured other than cession of the Dodecanese.[22]

21. This step, of course, meant the abdication of any possible claims on Turkish territory.
22. For a detailed discussion of the claims of Greece, see Xydis, pp. 23, 39, 96, 99, 182, 198–206, 210, 221–22, 270–71, 277–84, 299, 326–29, 363–64, 375–79, 384, 408–09, 420–22, 693.

The Greek government claimed nothing from Turkey, since a Western orientation and claims to the north had required Greece to align herself and coordinate her defenses with Turkey. Feeling the full force of the ominous Soviet threat, Turkey did not object to the ceding of the Dodecanese to Greece, notwithstanding the presence of a sizable Turkish minority in these islands.[23] The Greek government soft-pedaled, also, the Greek claim to Cyprus. When it was—infrequently—mentioned, it was always described as an affair to be settled strictly between Greece and Britain. This can be attributed to the need for Britain's support, which was considered of vital importance to the very existence of Greece as an independent, Western state.

The Communists, who were oriented toward the U.S.S.R. and East Europe, wished to see Greece take her place among the newborn generation of East Europe's "People's Democracies." [24] The early postwar Greek Communist objectives[25] emphasized a policy of equal friendship or bilateral orientation toward East and West alike. They were opposed to the resurgence of fascism in Greece and to the betrayal of claims such as Cyprus and Eastern Thrace to placate the British and the Turks. They heralded a struggle against a foreign-imposed reestablishment of monarchy in Greece. The secretary of the Greek Communist party, Nicos Zachariades, upon his return to Greece in May 1945 from internment in Germany, caustically described Greece as a "colony for foreign interests." [26] He admitted that Greece's location was vital to Britain's interests and said that he would be willing to negotiate on an equal-to-equal basis: i.e. Greece should extend strategic privileges to Britain if the latter provided for

23. With the relaxation of Soviet pressures, Turkey is not currently willing to look the other way in the case of Cyprus' union with Greece. The Turkish minority in Cyprus is smaller (as a percentage) than in the Dodecanese.

24. To illustrate the Communist point of view for this period the following works, or collections of documents, may be perused: National Liberation Front (EAM), White Book: May 1944–March 1945 (Trikkala, Greece, Greek American Council, 1945); Yugoslav Office of Information, Book on Greece (Beograd, 1948); Yugoslav Information Center, The Greek Partisans Accuse (New York, 1950); John Petsopoulos, The Real Causes of My Expulsion from the Greek Communist Party (in Greek) (Athens, 1946); John Petsopoulos, The National Matters and the Greek Communists (in Greek) (Athens, 1946).

25. Xydis, p. 89.

26. Ibid., p. 93.

cession of the Dodecanese and Cyprus to Greece. The Communists advanced their own brand of national claims, vociferously demanding the return of Cyprus from Britain and Eastern Thrace from Turkey, while playing down any claims against the "People's Democracies" of the North, and even denouncing chauvinist Greek claims against Albania and Bulgaria.[27]

In this acutely bipolar Greek political situation, foreign influences, pressures, and presence were quite necessary to tip the political balance. On one side was the legally established government of Greece, representing about 80–85 per cent of the Greek population as the internationally observed elections of 31 March 1946 had demonstrated.[28] On the other side was the well-organized and determined Communist minority. The noncommunist government was suffering from political divisions (the heritage of over thirty years of liberal vs. monarchist struggles). It was confronted with insurmountable economic problems and dislocations, a destroyed and devastated nation, a hungry, homeless, and mistrustful population, and a countryside dominated by well-organized Communist bands. Faced with such overwhelming odds, Greek nationalist politicians felt that without British support, and even intervention, Greece was sure to fall into Communist hands.

British policy regarding postwar Greece and Turkey was quite firm and definite. Both nations were to be kept within the British sphere of influence. They were vital to British interests and preeminence in the Mediterranean.[29] The British demonstrated their intent to keep Greece noncommunist and outside the Russian sphere of influence through their military presence in Greece, their massive military assistance up to 31 March 1947 (when the United States took over), and their economic, political, and administrative advice. This in nu-

27. See Petsopoulos, *The National Matters and the Greek Communists*, pp. 36–41.

28. Xydis, pp. 184–85. The Communists decided to boycott these elections and recommended abstention to their supporters. The British, French, and American observers (the Soviets had been invited and had refused to send observers, apparently to prevent similar situations in Soviet-controlled countries) reported that an estimated 15 per cent, at most 20 per cent, of the voters had abstained from this election. This places the noncommunist voters in the vicinity of 80 to 85 per cent of the total.

29. Ibid., pp. 43, 54–55.

merous instances necessitated intervention in Greek national political affairs, as well as on technical and administrative matters.[30] The presence of British troops in Greece, however, was welcomed by the Greek nationalists, as providing the best guarantee against threatened territorial encroachment from Greece's northern Communist neighbors. This trend of thinking carried well into the 1950s. Foreign (British or United States) bases and troops were actually solicited by Greek politicians because their presence could serve both as an anti-invasion deterrent and as a trip-wire for further big power assistance and involvement against any encroachment on the territorial integrity of nothern Greece.

British, and later American, intervention in Greek politics during the late 1940s was quite significant. The British, Americans, and French, for example, supervised the Greek elections of 1946 and the subsequent plebiscite regarding the desirability of reestablishing the monarchy. This supervision was to insure that the elections were free and the voters not intimidated by any political party. Members of the British and later the American economic and military missions attended meetings or were informed on day-to-day affairs of policy-making organs of the Greek government. Although these missions did not have final veto powers, they exerted tremendous influence, through advice and guidance, over the course of events in Greece.[31]

30. Ibid., pp. 113, 131, 144, 152, 194–95. For purposes of illustration, Xydis, on p. 144, describes the relationship of the Greek Supreme Council of National Defense and the Council of the Chiefs of Staff (established on 15 December 1945) with the British authorities. The Greek Supreme Council of National Defense was set up with the provision that the heads (or authorized representatives) of the British military, naval, air, and gendarmerie missions would be allowed to participate in its deliberations without vote. The British mission in Greece was to be kept informed on all matters of policy in order to insure coordination. The opinions of the British Chief of Mission were to be secured prior to the signing of any laws or decrees. If there were disagreements between the Council's views and those of the British mission, they were to be referred to the Greek Premier, who would have to consult the British ambassador if his position were contrary to that of the British mission's chief.

31. For a discussion of the wide authority enjoyed by the American mission in the 1947–49 period see William Hardy McNeill, *Greece: American Aid in Action 1947–56* (New York, The Twentieth Century Fund, 1957), pp. 35, 60–62. McNeill, in a characteristic quotation, states: "These agreements gave very wide authority to American representatives, so much so that the Greek government itself was thenceforth unable to make any important decision without their approval. At the time [1947] there was little objection. The Greeks knew they needed help, and were not inclined to quibble over details" (p. 35).

The British and American interventions of the late 1940s, when the Greek government was threatened with destruction by the rebelling Communists, remained either unnoticed or unopposed by Greek politicians and the Greek press. This was quite contrary to the situation of the 1950s, when fewer and subtler instances of influence and intervention met with extreme sensitivity and touchiness on the part of the noncommunist politicians, press, and public. Once the Communists had been decisively defeated and the Greek nationalist government firmly established in power, and as both aid and the organizations administering it decreased in value and size, respectively, United States and British intervention diminished or ceased.

Civil War and British Withdrawal

As the European phase of World War II drew closer to an end, with Nazi forces meeting with disastrous defeats at the hands of the Allies on both fronts, the Greek Communists increased their determination to transform Greece into a "People's Democracy" by sheer force of arms. The decision to launch "Round Three" (the last massive Communist guerrilla effort to gain control in Greece in 1946–49), was reached as early as December 1945, and at the latest by February of 1946.[32] As the postwar conflict of interests and ideologies between the U.S.S.R., on one hand, and the United States and Britain, on the other, became increasingly apparent, the Greek Communist line and demands grew proportionately harder and uncompromising.

Britain was beginning to show, and to publicly admit, signs of weariness caused by economic difficulties, and contemplated whether she would soon have to cease aid and support of Greece and Turkey. The United States, still vacillating between a policy of global cooperation and an increasing awareness of the Soviet threat, was not taking definite steps to fill Britain's shoes in either Greece or Turkey. A power vacuum was developing in the Eastern Mediterranean, which the Soviets were quite eager to fill by increasing their pressures and those of their "satellites" against Greece and Turkey, and by using the well-armed and well-supplied Greek Communist guerrillas in a direct bid to take over power in Greece. This, in turn, would cut off Turkey from Western Europe and would squeeze her into capitulating

32. Xydis, pp. 138, 181.

to Soviet demands regarding bases in the straits and territorial claims against Turkey's northeastern territories.

The minimum Greek Communist demands which would have precluded their resorting to an armed contest and, perhaps, could have insured their political cooperation within the framework of parliamentary democracy, were the following:[33]

1. Annulment of the results of the plebiscite which provided for the return of King George II to Greece, and suspension of the King's imminent return to the country.

2. Formation of a new coalition government to include EAM representatives.

3. General amnesty for Communist political prisoners.

4. Assumption of a foreign policy of equal friendship toward the Big Three (United States, Britain, U.S.S.R.), as well as friendship for the People's Republics of Eastern Europe.

5. New elections (the elections of March 1946 were boycotted and contested as fraudulent) to elect a new constituent assembly.

6. A new plebiscite to determine the disposition of the question of the Greek monarch.

7. The last demand, which pervaded all of the above six and was considered the most important, provided for the evacuation of all British troops and missions from Greece.

The Communists undoubtedly felt that their bargaining power would be increased one hundredfold if the British were to evacuate Greece. Naturally, these seven demands were not met and the Communist guerrilla bands, operating from "privileged sanctuaries" in Albania, Yugoslavia (especially), and Bulgaria, increased their tempo of attacks throughout the second half of 1946.

The year 1947 found Greece in the midst of a full-scale anti-guerrilla war, confronted with the decision of the British to stop supporting the Greek armies with money and equipment after 31 March 1947 and, further, to withdraw British troops from Greece. The northern Communist neighbors of Greece in the meantime had launched a massive anti-Greek government propaganda offensive,

33. Outlined in *Rizospastis* (Greek Communist Athens Daily) of 12 September 1946. Included in Xydis, p. 301.

accusing it of enforcing fascist and other oppressive measures and practices. The Greek economy was on the verge of utter collapse. The noncommunist politicians (Themistocles Sophoulis, Liberal, and Constantine Tsaldaris, Conservative, being the protagonists) were bickering and refusing to cooperate, still nursing old, traditional grudges. Large areas of rural Greece had fallen under direct control of the Greek Communists, and the situation was daily deteriorating. This was the tragic state of affairs when President Truman's historic decision to launch the Truman Doctrine was made in March of 1947. American intervention was the *deus ex machina* that disentangled the hopelessly complex postwar Greek tragedy, and returned Greece to relative stability.

The Background of Greek-American Relations

Greece's relations with the United States before World War II had not been at all extensive. Diplomatic relations were first established in 1833, shortly after the modern reappearance of the Greek nation. The traditional policy of American isolationism affected nineteenth-century Greek-American relations which, although warm, remained quite superficial. The increasing number of Greek immigrants pouring into the United States from 1890 to 1921 provided a great stimulus to the scope of Greek-American relations. Greek immigrant remittances from the United States became one of the chief compensations for Greece's habitually unfavorable balance of trade.

Before World War II the United States did not consider the Mediterranean Sea as an area directly related to its political and economic interests. In the late 1940s, however, the United States departed from precedent and deployed its naval forces in the Mediterranean on a continuing basis. There were many reasons contributing to this, chief among them the gradually growing suspicions and fears of Soviet expansionist objectives and the great importance assigned to Middle Eastern oil reserves and their access routes. The United States naval policy was also strongly influenced by Britain's willingness[34] to share the burden of maintaining control over the Mediterranean Sea and was propelled by the catalytic effects of Secretary of the Navy For-

34. This willingness perhaps stemmed from her inability to maintain primacy in the Mediterranean without American help.

restal's pressures favoring an expanded strategic role for the American navy. The modest and experimental cruises of early 1946 gradually developed into today's powerful, permanent force known as the Sixth Fleet.[35]

The attitude of the State Department regarding Greece, as late as June 1945, in no way forecast the massive role that the United States was to play in that country a year and a half later.[36] Greece was considered to be traditionally bound to Britain more than to the other Great Powers, and the United States had consistently refrained from any intervention in Greek political affairs. Greece was a "bridge" between Europe and the Middle East. The United States should, therefore, assume the role of mediator in disputes of Britain and the U.S.S.R. over the Greek question. Republicanism was recommended as the best form of government for Greece, suiting the temperament and traditions of that country.

American interest in postwar Greece mounted quickly after 1945 and was manifested in numerous ways. On 20 August 1945, for example, the United States announced its intention to send observers to the forthcoming Greek elections in accordance with the Yalta Conference decisions.[37] Then came a series of friendly visits of American ships, signifying interest and friendship. The battleship *Missouri* visited Athens in April 1946, and the aircraft carrier *Franklin D. Roosevelt*, with escorts, early in September 1946, followed by the aircraft carrier *Randolph* on 6 December 1946.[38]

Greek politicians, with the knowledge and blessing of the British, made numerous attempts through talks, notes, and visits to secure American economic and, if possible, military aid.[39] The American hesitation to respond to these pleas was based partly on the fact that Greece was considered a British concern, and partly on the difficulty of convincing Congress to authorize large amounts of aid to that or any other country. Ambassador to Greece MacVeagh, in a meeting

35. Xydis gives an excellent account of the factors, trends, and events which led to America's historic decision to keep naval forces in the Mediterranean and habitually show the flag as a gesture of interest and support in various friendly ports of call. See pp. 159 ff., 267 ff.
36. Xydis, p. 105.
37. Ibid., p. 126.
38. Ibid., pp. 170–71, 186–87, 291, 423.
39. Ibid., p. 261, e.g. the Venizelos mission to Washington in August 1946.

with King George II, set the preconditions which should materialize before the United States extended any aid to Greece.[40] He felt that the American public should be convinced by deeds that the Greek government was not oligarchic and reactionary, that democratic institutions were not stifled, and that all noncommunist Greeks were united. Therefore, he recommended the adoption of such measures as broadening the Greek government, moderation toward the Center and Left, and the immediate reorganization of the Greek army. This, occurring in October 1946, constituted an early instance of American advice concerning Greek politics, a function which had previously been reserved for the British.

The Truman Doctrine

In 1947, with the deterioration of the Greek government's position in the guerrilla war, and the contemplated British termination of aid, events dramatically led to the announcement of the Truman Doctrine. In January 1947, an American economic mission arrived in Greece to conduct a general survey of political and economic conditions. Then, on 23 January, a broader coalition government was sworn in, under Demetrios Maximos, including cabinet members from seven noncommunist political parties. Thus, at least superficially, American preconditions for aid were met by broadening the composition of the cabinet. On 21 February the British Ambassador in Washington informed the United States that Britain could no longer provide aid and support to Greece and Turkey.[41] On 12 March 1947, President Truman delivered his famous "Aid to Greece and Turkey" speech to the joint session of Congress. This was a decisive endorsement of the new role of world leadership for the traditionally isolationist United States which had begun with the proclamation of the Marshall Plan.

From the Greek viewpoint, the Truman Doctrine meant that a new breath of life would be blown into the tiring government's efforts to prevent Greece from becoming communist. There was, however, the realization that, of necessity, there would be some limitation of Greece's sovereign rights. The Minister Councilor of the Greek

40. Ibid., pp. 400–01, pp. 403–05.
41. Ibid., p. 475.

Embassy in Washington, Economou-Gouras, reported to his home office that "although the United States Government had no desire to intervene in Greek internal affairs, it recognized, nevertheless, that the full implementation of the proposed plan could not but involve some kind of *interference in these affairs.*" [42] Therefore, the full cooperation of the Greek government was requested. "This cooperation [was to] rest on the assurance that the suggestions of the United States Government would be followed. If, for instance, a tax was proposed, the Ministry of Finance should not reject this proposal." Economou-Gouras added further that "the United States Plan would be accompanied by *a limitation, in some measure, of the sovereign rights of Greece.*" This limitation, however, was to be balanced against the prospect of the tragic danger of the Greek nation being overrun by the Slavs. Considered against the background of the British withdrawal, "U. S. intervention appeared like 'A Plank of Salvation.' " [43]

The massive quantity of American aid which poured into Greece following the proclamation of the Truman Doctrine is a matter of record. From May 1947 to June 1956 this aid has been estimated in the amount of $2,565 million—the highest per capita aid received by any underdeveloped country in the postwar period.[44] Notwithstanding this gigantic American aid and technical assistance, the bloody civil war extended for over three years (from early 1946 through August 1949) and cost Greece incalculable moral and material damage.[45] After numerous, vigorous, and sustained offensives, the

42. Ibid., p. 479 (emphasis supplied).
43. Ibid., p. 480 (emphasis supplied).
44. Ibid. From the end of World War II until June 1961, aid to Greece was reported by the *New York Times* of 18 March 1962 as totaling $2,950 million.
45. The following statistics may be found in Xydis, p. 541. He quoted pp. 662–67 and 670 from D. Zafiropoulos, *The Antiguerrilla Struggle* (in Greek) (Athens, 1956).
   a. *Casualties of the Greek Armed Forces:* 43,392 Men
      8,440 killed
      29,496 wounded
      5,446 missing
   b. *Civilian Casualties:* 5,219
      4,288 murdered
      931 killed by mines
   c. *Guerrilla Casualties:* 38,421 (Prisoners surrendered not included)
   d. *Communist Destruction Toll:*
      746 road bridges
      438 railroad bridges, several railroad tunnels and stations, many miles of

Greek National Army scored a final and decisive victory over the Communist Democratic Army. Various factors accounted for the Communist defeat. Foremost among these was the effectiveness and determination of the Greek armed forces, boosted by the massive assistance they enjoyed, directly and indirectly, from the United States as a result of the Truman Doctrine and the Marshall Plan. Another major factor was the sealing of Yugoslavia's frontier, following the Tito–Stalin dispute, which denied the Communist guerrillas the use of Yugoslav soil as a "privileged sanctuary." This enabled the Greek forces to concentrate on insulating the Greek-Albanian frontier, and left open only the Greek-Bulgarian frontier which was too distant from the Communist base of operations in the Pindus Mountains (in Greek Epirus) to be of any military significance. Thus Communist guerrilla supply lines were cut, with commensurate loss in their tactical effectiveness.[46]

The "Democratic Army" suffered a tremendous blow to its standing with Greek public opinion after it tacitly approved a plan for the establishment of an "Independent Macedonian People's Republic."[47] This action in effect abdicated all rights over Greek Macedonia. To the average nationalistically minded Greek, it amounted to treason. The effect of such a development was to improve the morale and determination of the anticommunist Greek army. Also, great frictions were created within the Greek Communist party itself, as well as within the Democratic Army, stemming from the reaction of nationalist-minded Communists,[48] who were equally opposed to the loss of a large and important Greek territory.

After its defeat, the Greek Communist party continued its opera-

road and railroad lines.
e. *Dislocations:* 1/10 of the Greek population had to move to urban areas of the country, thus creating serious economic, social, and psychological problems. These 700,000 refugees absorbed damages valued at $186,739,548.
f. *Private Property Destroyed:*
24,626 houses totally destroyed.
22,000 houses partly destroyed.
100,000 houses damaged through abandonment.
g. Finally, 28,000 young Greek children were abducted in countries behind the "Iron Curtain."
46. See McNeill, *Greece: American Aid in Action*, p. 42.
47. The approval was publicly voiced in a broadcast of "Radio Free Greece" on 1 March 1949. See McNeill, p. 43.
48. Ibid., p. 44.

tions in exile. It has strictly toed a pro-Soviet Union line and its positions have reflected all the neurotic fluctuations of Soviet foreign policy. For example, after the Soviet 20th Party Congress and the launching of Khrushchev's famous "peace offensive," Greek Communist views moderated considerably. The ultimate objective of transforming Greece into a "People's Democracy" was suspended in favor of an intermediate policy advocating neutralism and nonalignment for Greece.

The Greek Communist party has enjoyed a great identity of views[49] with the quasi-communist EDA party established in Greece in August 1951.[50] The extent of differences and similarities between EDA and Greek Communist views could be established by an exhaustive content analysis of EDA political positions and Greek Communist party positions as broadcast daily from the party's radio station-in-exile. Although this type of analysis is beyond the scope of the present study, it would be quite useful in a final assessment of EDA's work as an opposition party in the Greek political spectrum.

Postwar Greece was caught in the morass of Soviet-Western antagonisms. The Greek government's national claims, directed primarily against Germany's World War II allies in the Balkans, were neutralized by Soviet opposition, since the Soviets had inherited all the Nazi "satellites." The Greek Communists, for their part, pressed for claims directed against countries (e.g. Britain and Turkey) whose friendship was deemed indispensable by the Greek government, if Greece were to survive an attempted Communist take-over. The early postwar Greek governments had a many-pronged problem. They faced a massive task of reconstruction and development in a devastated nation, while still prosecuting a war against the foreign-supported and well-armed Greek Communist guerrillas. Politically they strove to achieve unity among the divided noncommunist factions and at the same time to preserve a semblance of democracy to satisfy the apprehensive British and Americans. And in the economic sphere

49. For a more detailed discussion on this point, see ibid., pp. 198–203.
50. EDA stands for "Unified Democratic Left." This party was established by John Passalides to fill the vacuum created by the outlawing of the Greek Communist party.

the government was caught between pressures for increased wages on the one hand and for control of inflation on the other.

The war against the Communists was won and the Greek people, having paid the bloody toll of national and international political conflicts, looked to the 1950s with a deep longing for peaceful, progressive reconstruction and development. The Communist dangers were not altogether wiped out, however. The Greek Communists had vowed that some day they would return for the "fourth and final round of conflict." [51] Albania and Bulgaria, supported by the Soviet Union and other East European countries, continued waging ruthless anti-Greek government propaganda campaigns. Yugoslavia, fortunately for Greece, reduced her pressures after the famous Tito–Stalin dispute of 1948.

One of the basic policies of Greek postwar governments was to secure a peacetime alliance with one or more of the great Western powers, especially Britain and the United States. It was not until 1952, however, and the formal admission of Greece into NATO, that this fervently pursued Greek objective was realized. This, in part, explains the great sense of urgency and the attitude of unconditional acceptance of terms with which Greek noncommunist politicians accepted their country's entry into NATO.

During the long years of the Greek Civil War, the United States supported a Sophoulis/Tsaldaris (Republican–Royalist) coalition government which attempted the huge task of clearing the Greek Mountains of the rebellious guerrilla forces. During the course of the late 1940s there were numerous instances of reluctant American intervention in Greek political affairs,[52] intervention deemed necessary to the goal of a decisive military victory over the Greek Communists. The challenge of the 1950s was to consolidate this victory in the economic, social, and political fields and to project Greece as a "showcase" of the results of unencumbered democratic development.

The Americans in the early 1950s were disillusioned with the tradi-

51. "Free Greece" radio warned that "The Democratic Army has not laid down its arms, it has only put them aside." *New York Times*, 18 October 1949, quoted in Stavrianos, *Greece: American Dilemma*, pp. 204–05.

52. See ibid., pp. 187–88, 218. Stavrianos covers the period of 1940–51, perhaps indulging in some overcriticism of the Greek noncommunist politicians. On this topic see also McNeill, pp. 35, 60–67.

tional antagonisms and disputes of Greece's old political guard. There was a vacuum created for a new force, to be led by a strong, independent, and nationally respected man, around whom all Greek non-communists could rally. Such a man was found in the person of Marshal Alexander Papagos, who had led the Greek forces in their successful operations against the Communists. His rise to power and the support he received from the United States will be the concern of subsequent chapters.

Chapter Two
Some Preliminary Viewpoints
Regarding Greece's Participation
in NATO

Greece applied for admission to NATO in August 1951. The government initiating this momentous policy was headed by General Nicholas Plasteras, and was a coalition of the two major Center parties of that period, called Liberal and EPEK[1] (National Progressive Union of the Center). Greece gained formal admission to NATO, along with Turkey, on 18 February 1952.[2] The two countries formed the southeastern flank of the NATO alliance, and contributed significantly to the strength of the conventional armies of NATO, which were quite inadequate in comparison with their Soviet counterparts. In 1952 Greece had ten combat-ready divisions, while Turkey had approximately twenty-five.[3] In addition the Greek army had successfully defeated a well-organized communist rebellion which had enjoyed the wide support of Greece's northern Communist neighbors. It was the only European army which had successfully fought a full-scale war against the Communists.

The Greek armed forces were placed under major NATO commands soon after the formal ratification of the accession treaty: the army and air force under the general command of Allied Forces Southern Europe (AFSOUTH) in Naples, Italy, commanded by an American general or admiral;[4] the land forces, in turn, under the direct com-

1. EPEK was founded by General Nicholas Plasteras in December 1949.
2. For details on Greece's entry into NATO see infra, pp. 45–46.
3. George F. Eliot, "Military Evaluation of Greece's and Turkey's Forces," *Vema*, 26 March 1952, p. 1.
4. James S. Russell, "The Strategy of NATO and Greece," *International Relations*, November 1962, p. 29; J. F. R. Seitz, "AFSOUTH in NATO," *Army Information Digest* (October 1962), p. 40; see also *The Organization of NATO* (in Greek), NATO Handbook (Paris, NATO Information Service, 1962).

mand of the Allied Land Forces Southeastern Europe (LANDSOUTH-EAST) in Izmir, Turkey, usually headed by an American general; the Greek air force together with Italian and Turkish air forces under AIRSOUTH, with headquarters in Naples, commanded by an American general. Both LANDSOUTHEAST and AIRSOUTH were subordinate commands of AFSOUTH. The Greek navy elements assigned to NATO were placed under the command of Allied Forces Mediterranean with headquarters in Malta. This command is usually assigned to a British admiral and its mission is to guard and control the vital sea lanes of the Mediterranean.

The assessment of advantages and disadvantages accruing to Greece as a result of NATO participation is a difficult task at the present time, because much useful information is classified for security reasons. Also, the decision as to what constitutes an advantage or disadvantage for Greece is dependent on one's political viewpoints and beliefs; at best the author can present a series of varying political evaluations of the merits and demerits of Greek membership in NATO.

By and large the Greek nationalists, who form the great majority of the Greek people and who are represented by the conservative Right or the liberal Center parties, considered NATO participation axiomatically advantageous for Greece, and a vital foreign policy. They felt that Greece through NATO could secure its territorial integrity and increase its chances of maintaining national independence.[5] The Communists,[6] on the other hand, questioned the wisdom of this policy and considered that it would serve Greece's interests to abandon NATO and pursue a policy of nonalignment, and preferably benevolent neutrality, toward Eastern Europe and the Soviet Union.

Advantages of NATO Membership: The Nationalist View

The Center and Right parties, representing nationalist elements in Greece, have supported the policy of Greek participation in NATO for many reasons. To start with, they assumed that Greek participation in NATO was necessary not only because of traditional and ideological

5. Chapters 3 through 13 illustrate in detail the positions of the Greek political parties toward NATO and their occasional fluctuations.

6. For the purposes of this study, the Communist political viewpoint will be represented by actions and positions of EDA, rather than the outlawed Communist party which is operating in exile in Eastern Europe and the U.S.S.R.

affinities with the free Western world, but also because of geographic and strategic necessities. That is, Greece's geographic location and her vital need to maintain freedom of resupply from the sea required her to cooperate with the West (which controlled the Mediterranean). These factors did not even permit the consideration of neutrality.[7] This general position was shared by most authorities, whether military, political, or press commentators.[8]

Another key factor cited by noncommunists in support of NATO membership was the unprecedented security which Greece would enjoy under the NATO umbrella. According to the provisions of the alliance,[9] if Greece were to be attacked she would enjoy the support of fourteen other nations which comprised the strongest united force in the world. This, therefore, "guaranteed" territorial integrity for Greece, a luxury which she had not been afforded in recent history. It also would afford the Greeks peace of mind and free them to concentrate on economic development. In the area of material benefits, military and economic aid were considered powerful incentives to NATO membership. Greece had enjoyed and would be enjoying large quantities of military aid from the United States in the form of war material for the army, navy, and air force, amounting to between $100,000,000 and $200,000,000 yearly.[10] Also, large quantities of economic aid, usually commensurate with the degree of military and po-

7. There have been occasional fluctuations from this clear-cut pro-NATO position, primarily caused by the Cyprus dispute or by complaints about the high military costs necessary to meet NATO-determined defensive requirements.

8. E.g. Gregory P. Kassimatis, "Rules and Methods of Foreign Policy," *International Relations*, Athens (February 1963), p. 45; Gerasimos Lyhnos, "The Independence of the Great Powers and the International Environment of Greece," *International Relations*, Athens (May 1963), p. 33; Evangelos Averoff, "The Collision of the Two Worlds from the Athenian Observation Post," *International Relations*, Athens (February 1963), p. 5; Spyros Markezinis, "Forward Diplomacy," *International Relations*, Athens (November 1962), p. 6; Sophocles Venizelos, "Greece Amid International Developments," *International Relations*, Athens (February 1963), p. 34; NATO: *Pact of Peace and Friendship of Nations* (Athens, Atlantic Treaty Association, 1962) (hereafter referred to as NATO–Greek ATA); and National Defense School, "Geostrategic Position of Greece: The Importance of Greece for NATO and the Soviet Union," Study No. 5 (Athens, undated).

9. This refers to Article 5 of the NATO treaty which declares that an attack on the territory of one signatory will be construed as an attack upon all of them. For the entire text of the NATO treaty, refer to Appendix B.

10. K. A. Alexandris, "Accounting of a Decade," NATO–Greek ATA, pp. 15–16. See also figures on p. 28 above.

litical affinity, would be pouring into the developing and war-ravaged nation. A major hope expressed by Greek noncommunist politicians was that stronger Western European nations (such as Britain, France, or West Germany) would relieve the United States from the burden of continuing economic aid to Greece.[11] They believed that without postwar economic and military aid Greece would have been well behind its present stage in economic development.[12]

There were numerous other advantages which justified Greece's permanent participation in the NATO alliance. For instance, they pointed to the army which had been modernized not only in equipment but also in tactics and strategy thanks to NATO. Combined NATO exercises, in which Greek forces have participated regularly, were considered invaluable in this respect. Of greater importance, they felt, was the NATO infrastructure which had benefited Greece not only militarily but also industrially and economically. For example, many of the roads, airports, and port facilities that had been erected at minimal cost to Greece were enhancing the base for industrial expansion and helping to curb the chronic unemployment problem.[13] NATO proponents also considered that common Greek and Turkish participation in NATO would improve the conditions for friendly cooperation between the two nations. Greek-Turkish friendship was earmarked as a cornerstone of Greek foreign policy, essential for effective defense against a common external enemy[14] such as Communist Bul-

11. This hope has partially materialized with the establishment (May 1962) of a NATO-sponsored Consortium for Greece, whose purpose was to study the country's economic conditions and recommend ways and means through which NATO could assist toward their amelioration. This subject is discussed in greater detail below; see pp. 144–45, 173–74.

12. M. Melas, "Greece and NATO," NATO-Greek ATA, p. 31; and Alexandros Merenditis, "A Decade Since the Greek Entry in the Atlantic Alliance," NATO–Greek ATA, p. 56.

13. A. Tziras, "A Very Noteworthy Anniversary of Greece," NATO–Greek ATA, p. 34; Alexandris, "Accounting of a Decade," p. 15; Athanasios Frontistis, "The Defensive Problem in the Greek Area," International Relations, Athens (November 1962), p. 33; see also NATO Information Service, Functions of NATO Activity: Defensive Production and Infrastructure (Athens, undated).

14. It should be noted that recent trends of political writing in Greece deemphasize the "threat" from Bulgaria and other communist nations. These writings urge the development of friendly relations and economic cooperation with East Europe and the U.S.S.R.; see the discussion below in Chapter 12, p. 148, and Chapter 13, pp. 174, 180, regarding these current attitudes.

garia, which would enjoy the backing of the Soviet Union.[15] Friendly relations with Turkey would also free Greece to concentrate on defending against military and political inroads from other countries of the Communist north. Realities did not correspond with this pious wish, however, for the relations of Greece and Turkey throughout the 1950s have been seriously damaged, primarily by the Cyprus issue but also by the territorial waters issue, economic competition, and a score of other differences.

Finally, NATO defenders discerned some long-run, yet quite vital, advantages in Greek–NATO association. Close cooperation through NATO in numerous spheres of human endeavor would gradually arouse a new supranational outlook in Greek government circles as well as among the general public: namely, the ability to consider pan-European or pan-Atlantic federative plans, and the abandonment of narrow nationalistic attitudes which had so often in the past been the cause of damaging disputes or even conflicts.[16]

Disadvantages of NATO Membership: The Nationalist View

Certain disadvantages associated with Greece's participation in NATO are often discussed in Center or Conservative literature. First and foremost in the minds of most Greeks is the conflict of military preparedness with the desire for economic development. They feel that large military expenditures (running in the vicinity of 50 per cent of the budget), which Greece spends yearly in order to maintain her defensive stature within NATO, have hindered the rate and effectiveness of economic development. It is obvious that this conflict will continue to be considered a disadvantage unless or until NATO, or a few of its stronger members, see fit to assist Greece in this respect and permit her to devote a larger portion of her budget to productive developmental uses.[17] It is generally felt that economic cooperation among

15. A. Merenditis, "Comparison of Greece and Bulgaria," *Vema*, 8 April 1960, p. 1; A. Merenditis, "Effects in Greece of the U-2 Incident," *Vema*, 14 May 1960, p. 1; G. A. Daskarolis, "The Paragon 'Greece' Within the System of Collective Security of the Free World," *Vema*, 13 September 1959, p. 7.

16. G. Daskalakis, "Democracy for Growth," NATO *Letter* (Pris, NATO Information Service, March 1963).

17. Alexandris, "Accounting of a Decade," p. 17; G. Kassimatis, "NATO and Greece," NATO–*Greek* ATA, p. 24.

NATO allies is not complete, and that a more just allocation of military burdens would benefit not only the poorer allies but the entire alliance.[18]

There is also less than complete confidence in the credibility of the American nuclear deterrent and a fear that Greece would suffer irreparable damage in case of a nuclear war. These fears are nurtured by the protracted political disagreements existing among the larger NATO members; e.g. the United States vs. France, the West German ambitions for reunification, or the British and French insistence on separate (independent) nuclear striking forces. Greece, representing the small nations' point of view in the NATO alliance, would like to see greater political coordination and consultation in NATO as well as greater military integration.[19]

Other disadvantages include the frequent complaint that Turkey is afforded preferential treatment by NATO or the United States, especially with regard to aid (military and economic), of which it receives the lion's share.[20] Equal treatment by NATO of all "underdeveloped" NATO partners (e.g. Greece, Turkey, Portugal, and Iceland) is therefore earnestly advocated in Greece.[21]

The nationalists (liberal or conservative) are in general agreement on the areas where the NATO alliance needs to be strengthened in order to survive the tests of a multiphased Soviet offensive. The primary need, often mentioned, is for NATO to transcend the bounds of a purely military cooperative organization and approach the status of an "Atlantic Community." [22] For example, Gregory Kassimatis, Greek Minister of Education of the latest ERE government (May 1963), has pointed out that "defense, as a part of politics, is unbreakably con-

18. L. Makkas, "The Political Crisis of NATO," NATO–*Greek* ATA, pp. 40–41. The subject of the effect of military expenditures on Greek economic development is a vital one. It is touched upon in every major foreign policy debate, and this study covers its ramifications in greater detail in the following chapters.

19. Ibid., pp. 40–41; Melas, "Greece and NATO," p. 30.

20. The figures in Table 1 are self-explanatory. Sharp decreases in the amounts of both military and economic aid to Greece in the early 1960s were not matched proportionately in Turkey. This was especially the case with economic aid. Units are in millions of dollars.

21. Alexandris, "Accounting of a Decade," p. 18. For more on the subject of preferential treatment toward Turkey, see infra, Chapter 10, p. 121.

22. Alexandris, pp. 17–18; D. G. Daskalakis, "The Atlantic Community: Expectations and Realities," NATO–*Greek* ATA, pp. 44–45.

selected to host a base for missile warfare training.[27] Thus most Center/Right authorities have concluded that if Greece were to be lost to NATO, the results would be catastrophic indeed on the southeastern sector of the alliance and, by extension, for all of NATO. The Center/Right viewpoint is that Greek participation in NATO is mutually beneficial, for the country as well as the alliance, and is necessitated by strategic, geographic, economic, cultural, political, and ideological affinities which Greece and the Western NATO nations share.

Greek Communist Attitude toward NATO

The Communists, as represented in Greece by EDA, do not attribute any advantages to NATO participation. They question all the premises upon which Greece has based her alliance with the West.[28] Generally, they emphasize the following positions:

1. EDA sees no threat from East European Communist nations compelling Greece to arm heavily and associate herself with "the aggressive American alliance—NATO." [29]

2. Greek participation in NATO prevents the conclusion of agreements and settlements with Albania and Bulgaria (which offer peace plans constantly), thus perpetuating a hostile situation which the nationalist government is using as a pretext to justify NATO association and continued armaments.[30]

3. Greece has lost her sovereignty and independence as a result of the United States and NATO presence on her soil; e.g. the 1953 agreement to cede bases to the United States has ended all independence for Greece.[31]

27. Sergios A. Gyalistras, "The Tenth Anniversary of Greece's Entry in NATO," NATO–Greek ATA, p. 57; S. Koundouros, "The Training Center of Crete," *International Relations*, Athens (February 1963), pp. 25 ff.

28. For a comprehensive book about the EDA position, see Michael Kyrkos, *Greece and NATO* (Athens, 1961); also see sections on EDA positions in subsequent chapters.

29. Kyrkos, p. 21.

30. Ibid., pp. 16–17. This did not prove an accurate prediction. Greece and Bulgaria signed an agreement settling most of their outstanding disputes on 9 July 1964. There is currently a sincere atmosphere of détente in the relations of these two countries in spite of Greece's membership in NATO.

31. Ibid., pp. 27–28. For a detailed discussion of this agreement, see infra, pp. 77–89.

4. Valuable trade with natural East European and Soviet markets is not materializing because of American pressures preventing Greece from trading with Communist nations.[32]

5. Greece is exposed to frightening dangers of nuclear retaliation by playing host to American "offensive" nuclear weapons. The United States would never fight a nuclear war on its own territory but rather in Europe, and Greece would be one of the earliest victims.[33]

6. The Greek nationalist governments systematically negate peace plans for a denuclearized Balkan peninsula, thus perpetuating the dangers of a nuclear holocaust.[34]

7. American aid to Greece is coupled with economic "guidance" which seeks to perpetuate the "advanced industrial vs. raw-material-producing backward nation" relationship between the two countries, in accordance with American economic interests. The United States stifles all Greek efforts for immediate industrialization.[35]

Given all these assumptions, it is advocated that Greece should abandon NATO, maintain a policy of nonalignment such as that pursued by Nasser and Tito, expand her economic cooperation with East Europe and the Soviet Union, and diminish military expenditures to the minimum, pouring the difference into productive, industrially feasible projects.[36] The EDA position becomes suspect because it fails to recognize any advantages accruing to Greece as a result of NATO membership,[37] even if, for the sake of argument, it were assumed that the proposed list of disadvantages was realistic. It is also interesting to see that time has already disproved many of their above predictions, made as late as 1961.

32. Kyrkos, pp. 40–41.
33. Ibid., pp. 24–25.
34. Ibid., p. 26.
35. Ibid., pp. 40–41.
36. Ibid., pp. 16–17.
37. For example, territorial insurance against Greece's traditional northern antagonist, Bulgaria. This aspect is covered in greater detail in Chapter 1, pp. 13–16.

PART II: INFLUENCE

Chapter Three
The Treaty of NATO Accession in the Greek Parliament

C. L. Sulzberger wrote in the New York Times on 9 March 1952, that the North Atlantic Treaty "so far as the United States is concerned began in Greece and Turkey."[1] The Truman Doctrine, proclaimed as early as 12 March 1947, marked the realization of the Western world and particularly the United States, that collective security was mandatory if the Western democratic system of government was to be protected against Communist penetration. Greece and Turkey did not become original signatories of the North Atlantic Treaty primarily because of British objections and, to a lesser extent, the objections of the Scandinavian and Benelux nations. Britain's objections were based on desires to link Turkey and Greece with a Middle Eastern regional defensive arrangement which would be primarily under British leadership.[2] The Scandinavian and Benelux nations objected[3] primarily because they feared involvement in the anticommunist guerrilla war which was raging in Greece and because they feared that Greek and Turkish membership in NATO would reduce their own shares of military supplies from the United States.

The single most important factor which overcame British and other European opposition to Greek and Turkish entry into NATO was America's outright sponsorship of this project.[4] Other factors which

1. Quoted in Dimitrios G. Kousoulas, The Price of Freedom: Greece in World Affairs, 1939–1953 (Syracuse, Syracuse University Press, 1953), p. 184.
2. Ibid.
3. See Joe R. Wilkinson, "Denmark and NATO: The Problem of a Small State in a Collective Security System," International Organization, 10 (1956), 390–401; Tim Greve, Norway and NATO (Oslo, Oslo University Press, 1959).
4. Kousoulas, The Price of Freedom, pp. 185–89; see also "Review of Events in 1951," Eleftheria, 3 January 1952, p. 11.

softened this opposition were the first nuclear explosion by the
U.S.S.R. in September 1949, the Korean War, the intensification of
Soviet pressures on Tito's Yugoslavia, and the political deterioration
in the Middle East (especially the Iranian oil crisis).[5] Once British
support was finally enlisted, the misgivings of other NATO members
were easily pacified and the North Atlantic Council signed a protocol
in London, on 22 October 1951, which proclaimed the intention to
admit Greece and Turkey into NATO. The impact of this policy was
manifested by the immediate and acute negative reaction of the Soviet Union. It protested, it threatened and pressured Greece and especially Turkey, and generally considered the two-nation NATO accession a hostile act toward the Soviet Union.[6]

By 15 February 1952, the Greek-Turkish entry protocol had secured ratification by all twelve member nations. The atmosphere in
Greece was one of jubilation over NATO association. Opposition was
voiced, however, to having Greece and Turkey placed under Italian
military command. Also, a strong case was made in press reports for
acceptance of a principle on member contributions wherein each
member would expend funds in proportion to its economic capability.[7] On the positive side, it was argued that Greek-Turkish friendship would be considerably strengthened by the impending NATO association.[8]

NATO Accession Debated in Parliament

The debates in the Greek Parliament concerning the ratification of
Greek accession to NATO are illustrative primarily of the great eagerness with which the Greek political world (with the exception of the
Communists) welcomed association with the powerful Western alliance.[9] So great was this eagerness that the formal invitation to join

5. Kousoulas, pp. 185–88.
6. For more details on this subject see ibid., p. 188.
7. "What Greece Wants" (Editorial), *Eleftheria*, 17 February 1952, p. 1.
8. "Talks in Turkey Between Venizelos and Turkish Foreign Minister,"
Eleftheria, 2 February 1952, p. 1.
9. *Official Minutes of the Meetings of Parliament* (Athens, 1952) (hereafter
referred to as *Minutes*); the statements of the following political figures in
Parliament are indicative of enthusiastic support for Greek accession to NATO:
Alexandros Papagos (Chairman of Synaghermos [Right]), p. 571; Konstantinos
Tsaldaris (Chairman of the Populist [Right] Party), pp. 571–72; Nicolaos
Plasteras (Chairman of EPEK [Center] and Prime Minister), p. 573; George

NATO was ratified by the King within hours after its receipt and on the following day, after a short and superficial discussion, by the Greek Parliament.

The coalition government of Plasteras–Venizelos, comprised of elements of the Greek liberal Center, should be given the credit (or blame, in the view of certain political elements) for initiating and successfully completing the project of securing Greek membership in NATO. The approach of the Center government parties, as well as the major party of the conservative Right (Synaghermos) toward NATO membership was "don't look a gift-horse in the mouth." NATO membership for Greece was considered such a good thing that even prolonged debate on the subject was discouraged for fear of insulting the Western allies.[10]

On 18 February 1952, George Varvoutis, the Deputy Foreign Minister of the Plasteras government, introduced the treaty for Greek accession to NATO in Parliament. He hailed this treaty's "historical" importance and amplified some of its general ramifications. Greece, according to Varvoutis, was joining a large military organization dedicated to the defense of liberty, and in support of the ideals outlined in the famous Atlantic Charter of Franklin Roosevelt and Winston Churchill.[11]

Greece would have both rights and obligations under this treaty. Among the basic rights would be an equality which would afford Greece international dignity, and foreign aid which would allow the nation to develop its badly war-damaged economy.[12] Among the obligations, Varvoutis included rising military expenditures and certain "inescapable influences" which would result from international association and cooperation. However, these influences would act upon all fourteen member nations "equally." [13] The Parliament was informed

Varvoutis (Deputy Foreign Minister [Center]), p. 569; Alexandros Baltatzis (Chairman of Agrarian [Center] Party), p. 573; Sophocles Venizelos (Chairman of Liberal [Center] Party and Vice Premier), p. 492; Panayotis Kanellopoulos (leading member of Synaghermos [Right]), p. 494.

10. Kanellopoulos, *Minutes*, p. 494.

11. Varvoutis, *Minutes*, p. 570.

12. Ibid.; also Gerasimos Lyhnos, *Minutes*, p. 571; Lyhnos, for example, stated in Parliament that Greece would be standing "for the first time" next to the Western nations "as an equal among equals,"

13. Varvoutis, *Minutes*, p. 575.

that Greek and Turkish entry into NATO did not materialize without the opposition of some of the original member nations.[14]

The reaction of the opposition parties was generally marked by unqualified approval of the NATO accession treaty, with the exception of the Communists, who registered their unqualified rejection. Marshal Papagos' Synaghermos, the major opposition party in Parliament, voiced its enthusiastic support of the treaty and, in the light of NATO participation, stressed Greece's need for a strong government to carry out the new and more important international role.[15]

In addition to the Communists, there was one other voice cautioning, if not dissenting, and questioning the wisdom of the timing and the terms of the NATO association agreement. Konstantinos Tsaldaris, the leader of the Populist party and an ex-Prime Minister of the late 1940s, expressed considerable doubt.[16] He noted that the government and the Synaghermos opposition, in their great jubilation over the attainment of the treaty, were neglecting to seek the best terms of entry and were not adequately prepared to join the NATO alliance in full understanding of its many ramifications. In this connection, Tsaldaris felt that Greece and Turkey, whose combined armies numbered about "600–700 thousand men," comprising the largest West European land force, should have negotiated entry into NATO as a unit, thus securing much better terms of entry as well as maintaining a stronger voice within NATO.[17]

Tsaldaris posed certain basic questions, seeking to determine what NATO's reaction would be should Greece be attacked by another nation. He pointedly asked the Deputy Foreign Minister if other NATO partners would be "automatically . . . obligated" to come to Greece's assistance in case of attack.[18] Varvoutis, in his reply, evaded the core of this question and went on to discuss other aspects of the treaty.[19] Tsaldaris, developing further his reservations vis-à-vis NATO accession, stated that NATO participants should know "that a certain degree of sovereign rights has to be granted to a general authority which will

14. See pp. 45–46 above.
15. Papagos, *Minutes*, p. 571; Kanellopoulos, *Minutes*, p. 494.
16. Tsaldaris, *Minutes*, p. 571.
17. Ibid., pp. 492–93.
18. Ibid., p. 75.
19. Varvoutis, *Minutes*, p. 575.

oversee the affairs of that community—(NATO)." He asked Venizelos to expound on the "directives" to be expected from NATO which would "determine" the future policies of Greece and, primarily, what these directives would be concerning the close and "absolute" political and military cooperation between Greece and Turkey as one "community" within NATO.[20]

Sophocles Venizelos, the Foreign Minister of Greece, sought to reply to the questions posed by Tsaldaris. The nature of his responses suggests to the analyst that his government did not indeed know much about (or care to discuss publicly) the conditions under which Greece was joining NATO. Regarding NATO directives, Venizelos informed Tsaldaris that a member nation could not enter into separate agreements with other member nations. Separate agreements would only be possible with nations outside NATO. Venizelos was undoubtedly grossly misinformed on this particular point, because there is nothing in the NATO treaty preventing NATO members from entering into bilateral agreements with other member nations, unless these agreements conflict with the North Atlantic Treaty (Article VIII). In response to Tsaldaris' criticism that Greece and Turkey should have negotiated a common front prior to NATO entry, Venizelos' reply again indicated uncertainty about the consequences of NATO participation. He said, in effect, that before Greece could make an agreement with Turkey, it should first "learn" the obligations which would flow from NATO participation.[21] This he stated on the floor of the Parliament ten days before the formal and final ratification to NATO membership was granted. It appears from Venizelos' replies that Greece entered NATO without really knowing what to expect in terms of obligations.

The eight-man EDA parliamentary team, representing the Communist point of view, opposed Greek participation in NATO, as was to be expected. John Passalides, leader of EDA, stated from the podium in the Parliament that the Greek government's foreign policies should reflect the philosophy of its internal policies. The Plasteras government had been elected, according to Passalides, on a promise to bring about "pacification" for the nation of Greece, torn by civil war. It

20. Tsaldaris, *Minutes*, p. 492. This is indicative of Tsaldaris' apparent willingness to follow NATO directives.
21. Venizelos, *Minutes*, pp. 492, 493.

should, therefore, follow suit on a policy of international pacification, which to the Communists meant neutrality and nonalignment. They cautioned that, as in 1922–23, Greece through NATO would once more be sacrificed for the big Western interests in Middle Eastern oil.[22]

The brevity of the discussion, the speed of passage of the treaty, the general agreement that NATO membership was of historical importance, and the unwillingness to consider bargains for securing easier terms for Greek participation, suggest the great importance which Greek political leadership placed on NATO membership and concomitant considerations, such as the Western nations' "guarantee" of the territorial integrity and political independence of Greece, and the prevention of any possible reemergence of attempts for Communist takeover.

The debate in Parliament was indicative of the realization by many political leaders of the Right and Center that collective security necessarily brings about some limitations in sovereignty and national independence. Entry into NATO, therefore, aroused among some deputies expectations of inflowing NATO "directives" in the field of foreign policy.

In 1952 Greece was heavily subsidized by American economic, technical, and military aid. As a result, many have argued that the Western alliance's leading nation exerted considerable influence in Greece and that Greek participation in NATO was a by-product of extremely close Greek-American relations.[23] The next three chapters are devoted to a discussion of political reaction to this alleged United States interference and influence in Greek politics.

22. Passalides and Kyrkos, *Minutes*, pp. 572–73.
23. Varvoutis, *Minutes*, p. 569.

Chapter Four
Greece
and American Influence

National sovereignty in its unlimited form denotes that one of the prerequisites of being a full-fledged nation-state is independence from controls and influences or directives of other nations. In practice, however, and especially when applied to small nations, the term "national sovereignty" [1] loses some of its rigid theoretical properties. The fact of international relations, whether friendly or hostile, presupposes some degree of abandonment of absolute sovereignty, be it self-imposed or necessitated by circumstances. Relations between large nations on one hand and smaller ones on the other, whether in the economic, political, or military spheres, bring about certain pressures and commitments which dictate flexibility and noninsistence on absolute independence by the smaller nations. Whether Greece belonged to NATO or not, it would still, by virtue of its small size and relative weakness, have to compromise its insistence upon pure independence in order to secure better economic terms with a given nation, or to avoid conflict with another, or to gain the pledge of support of a third nation. We will try to determine, on the basis of public political commentary, the extent to which Greek-American asso-

1. For a detailed discussion of political and legal interpretations of the term "national sovereignty," refer to the following: Hans J. Morgenthau and Kenneth W. Thompson, *Principles and Problems of International Politics* (New York, Alfred A. Knopf, 1960), p. 134; Philip C. Jessup, *A Modern Law of Nations* (New York, Macmillan, 1959), pp. 1, 40–41; Quincy Wright, *Contemporary International Law: A Balance Sheet* (New York, Doubleday, 1955), p. 21; Hans J. Morgenthau, *Politics Among Nations* (New York, Alfred A. Knopf, 1954), pp. 287–308.

ciation influenced the course of events in Greece more than would be natural in a traditional alliance.

Greece and Turkey gained entry into NATO thanks to the support and initiative of the United States.[2] As soon as the accession treaty was ratified, critical reports publicizing allied dissatisfaction with the weakness of the coalition Plasteras–Venizelos government began appearing in the Greek press. The daily paper, Vema, then opposed to the Center coalition government and championing the cause of General Papagos, reported concern throughout NATO that the Greek government, which was undergoing a grave political crisis, was indeed weakening the entire alliance.[3] The seriousness of Greece's internal political crisis was thus increased by the articulation of such concern and dissatisfaction.

The major concerns of Greece in the early part of 1952, and indeed throughout the 1950s, were to bring about the rapid reconstruction of the war-ravaged country, to continue the burgeoning economic development, and to prevent Greece from falling under Communist control. In all these basic objectives, the United States had, through its well-known policies commonly referred to as the Truman Doctrine, come to the aid and assistance of Greece. Billions of dollars were poured into the country in the form of military and economic aid from 1947 on.[4] The results justified the expense. The Communist guerrilla forces, which had enjoyed sizable support from Greece's Communist northern neighbors, were decisively defeated in 1949. Following the conclusion of the civil war, great strides were taken in the difficult task of reconstructing the war-torn nation.

The large amount of American aid to Greece brought about greater American involvement in affairs which would otherwise have been considered strictly domestic. A number of studies have been conducted dealing with United States aid administration or maladministration in Greece and analyzing its effects.[5]

2. Varvoutis, Minutes, p. 569.

3. "Greece Following Her NATO Accession as Equal Member Causes Allied Concern Due to Crisis Undermining Her Internal Front," Vema, 27 February 1952, p. 1.

4. For more details on aid see supra, pp. 27–28.

5. C. A. Munkman, American Aid to Greece (New York, Praeger, 1958); W. H. McNeill, Greece: American Aid in Action.

A Case Study of American "Intervention" in Greece

An analysis of Greek political reaction to United States involvement in Greece, as recorded in representative press organs, supports the view that American influences in Greece (whether justified or not) were quite significant and concrete, and were definitely responsible for numerous developments in that country. The events of 14–17 March 1952 illustrate one of the classic instances of what was considered, especially by the Center and Leftist parties, outright United States interference in Greek domestic political matters.

Greece was then governed by a coalition government comprised of members of two major Center parties. Newspaper reports in early March indicated that a serious political controversy had erupted over the electoral system to be used in future elections. The relatively youthful and dynamic conservative Rightist movement, called Synaghermos (Rally), was in favor of the "majority" or single-member district election system. On the other hand, two key members of the Center government, Sophocles Venizelos and Konstantinos Rentis, were seeking to reestablish the "simple proportional" system according to most newspaper reports. It was reported also that the ailing Premier, General Nicholas Plasteras, had discouraged this effort of his cabinet members.[6] While the controversy was at its peak, John E. Peurifoy, the United States Ambassador in Greece,[7] issued the following statement (which has since become notorious and well publicized):

6. "Plasteras for the Majority System," *Eleftheria*, 14 March 1952, p. 1; "Plasteras Personally Intervenes Against Proportional System," *Vema*, 14 March 1952, p. 1.

7. John Emil Peurifoy's career in the Foreign Service of the United States was ended abruptly by an automobile accident on the highways of Thailand on 18 August 1955, which took the life of Peurifoy and his young son. At the time, he was serving as American Ambassador to Thailand and had been preparing the groundwork which supported the Southeast Asia Treaty Organization. Peurifoy's primary mission in Greece was to consolidate democracy and to prevent the reemergence of communism. He was quite successful. Peurifoy is best remembered for his effective intervention in Guatemalan affairs (while he was Ambassador to Guatemala, 1953–54) which forced an agreement between two warring anticommunist factions and resulted in the overthrow of the Communist-controlled regime. His reputation as a leading State Department "trouble-shooter" is a matter of record. For additional information see *Current Biography Yearbook* (New York, H. W. Wilson, 1955), p. 433; also the *New York Times*, 13 August 1955, p. 1.

Because the American government believes that the reestablishment of the "simple proportional" election method, with its unavoidable consequences of the *continuation of governmental instability*, would have destructive results upon the effective utilization of American aid to Greece, the American Embassy feels itself obliged to make its support publicly known for the patriotic position of the Prime Minister Plasteras with regard to this subject.[8]

Premier Plasteras' condemnation of the simple proportional election method was thus given the stamp of American approval. This was considered by members of the Center and Leftist parties as clearcut and objectionable American interference in purely domestic Greek politics. The newspaper spokesman for the Prime Minister's (EPEK) party reported on 15 March that the Americans had clearly involved themselves in the acute Greek political controversy over the election system, which was strictly a domestic matter. The Center newspaper interpreted this American action, which it claimed had the enthusiastic approval of Synaghermos leaders, as prearranged between American diplomats and members of Synaghermos and designed to serve as the beginning of a series of forceful American efforts to unseat the Center government and bring General Papagos to power.

Members of the press interviewed Peurifoy and asked him whether his announcement could be interpreted as interference in Greek domestic politics. His reply was quite inconclusive: "I think that the Greek *public* must be assured, and will believe very soon, when it observes the development of events, that I am working for the benefit of Greece." [9] The editorials of most middle-of-the-road and leftist newspapers interpreted Peurifoy's reply as a tacit acceptance of the fact that such interference was intentional.

THE CENTER'S REACTION   A typical reaction of the Center movement toward the "American interference" was illustrated in one of *Eleftheria's* editorials.[10] The editor pointed out that a dispute on the

8. "U. S. Announcement Against the Proportional System," *Eleftheria*, 15 March 1952, p. 1 (emphasis supplied).

9. Ibid. (emphasis supplied). The interesting feature of Peurifoy's reply is that he was appealing directly to the Greek public as if he were a local politician. This has been the pattern of operations with a number of other American ambassadors in Greece.

10. "The Americans" (Editorial), *Eleftheria*, 15 March 1952, p. 1.

subject of an appropriate election system for future Greek elections was purely a domestic affair. Therefore, the American Ambassador's endorsement of a given election system, regardless of the nature of his motives, constituted an "invasion" of Greek internal affairs. The American Ambassador was not the "guardian" of the Greek people's interests, and should not try to assume that role. The effects upon the Greek people of such invasions of privacy were indeed grave. The public was beginning to wonder "whether World War II marked the end of independence and freedom of small nations." The same editor observed with bitterness that in no other country allied with the United States or receiving aid from it "was there noted similar interference." In its editorial of 16 March 1952,[11] *Eleftheria* reached the peak of anti-American feeling with statements to the effect that the United States Ambassador had assumed a new role, that of "governor-general" and "sponsor" in the political life of Greece, expressing his preferences and chastizing or reprimanding those who opposed him. "In the name of what logic," argued the editor, "can a military alliance, which aspires to the fortification of the independence of nations, remove from its members even their political rights?"

The Greek government made official its chagrin over Peurifoy's activities in the following terse public announcement:

It is natural for the Government of the United States to be interested in the better utilization of aid supplied, for which we are grateful. It belongs, however, to the Greek people and government to decide with what election system the country will be administered, on the basis of our constitutional laws, a system enacted by the Parliament on the criterion of the nation's interest.[12]

THE CONSERVATIVES APPROVE   *Kathimerini*, the organ of Synaghermos, interpreted the same events from a different viewpoint. On 6 March 1952 it reported that, according to absolutely reliable information, a great controversy was brewing between the Center government and the American diplomats.[13] The existence of this controversy

11. "The Rights" (Editorial), *Eleftheria*, 16 March 1952, p. 1.
12. "The Communiqué," *Eleftheria*, 16 March 1952, p. 1.
13. "Relations Worsened Between the Government and American Diplomats," *Kathimerini*, 6 March 1952, p. 1

was reportedly substantiated by the actions of Venizelos in a visit to the United States. During his talks with Dean Acheson at the U. S. Department of State, Venizelos was supposed to have complained vigorously against the U. S. Economic Mission and its director, Roger Lapham. More specifically, Venizelos was said to have accused Peurifoy of exceeding the instructions of his government. Venizelos was reported also to have mentioned that in other nations receiving American aid, "interference" and "pressures" of the type exerted on Greece were either nonexistent or very limited. He had requested that Greece be treated the same way. He had sought, also, the removal from Greece of Peurifoy and Lapham, feeling that the men who would replace them could become accustomed to serving only in an advisory capacity to the Greek economic ministries. This would terminate the situation where American diplomats "govern Greek economics, while the government shoulders the responsibility." [14]

Synaghermos felt that the United States was rightly concerned about the disposition of its aid to Greece, and this concern was daily aggravated by the Center coalition government's inefficiency. Peurifoy's declaration was not considered interference, but rather a realization on the part of the United States that Greece needed a strong and capable government which only Synaghermos could offer.[15]

Kathimerini covered the Peurifoy incident in a favorable fashion. It reported that the American diplomatic representatives in Athens, following State Department instructions, were "determined to use *every means,* up to articulating a threat regarding temporary termination of aid, in order to dissuade the application of the simple proportional system." [16] Despite the Greek government's terse and loud complaints regarding Peurifoy's action, revival of the simple proportional system was more or less dropped by its sponsors, Venizelos and Rentis. *Kathimerini's* editorial of 16 March cryptically emphasized the point that the unwanted election system was averted "thanks to the drastic intervention of factors, which the government [was] *obliged to obey,*" but also expressed the fear that public opinion in

14. Ibid.
15. "The Declaration of Peurifoy," *Vema,* 15 March 1952, p. 1.
16. "American Announcement Obliges Government to Abandon Proportional System," *Kathimerini,* 15 March 1952, p. 1 (emphasis supplied).

Greece might react more violently than could be forecast.[17] Two years later, Rentis, in a speech delivered in Parliament, clarified the method of the successful American interference. He stated that Peurifoy had threatened the government of the Greek Center early in 1952 that he would terminate American aid to Greece if the "proportional" election system was adopted.[18]

THE LEFTISTS CONDEMN   The Leftist interpretation of these events was somewhat more emphatic than the Center's with regard to anti-American polemics. The spokesman paper for the Leftist movement and the outlawed Communist party, *Auge*, interpreted Peurifoy's action as one in a series of planned actions to erode and unseat the Center movement's coalition government and replace it with Synaghermos, the American-supported Conservative party, whose policies would best suit the interests of the United States.[19]

EDA Communists argued, citing numerous cases of American pressures, threats, and interference since the enunciation of the "infamous" Truman Doctrine, that the main lever for extracting obedience from Greek governments was the instrument of "aid." In every instance, the threat of aid termination, or sizable reduction, was used as a means of securing acquiescence to the "American Way." [20]

Auge quoted the Minister of Public Works, Theodoros Havinis, who "resigned in protest" on 17 March 1952, as saying, among other things, in his farewell speech to the Ministry's staff that Greece,

heeding necessity, accepted the limitation of her sovereign rights in order to secure economic assistance . . . Unfortunately we were deceived because we found ourselves in a worse fate compared to other friendly and enemy states [classifications as of World War II] which received proportional economic aid from our allies . . . Instead of recognition they [United States] have driven us

17. "In Reserve" (Editorial), *Kathimerini*, 16 March 1952, p. 1 (emphasis supplied).
18. "Rentis Wants American Intervention Investigated by United Nations," *Vema*, 16 March 1954, p. 6.
19. "The Americans in Greece," series of articles in *Auge*, commencing 22 January 1956, p. 1.
20. "The Americans in Greece," *Auge*, 12 February 1956, p. 4.

to a condition where the Minister, and I say this with bitter complaint, is nonexistent, not being able himself, nor the appropriate agency which he heads, to have an opinion and to make responsible decisions without the prior approval of other persons. Thus the Minister's initiative has been nullified to the point that he does not know whether his decisions will be executed or not. I protest, as a Greek and as a representative of the Greek people, for the unjust humiliation which occurs to our motherland and which I consider unacceptable.[21]

According to *Auge*, Peurifoy was instrumental in enforcing the single-member district election system, which, the United States hoped, would help create a two-party situation in Greece (i.e. a Conservative and a Center party), keeping the Communists out of the Parliament.[22] *Auge* condemned the Greek Center parties which, despite their loud protestations against American interference, had succumbed in the face of American pressures and adopted the single-member district system, thus allowing the United States to gain the position of "regulator" of the Greek state system and its procedures.[23]

The validity of the information which was used by each party to support its arguments is open, as it should be, to doubt as to objectivity or even veracity. However, a synthesis of the views presented through public statements indicates that the United States had had significant influence over actions taken in the Greek economic and military sectors and to a lesser extent in the political one. Official Greek circles were not overly sensitive to small American or allied inroads into what the theorist would classify as purely domestic matters. General Papagos' statement to V*ema* regarding possible American intervention in Greece is characteristic of the attitude the noncommunist politician was willing to adopt vis-à-vis the United States:

I like to state the unadulterated truth. *When we exist not only thanks to our own decision, but because the Americans exist, and*

21. Ibid., 2 March 1956, p. 6.
22. Ibid., 3 March 1956, p. 3.
23. "The Foreign Developments of 1952," *Auge*, 1 January 1953, p. 5.

they report to their citizens, under what type of logic can we deny them the right to have their own opinion? American aid is given for a specific purpose. It does not constitute charity, and neither would we as proud Greeks accept it as such. As a consequence, when its purpose is misunderstood we cannot claim its continuation. When for example the fighting strength of the Army wavers, or internal security is jeopardized, or the economic aid becomes, even in part, a favor to the few "insiders" of the Party, what must the Americans do? Congratulate us? More generally, this business of oversensitivity is out of place nowadays. We must understand that *we are members of a family of nations,* and this creates a new reality.

We would have spoken on the basis of different criteria in the 19th century, different ones during the interwar period, and others still today. *We will see that many things, exceptional according to theory, have become already rules of our public life.*[24]

If the attitude of the key political figures in Greece was not overly sensitive to American guidance or even interference; if the assertions of all three parties, regardless of their estimates of the situation, supported the thesis that American diplomats in Greece, in the interest of better disposition and utilization of aid, often pressured government or party leaders to follow a given course of action; if the common external enemy of communism threatening both Greece and the United States united the objectives of the military establishments of both nations within the framework of NATO; then it is safe to suggest that the United States, being the larger and stronger nation, influenced considerably the policies, whether external or internal, of the smaller state.

The "Peurifoy incident"[25] described in this chapter illustrates the

24. "Interview with General Papagos," *Vema,* 27 April 1952, p. 1 (emphasis supplied).
25. The "Peurifoy incident" is not an isolated case of interference in Greek politics. There are numerous other examples and only a few are mentioned here to illustrate a trend. Peurifoy, for example, was said to have criticized General Papagos' resignation as Commander-in-Chief of the Greek armed forces and to have strongly urged his immediate reinstatement. See "The Country Is Swiftly Driven to Disintegration and Destruction—An American Viewpoint," *Vema,* 22 August

credibility of this assumption and typifies the strong reaction of the Greek press to all practices which could be interpreted as intervention.

1951, p. 1. In another instance, in a speech delivered in Athens on 19 October 1951, he gave a series of detailed guidelines of actions which the Greek government "should" undertake in the economic and political spheres. See *Vema*, 20 October 1951, p. 1.

Chapter Five
The Fall of the
Center Parties' Government

As 1952 ran its course, the actions of the American diplomatic representatives in Athens continued favoring the establishment of a strong and stable government in Greece. Coalition governments were automatically opposed by the United States because they contained the seeds of instability. Only a strong government could implement the stern measures which the United States thought were needed to bring about economic development and the effective utilization of the large economic aid earmarked for Greece.

In its efforts to promote economic development and to reduce the burden of public expenditures for military maintenance and operational costs, the Center coalition government applied to NATO for $28 million in aid which would make up for the deficit in the national budget. This request was not favorably received in NATO circles, according to press reports.[1] Consequently the Center government considered the possibility of extricating itself from its economic straits by reducing the military budget by 500 billion drachmas (approximately $33.3 million).[2] This could be achieved by reducing the army's size from 140,000 to 120,000 men and the length of service from three to two years.[3] The American reaction to these intentions was quite negative because any reduction in size and length of service of the Greek

1. "No Response to Request for Special NATO Aid," Vema, 6 August 1952, p. 4.
2. The rate of exchange at that time was $1 = 15,000 drachmas.
3. "Admiral Carney in Athens," Vema, 28 August 1952, p. 1.

armed forces was considered as a serious weakening of the NATO south-eastern sector's force.[4]

The position of the Center government during this period was precarious indeed. General Papagos' Synaghermos was daily gaining momentum and attracting a number of prominent elements from the warring factions within the beleaguered Center movement. Following the departure from the ranks of the government, in mid-August, of two of EPEK's senators and their absorption by Synaghermos, it appeared that the government would be overthrown in a vote of confidence. This was averted by the accession of two sympathizers of the leftist EDA party (Kyrkos and Karamaounas) who abandoned EDA and joined EPEK. Thus it appeared that the entire Center government was maintained in power by two representatives whose position was considered far left of Center, if not actually Communist.[5] The reaction among members of Synaghermos to the fact that two "Communists" maintained a nationalist government in power was vehement indeed. More serious, however, was another manifestation of American influence in the vicissitudes of Greek political life.

In statements to the members of the Greek press Peurifoy indicated that, due to the rapid political developments and the fact that EPEK had replaced two of its members with ex-EDA leftists, it was his recommendation that the best thing for Greece would be to have new elections under the single-member district system as soon as possible. This way, he argued, United States aid could be best utilized by a strong government (not dependent on Communist elements) which alone could institute the unpopular but necessary anti-inflationary measures that were so vital to the effort of Greek economic regeneration. Peurifoy emphasized that the new elections would give the Greek people a chance to indicate their choice between the incumbent (Plasteras) and the major opposition contender (Papagos).[6]

4. "Serious Concern in Washington and Paris over Greek Government's Decision," *Vema*, 29 August 1952, p. 1.

5. Kyrkos was, for example, one of the most vocal opponents to ratification of the NATO accession treaty. See supra pp. 41–42, 50.

6. "Statement by Peurifoy," *Vema*, 20 August 1952, p. 1; "The United States Officially Declares Support of Immediate General Elections," *Kathimerini*, 20 August 1952, p. 1.

Leftist Reaction

The Leftist interpretation of the American role in the events in the fall of 1952 was very simple. Plasteras, according to *Auge*, was forced by Peurifoy to seek resignation. Peurifoy was quoted to have told Plasteras that, "your government under the present circumstances is objectively unable to respond to its mission and the *needs of allied policies*." [7] In effect, *Auge* argued, the American Ambassador threatened that if Plasteras and his government did not resign, the United States would cut its aid to Greece. This was the culmination of an American movement beginning as early as July 1950 which sought to undermine the Center coalition government, and to replace it by faithful elements of the conservative Right. [8]

The Communist interpretation of the American relationship to Greek politics was that there had been "clear-cut intervention by foreigners" in the affairs of all the postwar Greek governments, and that the Plasteras coalition government had become dependent on United States' direction. [9] This had resulted in military expenditures well above 50 per cent of the national budget, the forcible entry of Greece into NATO, and the continuation of Greek participation in the Korean adventure. Foreign trade was also stifled, being isolated from East European markets because of Western political pressures, to the detriment, of course, of the well-being of the Greek economy and people. [10] EDA felt that American influence over domestic Greek politics was responsible for the lack of prompt adoption of pacification measures (i.e. amnesty to Communist civil war participants). And foreign directives were said to be responsible for the acceptance of the single-member district election system by the Center parties. [11]

It is interesting to note that the Left did not distinguish between the objectives of the two noncommunist movements, Liberal and

7. "The Americans in Greece," *Auge*, 22 January 1956, pp. 1, 5 (emphasis supplied).

8. Ibid.

9. "Declaration of EDA's Parliamentary Team Submitted to the Parliament's Chairman," *Auge*, 24 August 1952, p. 1.

10. Ibid.; see also article in *Auge*, 7 September 1952, p. 1, on the effects of high military expenditures on the Greek economy.

11. "Declaration of EDA's Parliamentary Team Submitted to the Parliament's Chairman," *Auge*, 24 August 1952, p. 1.

Conservative; they believed that both were subservient to directives of the "allied factor." Any differences between them could only be within "the margins allowed by the intervention of the allied factor." [12]

THE CENTER'S VIEWS   The events of August–October 1952 which precipitated the resignation of the Center's coalition government brought the Center government parties to an unfortunate dilemma. The Center's basic policy of NATO participation and Greek-American association, primarily through the medium of United States aid, committed the small Greek nation to a purely pro-American position. On the other hand, the desire to gain more aid, or balance less aid with lower military expenditures, did not endear the Center's policies to American officials. The United States had pinpointed the year 1952 to initiate periodic and recurring reductions to the monies allotted for Greek aid.[13] The Center government's reaction to this was to respond with fewer military expenditures. This measure was considered only after comparing Greece to larger West European nations which were economically recovered and booming, and yet spending less proportionately on military expenditures than did Greece. The Center's position was that given this state of affairs, if American aid was cut or NATO aid was not approved, then the military budget should be reduced proportionately. This, the Center argued, should be a national policy and should not be opposed by Synaghermos, whose politicians were following a policy of "underbidding" the government to endear themselves to their allies.[14]

These sentiments were officially reiterated by George Kartalis (Minister of Coordination) in a speech to Parliament on 20 August 1952.[15] Kartalis explained additionally that the coolness existing between the Greek government and the members of the United States Embassy and Mission was caused by American pressures on the Greek government to lower the circulation of currency by 250 billion drachmas (approximately $16.6 million). This, he felt, would have

12. "Commentary by Stefanos Sarafis," *Auge*, 5 October 1952, p. 1.
13. "The Only Solution" (Editorial), *Eleftheria*, 17 August 1952, p. 1.
14. Ibid.
15. "Statement of Kartalis to Parliament," *Eleftheria*, 21 August 1952, p. 1.

led to suffocating effects on the Greek economy and the American advice had to be refused.[16] The Center parties admitted, following the Kartalis speech, that "basic disagreements" existed between Greece and the United States because the latter had reduced Greek economic development to a position of secondary importance, judging from its insistence on strictly anti-inflationary policies coupled with decreases in aid and continuation of the "staggering" defense costs.[17]

"Conservative" Synaghermos, a tag which members of that party would not accept judging from their statements of that period, became the chief target of the faltering Center government. Synaghermites were attacked for abandoning policies that were "strictly in the national interest," such as the reduction of military expenditures, in order to promote party interests. This they managed by adopting the "traitorous" approach of always offering the most favorable terms to the Americans or NATO in order to enjoy their support and influence.[18]

THE CONSERVATIVE VIEWS   The Synaghermos press, on the other hand, made no bones of the "fact" that its movement represented the best and healthiest elements in the Greek political world and could alone afford Greece the stable, strong government so badly needed. The Synaghermites claimed that they enjoyed indirectly the confidence and the support of the United States, which was interested in the best deal for the Greek people in terms of not only national security within the free world but also economic development and progress. This support, according to Synaghermos, was repeatedly demonstrated by American recommendations for immediate elections with the single-member district system.[19]

The conservatives accused the Center government of slipping into a "leftist" and "Bevanist" position of anti-American policies clearly contrary to the interests of Greece. Such was, for example, the "black-

16. Ibid.
17. "Basic Disagreements with the Americans," *Eleftheria*, 24 August 1952, p. 1.
18. "Non-Possumus" (Editorial), *Eleftheria*, 31 August 1952, p. 1.
19. "The United States Officially Declares Support of Immediate General Elections," *Kathimerini*, 20 August 1952, p. 1; "American Opinions Regarding the Political Developments in Greece," *Kathimerini*, 9 September 1952, p. 1.

mailing" policy of the Center government toward the United States whereby, if aid to Greece were reduced, Greek military expenditures would be reduced also.[20] The Greek Center government was said to be agitated by the "correct" and numerous American declarations in favor of speedy elections under a single-member district system, which could alone give Greece a stable and strong government. The Center was chastized for having characterized Peurifoy disapprovingly as the "regulator" of Greek politics, while repeatedly alluding to American interference in Greek domestic affairs which allegedly deprived the nation of its dignity and freedom. The conservatives charged the Center with adopting a purely anti-American policy in attempting to reduce the size of the armed forces.[21] Finally, it was asserted that the Center parties' design to promote instability and anarchy in Greece by returning to a simple proportional election system atrophied primarily because of American pressures; that is, a threat of decreased aid was used by the Americans as a regulatory valve to convince the Center elements to abandon support for the simple proportional system.[22]

Sampling the literature and the opinion of the three major political movements, it appears that each presented the "facts" in such a way as to support its basic political objectives. The conservative Synaghermos, feeling the dynamism of youth, maintained that it represented the best, healthiest, ablest, and most patriotic elements in the country, which supported progressive political approaches and were disenchanted with the political squabblings of the 1910–39 period. The Synaghermites felt that only they could give Greece a strong, stable government which would enjoy international respect and secure greater amounts of American aid. Synaghermos made it a

20. "Government Cultivates Anti-American Spirit," *Kathimerini*, 24 August 1952, p. 1. Interestingly enough, once Synaghermos was installed in power it adopted a similar policy of making a direct link between the size of Greek military expenditures and the size of foreign aid.

21. "The Government Is Agitated Following the Comments of the American Ambassador Recommending Speedy Elections," *Kathimerini*, 21 August 1952, p. 1. The allusion to status quo on the size of armed forces was obviously an appeal to overall United States objectives.

22. "Peurifoy's Step Upsets the Plotters' Plans Which Favored the 'Simple Proportional,'" *Kathimerini*, 12 September 1952, p. 1.

point to advertise as often as possible that it enjoyed American confidence and backing. Center accusations to the effect that Synaghermos was "underbidding" the Center in order to gain American backing were discarded as frustrated attempts to show United States favoritism toward Synaghermos, when in reality the United States was only making objective observations seeking to protect the best interests of Greece in terms of national security and economic development.

The Center parties manning the government had the dual problem of answering Communist and conservative allegations and accusations, and also paying the excessively high bills of running the government's program. If they proposed reduction in the ceiling of military expenditures they ran up against allied dissatisfaction and Synaghermite criticism; if they kept up military expenditures, they precipitated economic deficits and attracted Communist criticism. For their part, the Communists used every means possible to discredit the American presence in Greece, trying to convince the public that the Americans had taken over all responsibilities from the Greek government and were running the country to suit their own, rather than Greece's, interests.

The Plasteras–Venizelos government, bent by many pressures and criticisms, coupled with economic problems and a tendency of some of its supporters to "defect" to Synaghermos, resigned on 10 October 1952. It would be very hard to assess the degree to which American pressures accounted for this resignation. There is no question, however, from the account of events, that there was a measure of direct American and indirect NATO influence over the direction and outcome of Greek political developments in 1952. This influence was in favor of establishing political stability in Greece and adopting the single-member district election system which, as it happened, facilitated the rise of Synaghermos to power.

Massive aid [23] appears to have been the major incentive or instru-

23. The all-pervasive importance of American aid is very vividly illustrated in the words of Venizelos (then Prime Minister of Greece) who said: "on the handling of this matter [aid] depends the future of the country and the *survival* of the Greek people." *Vema*, 4 September 1951, p. 6 (emphasis supplied). Ambassador Peurifoy underlined dramatically the effect of American aid to Greece in "Message to the Greek People," *Vema*, 23 December 1951, p. 1.

ment through which the United States managed to generate the desired responses on the part of the Greek government. It could be suggested, therefore, that the effectiveness of American influence in Greece varied with the amount of aid which was extended at a given period.

Chapter Six
The Elections of 1952:
The Ascendancy of "Conservatism"

General elections using the single-member district system were conducted on 16 November 1952. The results gave Synaghermos the opportunity to form a government which enjoyed parliamentary support unprecedented in twentieth-century Greek history, with the exception of the almost absolute Conservative victory in the election of 9 June 1935.[1] Synaghermos secured 49.2 per cent of the popular vote, which meant 247 out of 300 (or 82.3 per cent) seats in Parliament.[2] This was one of the bonus effects of the much contested single-member district system. The election results were not contested by the Center parties; the Greek people had obviously given a clear-cut mandate to the Papagos movement to shoulder the extremely difficult task of governing Greece.

The Campaign and Election

Throughout the 1952 election campaigns, the nature of Greek-American relations continued to be a major foreign policy issue. NATO participation was treated by most candidates as a concomitant of Greek-American association. Synaghermos, under the leadership of Marshal Papagos, heralded a platform stressing Greece's need of a solid, strong government which alone could revive international respect for the Greek nation. Greece, under Synaghermos, would act in accordance with her United Nations and NATO obligations. Friendship

1. The Liberal party had abstained from this election, however.
2. For complete election results and statistics of twentieth-century Greek elections see Gregorios Dafnis, *The Greek Political Parties: 1821–1961*, pp. 179–90.

with Yugoslavia and Turkey would be promoted. The hard line toward Communists would be continued in order to prevent them from regrouping and possibly attempting to overthrow the nationalist Greek government. Finally, the Synaghermites claimed that unless Papagos was elected the United States would seriously reduce its aid to Greece, and Greek effectiveness in NATO would suffer.[3]

The Center parties considered as utterly absurd Synaghermos' claims that Greece's position in NATO would weaken without a Papagos government. They pointed out that entry into NATO had been clearly initiated and attained by a Center government.[4]

The leaders of the Center parties generally conducted a vigorous campaign and frequently addressed themselves to aspects of foreign policy.[5] They stressed the fact that thanks to the efforts of the Center governments, Greece was for the first time in her modern history enjoying external security. NATO was characterized as the best shield against the threat of international Communist infiltration. The Center leaders also reaffirmed Eleftherios Venizelos' time-honored policies of friendship toward Turkey and Yugoslavia and pointed out that excellent progress had been made in Greek relations with those two countries as well as with another neighbor and ex-enemy—Italy.

The leftist EDA stood for a policy of equal friendship toward all nations and peaceful political and economic relations with all (World War II) allies. EDA leaders accused both the Center and Synaghermos of having become foreign "lackeys," by attaching themselves to the United States and precipitating economically ruinous military expenditures.[6] They felt that Greece's participation in NATO had been predicated on the fabrication of the so-called Soviet threat primarily to maintain the oligarchic status quo in Greece.

EDA later attributed the outcome of the 1952 election to American

3. "Campaign Speech Delivered by Marshal Papagos to the People of Thessaloniki," *Vema*, 8 November 1952, p. 1; "Speech by E. Tsouderos at Crete," *Vema*, 11 November 1952, p. 6 (Tsouderos had "defected" from EPEK); "Report on Tsouderos' Radio Speech to the Greek People," *Eleftheria*, 5 November 1952, p. 4.

4. "Report on Stephanopoulos' Radio Speech to the Greek People," *Eleftheria*, 24 October 1952, p. 1.

5. "Pre-election Speech by General Nicholas Plasteras to the People of Thessaloniki," *Eleftheria*, 11 November 1952, p. 3; "Speech by S. Venizelos in Athens," *Eleftheria*, 15 November 1952, p. 5.

6. E.g. "Speech by Passalides in Thessaloniki," *Auge*, 11 November 1952, p. 1.

pressures and manipulations. It was argued, for example, that Plasteras had been forced by Ambassador Peurifoy not to accept EDA's offers of political cooperation under any circumstances, thus preventing the only effective competition with Papagos under a single-member district system. This point was allegedly admitted by Plasteras himself to the EDA leaders, John Passalides and General Stefanos Sarafis, when they approached Plasteras to seek his cooperation. He was quoted as having said that "his hands had been tied as a result of American pressures." [7]

EDA argued that the adoption of the single-member district system, which gave Papagos 49 per cent of the vote and three fourths of the seats in Parliament, served as the single most important method through which the United States influenced the political outcome of the 1952 elections in Greece. The result was that so-called national democratic governments, whether of the Center or of the Right, had brought about a miserable state of affairs for Greece, reducing her to a position of greater dependence than even that of bona fide colonies.[8]

It is interesting to note that the conservative Synaghermite press, in an effort to discredit the Center parties and especially Plasteras' EPEK, supported EDA's allegations regarding American pressures upon Plasteras' course of political action. For example, *Kathimerini* claimed that Plasteras resorted to a "secret deal" for election cooperation with the Communists (EDA), because American pressures against any alignment with crypto-Communists prevented him from cooperating openly.[9] The following quotation from an anti-Center, conservative editorial of the same paper seems to assume that American intervention in Greek affairs was a fact (in agreement with the Communist position), but a fact which was justified (contrary to the Communist position): "Why don't they [the Americans] interfere elsewhere and they interfere only here [Greece], why have they sent here multitudes of specialists and elsewhere they have sent five to ten?" [10] The same

---

7. "Elections of November 1952," *Auge*, 4 March 1956, p. 3.

8. "The Americans in Greece," *Auge*, 30 March 1956, p. 3. For the detailed EDA pre-election position, see "Speech by Passalides in Thessaloniki," *Auge*, 11 November 1952, p. 1, and supra, pp. 63–64.

9. "The United Parties Attempt to Hide Their Agreement with the Communists," *Kathimerini*, 29 October 1952, p. 1; "EPEK–Communist Cooperation," *Kathimerini*, 30 October 1952, p. 1.

10. "The Account," (Editorial), *Kathimerini*, 12 October 1952, p. 1.

editor answered this rhetorical question by saying that elsewhere the United States was dealing with organized governments with which rational communication was possible, while in Greece there was only chaos.

The student of events surrounding the elections of 1952 can only conclude that, despite interparty polemics, distortion of facts, and allegations, the American presence in Greece and the concomitant NATO accession had a significant and identifiable effect upon the course of action pursued by Greek political leaders during that period. American aid was once more in the forefront of political considerations. The voters were generally quite sensitive to any argument revolving around the magnitude and type of American aid, and Synaghermos exploited this sensitivity effectively. The analysis of Synaghermos' election campaign indicates that one of its chief selling points was its claim that, if installed in power, it could secure a larger portion of aid from the United States and NATO than could the Center's coalition parties.

The Conservative Program

Papagos formed his cabinet soon after the elections of 16 November and proceeded quickly with the task of administering his program. His government quickly became involved in two important, though hardly new, foreign policy issues: the size of defense spending and the question of alleged American interference in Greek internal affairs. Both issues were directly or indirectly related to the amount and type of American or NATO aid to Greece.

On 17 December 1952, Papagos read his government's program to the 300 members of the newly elected Parliament.[11] In the field of foreign policy he stressed such objectives as the perpetuation of peace through United Nations and NATO participation; Greek-Turkish friendship and cooperation in all functions so as to guarantee mutual security; efforts to cultivate better relations with Yugoslavia; a non-aggression policy toward Albania and attempts to solve the border

11. "Papagos' Presentation of Synaghermos Government's Program to Parliament," *Journal of Parliamentary Debates* (Athens, 17 December 1952), A, p. 10; see also "Statement to Press by S. Stephanopoulos (Minister of Foreign Affairs)," *Vema*, 22 November 1952, p. 4.

dispute; traditional friendship toward the Middle Eastern nations; realistic treatment of the Cyprus issue, considered basic to the lives of all Greeks;[12] closer friendship and cooperation with Italy and Western Germany; cooperation with France, Britain, and especially the United States, which should serve as the axis of Greek foreign policy; attempts to solve ethnic territorial problems through the United Nations and to support this organization wholeheartedly; deep understanding of obligations within NATO; and maintenance of the current strength of the military forces with the understanding that allied assistance in defense would be forthcoming when needed.

The Conservative position on defense spending, as expressed in its program declaration, changed considerably compared to what it had been throughout the previous year and the election campaign. Before the election, it was clear that Synaghermos supported a policy of maintaining the status quo on defense spending regardless of American aid fluctuations.[13] Papagos' post-election program, however, adopted a previously condemned position, asserting that the maintenance of a strong military establishment was directly dependent on foreign aid and assistance.[14] A probable explanation for this was that once Synaghermos came to power, Papagos realized that defense spending was indeed highly dependent on foreign economic infusions.

The Center parties, now in the role of the opposition, stated that they would not follow the Synaghermos policy of the "underbidder," running to the American Embassy and using it as a center of the opposition's anti-administration plots and machinations. The Center opposition pledged not to fabricate attractive foreign policy positions simply to gain American succor in its efforts to displace the ruling

12. Interestingly enough the Papagos government was the first Greek government to include the Cyprus issue in official program declarations. It is noteworthy because this party was later accused by both the Center and the Left of soft-pedaling the Cyprus issue in order to appease NATO partners. The Cyprus issue was to plague the Greek membership in NATO to the point of rupture, until its "settlement" in 1959.

13. "Speech by Papagos in Thessaloniki," *Kathimerini*, 8 November 1952, p. 1; "The Accounting" (Editorial), *Kathimerini*, 12 October 1952, p. 1.

14. The wording of Papagos' program on defense spending is closely akin to the Synaghermos-condemned Center position; Papagos said that Greece's "capabilities to continue contributing substantially in the future to the defensive effort are related by fate to the level of aid provided." See "Papagos' Presentation of Synaghermos Government Program to Parliament," *Journal of Parliamentary Debates*, 17 December 1952, p. 10.

party.[15] It accused the Synaghermos government, further, of continuing a policy of underbidding other NATO member governments in order to gain additional American support, often adopting to this end policies harmful to Greek interests; for example, the maintenance of the status quo on defense costs regardless of aid fluctuations.[16] John Zigdis, a spokesman of the Center parties, voiced great concern over excessive military expenditures in the following characteristic advice to Synaghermos: "Beware lest, under the vision of a deceptive military force, you lead Greece to economic collapse and her army together with her." [17] The Center formula prescribed that military expenditures should vary directly with aid supplied.[18] As a consequence, reports that the new defense minister, Panayotis Kanellopoulos, had made pledges at the Paris NATO conference to continue Greek military expenditures regardless of aid fluctuations were viewed with great alarm.[19] Finally, in the issue of American interference in Greek governmental functions, the Center cast aspersions on the Synaghermites for being told what to do by "foreign" elements. Venizelos, for example, in a speech delivered to Parliament on 18 December, stated that "outside forces acted decidedly in the selection of ministers." [20]

In summation, the positions of the three major political movements during the election period of 1952 were along the following lines. The Left was opposed to NATO participation and Greek–American cooperation because this policy would obligate Greece to continue large expenditures on military projects, thus stifling the rate of the nation's economic development. Also, the Left felt that NATO participation reduced Greece to a subcolonial status under NATO and especially the United States. Additionally, the Leftist opposition maintained that membership in the aggressive NATO alliance prevented normalization

15. "The Opposition Will Not Underbid," *Eleftheria*, 25 November 1952, p. 1.
16. "The Government Makes the Lowest Bid to NATO," *Eleftheria*, 16 December 1952, p. 1; also in the same issue, "Shameful Underbidders" (Editorial), p. 1.
17. John Zigdis, *Journal of Parliamentary Debates*, 18 December 1952, p. 17.
18. S. Papapolites, ibid., p. 25.
19. S. Allamanis, ibid., pp. 17–21.
20. S. Venizelos, ibid., p. 13. The term "outside forces" was not qualified as to whether it referred to elements outside the Greek government or outside the Greek state.

of relations with Greece's northern neighbors. Ironically enough, "bad relations with these neighbors" were used as the pretext for justifying large defensive expenditures against the alleged threat of northern "democratic" nations.

The Synaghermos position was firmly pro-Western and decidedly anti-Communist. Communism, it was argued, had threatened the existence of Greece as an independent nation and precautionary measures should be taken to prevent a future and perhaps more dangerous reemergence and attempt to seize power. Synaghermites believed that cooperation with the United States and active membership in NATO afforded Greece unprecedented guarantees against Communist incursions. As a result, the size and the excellent quality of the armed forces should be perpetuated not only to restore the wavering prestige of postwar Greece, but also to protect her from Bulgarian and Albanian, Soviet-supported designs, as well as to contribute to the defensive effort for free world security. It was the feeling of the Synaghermite leadership that Greece belonged culturally as well as ideologically to the ranks of the Western democracies. Thus Greece's membership in NATO was not interpreted merely as a policy of cold national interest, but also as one of moral and ideological compulsion.

The Center parties' position was basically in agreement with that of the conservative Right movement. Any differences could be attributed to, at most, variations in emphasis. The Center parties had initiated and seen through the policy of Western orientation and NATO participation. However, they manifested greater reluctance to continue excessive defense spending unless aided proportionately by the United States or other strong NATO allies, either individually or in concert. The Right–Center differences over defense spending were much more pronounced before the 1952 elections than after, when the position of the Synaghermos group seems to have converged with that of the Center. One explanation, purely in the realm of speculation, could be that Synaghermos made a pitch for a powerful defense establishment (regardless of aid considerations) in order to gain American and NATO backing and sympathies during the pre-election period. Once in power, however, it held, as the preceding Center government had done, that Greek defensive readiness was directly related to the amount of aid. If any other differences in the foreign policy positions of the Center versus the Right were discernible, it was in the attitude toward local and international communism. The Center parties tended to be more flexible and less severe toward communism than was the case with the Synaghermites.

In 1952, the first year of Greek participation in NATO, the alliance's influence on Greek politics was generally manifested indirectly through the medium of the American spokesman. The detailed effects on the organization, allocation, and procedures of the Greek military —which were probably considerable—are outside the direct scope of this study. The conservative election campaign strongly publicized, through its press organs, NATO member-nation views to the effect that Greece needed a strong and homogeneous government which, according to most reports, could be attained only through the single-member district election system. Synaghermos argued that only it was capable, as well as sufficiently cohesive, to give Greece such a government.

Chapter Seven
Reaction to the Installation of
American Bases in Greece

Military Agreement between Greece and the United States

On 12 October 1953 the Greek government announced the conclusion of a bilateral agreement with the government of the United
States concerning the use of Greek territory by American military
forces. This agreement, which was hailed by Prime Minister Papagos
as a historic modern Greek milestone, contained the following key
provisions:[1]

1. The United States was authorized to utilize such roads, railways,
and areas, and to construct, develop, use, and operate such military
and supporting facilities in Greece as appropriate authorities of the
two governments should from time to time agree to be necessary for
the implementation or furtherance of approved NATO plans.

2. The government of the United States was authorized to trans-
port, install, and quarter American personnel in Greece. American
armed forces and their equipment could enter, exit, circulate, or use
the land and air space in Greece and her territorial waters in accordance with provisions specified in technical agreements made by
appropriate authorities of both nations. American activities would be
exempted from any imposition of charges, duties, or taxation. Rates
charged for services rendered to American forces would not be higher
than those charged to the Greek armed forces.

1. "Agreement Between the United States of America and the Kingdom of
Greece Concerning Military Facilities," *United States Treaties and Other International Agreements 1953*, p. 2189. This agreement, related documents, and subsequent revisions are contained in Appendix C.

3. Machines, parts, and other supplies imported for the benefit of American forces in Greece or related to development of American bases there would be free of dues, taxes, custom duties, and inspection.

4. The United States could remove facilities or equipment installed in Greece under the terms of the agreement.

5. It was understood that the Greek government would compensate the United States for facilities or equipment not removed from Greece.

6. The American forces (military and civilian) and their families enjoyed the right of extraterritoriality.[2]

The immediate reaction in Greece to the terms of this agreement was swift as well as varied. General Papagos, representing the government and Synaghermos, termed the agreement beneficial to Greece in many ways. Closer cooperation and understanding with the United States would be guaranteed and Greek security would be enhanced more than ever.[3] Foreign Minister Stephanopoulos rejoiced because this great event would dispel all doubt regarding Greece's inclusion in NATO's defensive plans and would benefit Greece economically (since Greek labor would be employed in the development of American-financed facilities). Stephanopoulos asserted that the terms were

2. The term "extraterritoriality" was not mentioned in the text of the agreement. However, Article III enforces the following two documents which granted a very comprehensive type of extraterritoriality to American personnel in Greece:

(a) Article 1, Paragraphs 3a and 3b of the Greek Legislative Decree 694 of 7 May 1948. This Decree provides for extraterritorial "immunity from the jurisdiction of the Greek Civil and Criminal Courts" (Para. 3a), and exemption from all direct and indirect taxation (Para. 3b) for the members of the American Mission and their families.

(b) Memorandum of Understanding between the Governments of Greece and the United States of 4 February 1953. This Memorandum provides for extraterritoriality of U. S. property in Greece.

Appendix C includes the memorandum and its related documents, as well as a translation of Article 1, Paras. 3a and 3b of Legislative Decree 694. The agreement was revised on 7 September 1956, to delete all reference to the aforementioned Legislative Decree and apply provisions similar to the NATO status of forces agreements which were concluded in 1951. Thus, after September 1956, U. S. personnel no longer enjoyed extraterritorial rights in Greece. Appendix D contains the text of the revised Greece–United States status of forces agreement of 7 September 1956.

3. "Statements of Prime Minister Papagos and Foreign Minister Stephanopoulos on Agreement," *Vema*, 13 October 1953, p. 6; also "Papagos, Stephanopoulos on Agreement," *Kathimerini*, 13 October 1953, p. 1.

similar to those in agreements reached between the United States and France or England.[4] He stressed, further, that this agreement would neutralize Bulgarian arms superiority and enhance the defensive capability of Greece.

The military analysts forecast the effects of the agreement as excellent.[5] The American air force would be free now to support Greek tactical missions. The allies (United States), in demonstrating their determination to maintain a defensive stand on the northern frontiers of Greece, would be significantly strengthening the security of the beleaguered populations of northern Greece. Greece would no longer be abandoned to its fate in case of attack, as would have been the case prior to the Korean War and Western rearmament.

The overall Center position was one of caution mixed with partial disagreement. The Liberal and EPEK parties were chagrined at the "improper" manner in which the government concluded this agreement. The method of adopting this agreement was as follows: On 12 October, while the King was absent and the Parliament was not in session, the government, acting with lightning speed and without consulting or informing the opposition, announced the momentous agreement and then proceeded to call a ministerial meeting on an emergency basis which granted ratification to the measure in the absence of the King and the Parliament.

The various Center parties did not react identically. The Liberal party's approval was granted with relatively mild reservations on the matter of nonconsultation of the opposition and on the terms of the agreement, which were not considered as favorable for Greece as perhaps could have been obtained.[6]

EPEK, on the other hand, through its press, registered serious dissatisfaction with many of the terms of the agreement.[7] Both EPEK and the Liberals concentrated their criticism on its terms and provisions rather than on the wisdom or the concept of a Greek-American defensive pact. The agreement, it was argued, could create

4. Ibid. This of course was not the case with regard to the status of forces. U. S. forces did not enjoy extraterritoriality in France or England.
5. A. Merenditis, "The Cession of Bases to the United States," *Vema*, 14 October 1953, p. 1.
6. "Statement of Papandreou to the Parliamentary Committee on Authorizations," *Vema*, 23 October 1953, p. 4.
7. "The Agreement," (Editorial), *Eleftheria*, 14 October 1953, p. 1.

additional military obligations for Greece and the current obligations were deemed already excessive. A number of its provisions were considered detrimental to Greece's national dignity: e.g. the exemption from inspection of incoming and outgoing American personnel and equipment.[8]

There were other points where Liberal and EPEK views coincided. For example, both parties referred to Norway and Denmark which, while full-fledged members of NATO, had rejected similar American proposals for the cession of bases. They felt that Greece could have followed the same road. Then, there were such objectionable provisions as the one providing that the United States would be compensated by the Greek government for American facilities that were not removed from Greece once they were no longer needed. The granting of extraterritorial rights to American personnel was also resented. These rights were not granted to the Americans in similar agreements with Britain and France, so why in Greece? EPEK and Liberals both speculated that the extent to which Greek security would be enhanced could not be assessed before the location of American bases was revealed. For example, it was argued that if the bases were wholly insular, 80 per cent of the Greek population living on the mainland would not be afforded equal protection. Both parties questioned the timing of the agreement. Greece, instead of seeking needed economic assistance from the United States, was accepting military bases—especially during a period when an atmosphere of international détente was prevailing in the Balkans.

EPEK, to a greater extent than the Liberals, accused Synaghermos of scorning the interests of Greece and, for parochial political considerations alone, following a policy of international underbidding, always anxious to offer the best terms to the Americans without bargaining. EPEK's reaction, but not necessarily that of the Liberals, definitely indicated that the overall agreement infringed on Greek sovereign rights.[9]

Contrary to the opposition's assertions, the Conservatives stated that bases were not ceded but voluntarily given by Greece to the United States in order to promote Greek interests. The Conservative

8. "The Opposition Approves," Vema, 14 October 1953, p. 4.
9. "EPEK's Announcement on Agreement," Eleftheria, 15 October 1953, p. 6.

press argued that if some of the terms of the agreement appeared to make exceedingly generous concessions to the United States, these should be understood as necessary for the sake of "unity of the defensive effort." [10] Regarding the opposition's comments that the agreement was not in harmony with the "prevailing spirit of international détente" at that time, the Conservative position was that not words and promises but acts constituted détente. Neither the Soviet Union nor Bulgaria (the latter of immediate concern to Greece) had reduced its massive military establishment.[11]

A week after its announcement, the Greek-American pact was brought to the Parliamentary Committee on Authorizations for approval and enactment into law. The measure secured the approval of the Committee, which was comprised primarily of Synaghermos members. The reaction of the noncommunist opposition in committee debates illustrated significant differences of approach. Three Center parties, in addition to EDA, voted against ratification of the agreement.[12]

CENTER CRITICISM   All opposition parties disagreed with the "unconstitutional" procedure which was followed in the rapid ratification of the agreement. All the Center parties' leaders attacked some of the terms of the agreement.[13] The difference in approach lay in the fact that some leaders (e.g. Papandreou and Venizelos), although cautious of certain terms, endorsed the agreement in the interest of Greece's national defense, while others (e.g. Stelios Allamanis and Savas Papapolites) boycotted it, because they thought that the terms were unbearable and that NATO participation was enough guarantee for Greece's national defense.

10. "The Meaning of the Agreement," *Kathimerini*, 14 October 1953, p. 1.
11. "Stephanopoulos Answers Rentis on Agreement," *Vema*, 16 October 1953, p. 4.
12. Namely Papapolites' (EPEK), Allamanis' (Democratic Party), and Akritas' (Progressive Union). The first two parties are basic elements of the Greek Center Union Party which was founded in 1961, while Akritas was Deputy Minister of Education in the Center Union's government. (Akritas is now deceased.)
13. *Official Minutes of the Special Parliamentary Committee on Authorizations* (28 August 1953–29 October 1953; hereafter referred to as *Authorization Committee Minutes*) (Athens, 1954); K. Mitsotakis, p. 1358; E. Baklatzis, p. 1360; G. Papandreou, p. 1367; S. Allamanis, p. 1367; J. Zigdis, p. 1370.

Konstantinos Mitsotakis, one of the key spokesmen of the Liberal party, complained bitterly that the opposition was not informed of details of the agreement, thus being robbed of the opportunity to evaluate it properly.[14] He pointed out that Judiciary Order 694/1948,[15] which was included in the terms of the agreement, deprived Greek courts of jurisdiction over misdemeanors and criminal acts perpetrated by American personnel in Greece. Mitsotakis could not accept such concessions, in light of the fact that Greece was offering as many divisions to NATO as all the Western European allies combined.[16]

Emanuel Baklatzis, representing the EPEK point of view, shared Mitsotakis' criticisms. In addition, he pointed out that the sudden acceptance and the secret preparation of the agreement were unwise. Public opinion in Greece and abroad should have been prepared. The procedure followed created, undoubtedly, a "war preparation psychosis" among the East–West adversaries. Baklatzis also suggested that extraterritoriality should have been limited to the areas within American military installations.[17]

George Papandreou, who was later to become the number one man of the unified Center movement, favored the spirit of the agreement, seeing in it not provocation but prudent organization for defense which was the best guarantor of peace.[18] But he pointed out that the government had kept the opposition in thorough darkness as to the details of the agreement. He feared, therefore, that since the government was unwilling to compare the Greek-American treaty with similar treaties concluded by the United States and other NATO nations, Greece had suffered the imposition of unfavorable terms. Papandreou, notwithstanding his approval of the treaty, stated that if terms such as extraterritoriality, or compensation by the host nation, were special provisions for Greece and did not apply to other NATO nations, then it would be a mistake for Greece to accept and for the United States to impose these terms. This attitude was quite indicative of the apparent ignorance of Greek parliamentarians as

14. This attitude was shared by most Center spokesmen.
15. See Appendix C for a translation of the pertinent portions of this decree.
16. K. Mitsotakis, *Authorization Committee Minutes*, p. 1359.
17. E. Baklatzis, ibid., p. 1361.
18. G. Papandreou, ibid., p. 1366.

to the terms of treaties existing between the United States and Britain or France.[19]

Stelios Allamanis, the head of the Democratic party, was one of the sharpest critics of the Greek-American pact. His opening statement in Parliament clearly implied that the function of conducting an independent foreign policy had been taken away from Greece in the early postwar years.

> Dear Deputies, for the first time in this assembly, at least in the post-liberation period, the foreign policy of our country is being discussed.

> Indeed, due to the abnormal conditions and the extraordinary economic hardships of our country her foreign policy has been, during the recent years, *in absolute consonance* with those great powers which had assumed the responsibility of her economic support.[20]

Allamanis, desirous of seeing more initiative in Greek foreign policy, repeated most of the criticisms made by other Center parties' leaders. He justified his opposition to the treaty by pointing up the additional military costs which would be required for coverage and ground support of the proposed American military installations. He also warned that the agreement would take all initiative away from Greek foreign policy makers. He felt, for example, that the linkage of a small nation such as Greece to a superpower such as the United States would automatically reserve the decision-making control for the superpower. In addition, Allamanis feared that the association would often call for American concurrence on subjects of a purely internal nature. So the head of the Democratic party concluded that, although he was devoted to a purely defensive policy within NATO, he could not accept the terms of the agreement in question.

Another Liberal party critic of the pact, John Zigdis, pointed out some additional shortcomings. He felt that the agreement in question

19. No one, whether from the government or opposition, during the Committee's ratification debates had demonstrated any knowledge of the contents of comparable treaties between the United States and Western European nations.

20. S. Allamanis, *Authorization Committee Minutes*, p. 1367 (emphasis supplied).

gave excessive leeway to military and technical staffs by permitting them to negotiate most of the specific provisions and working steps. The danger was therefore great that, following negotiations among technicians, the government would be presented with a fait accompli which would be hard to reject.[21] Zigdis, prompted by the unequal terms of the agreement, noted that small nations hurt themselves in dealing with the big powers if their attitude was "this is my house, come in and do what you please." Had the Americans been confronted with more firmness they would not have insisted on special privileges, such as extraterritoriality, which could only poison good relations between Greece and the United States.

As a whole, the Center's criticism of the Greek-American pact was similar to the earlier Tsaldaris criticism of the NATO treaty ratification.[22] Both argued that although the treaties in question were good, much better terms for Greece could have been secured. Generally the Center parties were not averse to the concept of close Greek-American cooperation, but they thought that it could be secured at less exacting terms.[23]

CONSERVATIVE PRAISE   The Conservative counterarguments did not satisfy all the inquiries of the Center critics. The greatest blessing of the agreement, according to Panayotis Kanellopoulos,[24] Synaghermos' Defense Minister, against which all possible disadvantages should be weighed was that Greece's security would be "guaranteed." There would be no doubt any longer as to whether Greece would be defended if attacked. Kanellopoulos felt that the pact was a "reward" for Greece's faithful fulfillment of its obligations within NATO. The Greek-American pact, supplemented with a Balkan pact,[25] would

21. J. Zigdis, ibid., p. 1371.
22. See supra, pp. 48–49.
23. Also, it should be pointed out that the heterogeneity of viewpoint of Center leaders, such as Allamanis vis-à-vis Papandreou, should be kept in mind, considering that they are today members of the "homogeneous" Center Union party. The nature of such heterogeneous membership portends centrifugal tendencies in the foreign policy positions of this party.
24. P. Kanellopoulos, *Authorization Committee Minutes*, pp. 1353, 1365.
25. The Balkan Alliance was signed at Bled, Yugoslavia, on 9 August 1954. It was a military and political alliance binding Yugoslavia with Greece and Turkey. Although it has atrophied in recent years, it has not been abrogated. For more details on this subject see infra, pp. 93–94.

cement quite firmly the defense of NATO's Southern European front.

The Conservative counterargument to criticism over the possible repercussions of secret provisions in the agreement was to remind the critics that in accordance with Article 33 of the Greek Constitution secret provisions of a treaty could never reverse the publicly proclaimed ones.[26] The allegations that the agreement was concluded in a time of international détente were met with statements asserting that a policy of détente was a tactical phase in the Communist attack against capitalism, which was not backed by deeds but only by pious wishes for public consumption. The peaceful Communist overtures were dismissed as simply designed to confuse and undermine the defensive readiness of the Western world.[27]

Kanellopoulos, in defending the treaty and explaining its provisions on extraterritoriality, said that "it was necessary for reasons connected with *the greatest national expediency* to grant the right of extraterritoriality." [28] The Defense Minister refused to compare the Greek-American agreement with like agreements between the United States and Britain or France; Greece, he believed, should not be expected to predicate her policies toward the United States on those of other Western allies.

Foreign Minister Stephanopoulos[29] projected the pact as an integral part of Greece's membership in NATO.[30] Stephanopoulos argued that those who were opposed to the agreement should also be opposed to Greece's continued membership in NATO, since the two were closely interrelated. Then he made the startling announcement that if Greece refused to ratify the agreement, she would be expelled from NATO. Perhaps Stephanopoulos can explain the motive of this announcement, but it is clear that there is no provision in the NATO treaty which either forbids or requires a member to enter into bilateral agreements.[31] Summing up the Conservative argument, it appears that their chief

26. Konstantinos Vovolinis, *Authorization Committee Minutes*, p. 1355.
27. Ibid., p. 1356; also P. Kanellopoulos, ibid., p. 1363.
28. Ibid., P. Kanellopoulos, p. 1365.
29. Stefanos Stephanopoulos is one of the leading members of the Center Union today.
30. S. Stephanopoulos in *Journal of Parliamentary Debates*, Athens, 25 November 1953, p. 62.
31. Article 8 of the NATO treaty provides that member nations will not conclude any other treaties which are "in conflict" with the NATO treaty.

justification for conclusion of the agreement was the expected reinforcement of Greece's defense and security.

LEFTIST CONDEMNATION   The Leftist reaction again followed the
habitual anti-American pattern. EDA condemned the actions of the
Greek government leading to this agreement which permanently
committed Greece's foreign policy to unilateral action and robbed
it of all flexibility. The Leftists asserted that ceding bases to
the United States would destroy the last remaining vestiges of Greek
national independence. A foreign power was being granted co-sover-
eign rights in Greece. They did not accept the stoic rationalization
of the Synaghermos government that dependence was an imperative
of modern times. They questioned the alleged economic benefits for
Greece and saw only economic liabilities as a result of this agreement.[32]

They emphasized that American bases in Greece would be used
by strategic rather than tactical elements of the United States Air
Force, which would be offensive in nature and could expose Greece
to retaliatory nuclear holocaust. They accused elements of the Center's opposition of approving the agreement over very mild and mar-
ginal criticism. EDA's leader, John Passalides, reacted to the agreement
with fear, suspicion, and disgust.[33] He noted with bitterness that,
"contrary to colonial nations that were fighting to remove foreign
domination, the government of Synaghermos was turning the Greek
nation into a virtual colony. Instead of contributing to the promotion
of world peace it was ceding naval and air bases and turning Greece
into a war base for the United States." EDA, Passalides continued, was
the only group which had voted against Greek entry into NATO at
the Greek Parliament. Synaghermos and the Center parties were
equally responsible for pursuing a policy of subservience, first by joining NATO and then playing host to American bases.

A position very similar to that of EDA with regard to the agreement
was adopted by spokesmen of the Progressive Union, a small party
organized under the aegis of Loukis Akritas. He felt that the conclu-

32. "The Meaning of the Pact," *Auge*, 14 October 1953, p. 1; "Signing of
Greek-American Agreement Ceding Bases to the United States," *Auge*, 13 March
1956, p. 2.
33. "The Americans in Greece," *Auge*, 14 March 1956, pp. 3–4.

sion of the Greek-American agreement meant "utter abandonment of Greek independence" [34] and transfer of sovereignty from Greece to the United States.

To the average noncommunist Greek, the installation of American bases on Greek soil presented a dilemma and required some compromises. One alternative was to "go it alone," which would guarantee, in theory at least, a clear field of independence in foreign policy and especially in domestic policy. At the same time, however, Greece would be exposed to the dangers of internal and external communism without any pledges of support from the Western nations and especially the United States. The other alternative was to accept American and Western aid, in fact to welcome the American operational presence in Greece, which would guarantee Greek territorial integrity from external threats. The price for this protection was that Greece would be committed to an anticommunist policy and would, of necessity, be subject to some guidance and review in her external policies by her stronger, protective Western allies.

The Center and Conservative parties were agreed on the basic policy of Western, anticommunist orientation as shown by their endorsing NATO participation. Well over 80 per cent of the Greek voters supported this position and policy in most postwar Greek elections.[35] Political leaders of Conservative and Center parties chose the alternative of added security and economic assistance coupled with a small loss of sovereignty over what they thought would be the other alternative—namely, a transitional period of weak and independent isolation which would certainly invite Communist penetration and domination. Communist domination in Greece, they believed, would lead to nearly total loss of sovereignty to the Soviet Union which in no way would be commensurate to the minor losses within NATO.

In the post-World War II years, a new idea became increasingly acceptable in Greece, namely that unity in Western defense required international consultation, cooperation, and compromise. These were

34. "Statement by L. Akritas," *Auge*, 15 October 1953, p. 1; "Akritas' Statement," *Vema*, 15 October 1953, p. 6.
35. With the exception of the 1958 election (see Chapter 10 infra, p. 125), in which the Communists secured about 25 per cent of the vote.

postwar realities which should be faced and accepted. Theoretical adherence to policies guaranteeing unrestricted national sovereignty could not be blindly insisted upon. The Greeks were asked, in the interest of collective defense, not be be oversensitive to every minor infraction of pure sovereignty.[36]

Various forms of international community became increasingly acceptable to the Greek public and, in fact, began to replace age-old traditional ideologies which had been narrowly nationalistic for better or worse. Modern Greek youth in the nineteenth and early twentieth centuries had been brought up and nurtured to believe in *Megali Idea*[37]—a dream of regenerating Byzantine Greece and restoring it to its historical dimensions, not only territorially but culturally. Eleftherios Venizelos, a great modern Greek statesman who dominated the country's political destinies, was one of the men who nurtured this idea and one of the first who realistically decided to abandon it after 1923 and Greece's tragic defeat by the Turks in Asia Minor. Venizelos together with Kemal Ataturk began the cultivation of a new policy of Greek-Turkish friendship which meant the death of *Megali Idea* and of its converse applications in Turkey.

The mood of politicians in the post-World War II era, dictated by the times and circumstances, has quite emphatically endorsed the death of *Megali Idea*. The Greeks in search of a new "idea" looked upon supranationalist systems as more feasible and appropriate to the needs of small nations; hence, the great emphasis on and support for the United Nations and other collective organizations such as NATO and more recently the Common Market, of which Greece has become an associate member.

The Communists, who in postwar elections have drawn 10 to 20 per cent[38] of the Greek vote, have had an easy job. Not being

36. George Papandreou speaking in Parliament emphasized this trend as follows: "Since . . . the period of independence has passed, those who think that we can live in the current face of the world with the old understanding of sovereignty are wrong. But as it is certain that the period of independence has passed, it is equally certain that the period of subjugation applies only to the Iron Curtain and not to the free peoples." *Authorization Committee Minutes,* p. 1367. For similar views expressed by General Papagos, see supra, pp. 58–59.

37. *Megali Idea* = The Grand Ideal.

38. This vote is not necessarily all Communist. Often EDA has gained the support of dissatisfied voters who were disenchanted with the disunity and

afforded the arduous task of governing and administering Greece, they could with impunity be severely critical and entirely opposed to all nationalist pro-Western policies. EDA's criticism, while in part correct, lost all aura of responsibility because it failed to recognize that there was any good in any of the policies associated with NATO and Western orientation. By indiscriminately condemning every aspect of pro-Western policies and praising the benefits of Eastern cooperation, EDA was indeed advocating the abandonment of a pro-Western orientation, adoption of a transitional "neutralist" policy, and an ultimate pro-Eastern orientation. In praising the regimes of the "Eastern Democracies" and in not recognizing their status of political dependence on the Soviet Union, EDA was more or less allowing its critics to infer that if it ever came to power, it would allow the Greek nation to assume a "satellite" status.

The crucial question to be asked here was what indeed could be inferred to be in the best interest of the Greek nation? Western orientation, strict neutralism and nonalignment, or Eastern orientation? At least 80 per cent of the Greeks endorsed a Western orientation. This was based on not only cultural affinities but also geopolitical imperatives and economic and military considerations. Noncommunist Greece felt itself threatened by Communist neighbors—Albania and especially Bulgaria—who not only wanted to see communism mature in Greece, but also nursed territorial aspirations for large parts of northern Greece. To remain neutral, or worse still to seek an alliance with those states, appeared to be politically imprudent.

lack of cohesiveness of the Center parties. EDA also has sought to identify itself with a leftist, democratic center, rather than a purely Communist position.

PART III: REACTION

would not commit the Greek nation to acceptance of nuclear weapons prior to securing legislative approval. Generally, Averoff indicated that the whole matter was blown way above its proper proportions by politicians who wanted to make gains by spreading rumors and fears of nuclear destruction among the Greek public.

The Liberal party's position on nuclear bases was enunciated in more definite terms by Sophocles Venizelos in the same series of parliamentary debates.[13] The Liberals maintained that NATO should pursue a policy of "catholicism," i.e. insure that bases were accepted by all member nations rather than a selected few. If certain NATO nations, such as Norway, refused to accept bases on their territories, then Greece should follow suit. If nuclear bases were to be installed in Greece, they should be located on the mainland rather than the islands, thus insuring security for the entire country.[14]

Venizelos also argued that the Karamanlis government, commanding only a minority of Greek votes (a majority of parliamentary seats, however), was not representative enough of the Greek public to enter into an agreement binding Greece on such an important and far-reaching international commitment as the acceptance of nuclear missiles. The Karamanlis government should, therefore, resign, proclaim new elections, and permit a majority, responsible government to negotiate the matter of nuclear bases.[15] An immediate acceptance of bases by the Karamanlis government might be negated by the successor government, reflecting adversely on the international prestige and good faith of Greece; or immediate acceptance of bases could become a cause of civil conflict for the majority of Greeks who were opposed to hosting NATO nuclear bases without gaining certain concessions on the Cyprus issue.

Venizelos concluded by emphasizing the Liberal party's discontent

13. S. Venizelos in ibid., 21 January 1958, pp. 465–69.

14. This illustrates an often-repeated Greek view that the allies, in case of war, will abandon the Greek mainland and only seek to maintain control over certain strategically located Greek islands, especially Crete. This fear is reinforced by Greek experiences during World War II, when the mainland was more or less abandoned to the Germans, while the British made a monumental effort to hold on to the island of Crete.

15. A new dictum, which was often to recur, was being coined here by Venizelos; namely, that participation in NATO or other major international organizations required that Greece should be ruled by a strong, representative government before entering on long-term international agreements.

over the preferential treatment afforded to Turkey, as compared to Greece, by the United States and NATO. Although equal sacrifices were expected of both nations, military aid to Greece was slashed 40 per cent while Turkey's was reduced only by 3 per cent.[16]

The position of most other Center parties on the subject of missile bases ranged within the limits set by Venizelos for the Liberal party. The Democratic party's chairman, Stelios Allamanis, registered his condemnation of the possible installation of nuclear bases in Greece. He argued that there was no obligation for Greece to accept such bases under the NATO agreement.[17] He saw no direct benefit to Greece's defensive mission through the installation of IRBMs because these missiles could not be used against short-range Bulgarian targets where they would be needed most. Further, the installation of nuclear weapons in Greece would invite nuclear retaliation. The nation, being poor, would be in no position to undertake the costly program of developing an adequate passive defense against nuclear blast, radiation, and fallout. He therefore considered the acceptance of nuclear missiles under all these circumstances highly inadvisable.

Savas Papapolites, heading the waning movement of EPEK, reiterated Allamanis' argument and suggested that his acceptance of nuclear missiles could only be secured if terms and concessions in the clear national interest of Greece were gained,[18] i.e. granting of self-determination to the Cypriotes.

The Agrarian party restated its position, in favor of remaining with NATO and the Western world's defensive system, but opposed any agreement limiting Greece's sovereign rights. It was implied that installation of missile bases whose missiles were not under the control of the Greek armed forces constituted a limitation of sovereignty.[19]

In 1958, the Center parties as a whole, through their leaders or press organs, adopted a very definitely negative position on nuclear bases compared to ERE, whose attitude was one of postponing a decision until the actual time when nuclear bases were offered. Center leaders, prompted by the great disillusionment resulting from British

16. Ibid.; in this connection, see also "The Unjust Reduction of American Aid to Greece," Vema, 14 January 1958, p. 1.
17. S. Allamanis in Journal of Parliamentary Debates, 21 January 1958, p. 477.
18. S. Papapolites in ibid., 21 January 1958, p. 489.
19. "Agrarian Party Position," Eleftheria, 22 January 1958, p. 5.

and American policies toward the Cyprus question, were not very well disposed toward assuming additional collective security obligations; it was considered idiotic to assume obligations which, although necessary for the strategic interests of the entire Atlantic alliance, tactically exposed Greece to great nuclear dangers and increased the grounds for effective anti-Greek propaganda on the part of the Soviet bloc, given the Western stand on the Cyprus issue.

Elias Tsirimokos,[20] then a member of the executive committee of the Greek Democratic party and presently a highly controversial Center Union figure, reflected additional Center arguments in opposition to the acceptance of missile bases. In a short article published in Vema, he argued that opposition to nuclear weapons installations in Greece should not be interpreted as advocacy of an anti-NATO policy or recommendation for Greek disengagement from this defensive alliance. It only signified concern about the "rash" American leadership of the Western world which could possibly lead to worldwide destruction. Another argument advanced by Tsirimokos was that installation of nuclear bases would mean the end of Greek national independence since the decision to fire these missiles clearly rested with the authorities of the United States. Countries hosting such bases under these provisions would be, in effect, abdicating the "basic and fundamental sovereign right to declare or not declare war at will." [21] Tsirimokos finally, as a representative of the left flank of the Center parties, stated that the larger NATO nations should retain the primary responsibility for the defensive readiness of the entire alliance. They should be the first, therefore, to host nuclear missiles.[22] This was directed

20. Elias Tsirimokos, one of the founding fathers of the Center Union party, has been in the forefront of controversy ever since the party came to power after the elections of February 1964. Tsirimokos at first became disaffected with George Papandreou for not giving him the position of Chairman of the Greek Parliament. More recently, during the Greek political crisis which began in July 1965, Tsirimokos separated from the majority of the Center Union party and accepted a bid from King Constantine to form a government. This is indeed ironical because a comparison of the backgrounds of the two men would show Tsirimokos as the more likely of the two to be antimonarchist.

21. E. Tsirimokos, "Reasons Against Installation of Nuclear Bases," Vema, 16 February 1958, p. 6. According to Tsirimokos, Aneurin Bevan had also reflected great concern in Britain over American leadership of the Western world.

22. Tsirimokos had in mind, undoubtedly, similar reservations expressed by France and Germany at the time with regard to the terms and conditions of installation of missiles on their national territories.

primarily at France's reluctance to accept nuclear missiles without the right to control their firing.

An excellent presentation of the Center parties' position was given in two editorials of *Vema* by its owner and manager, Christos D. Lambrakis.[23] Lambrakis evaluated the nuclear bases controversy in Greece in the light of its relation to the disposition of Cyprus. Because of Cyprus, Lambrakis argued, the Greek public was upset, confused, disillusioned, and divided as to the future external political orientation of Greece. So the matter of nuclear base installation became a major political controversy rather than a strategic and military problem to be evaluated by technicians in appropriate functional fields. Communist propaganda against the bases, according to Lambrakis, "found psychologically fertile ground in almost the *entire* Greek people, regardless of their ideological or party position." [24] The question of acceptance of nuclear bases was posed during a time when all Greeks felt that their allies were treating them highhandedly, underestimating the Greek defensive contribution and propagandizing against Greek efforts to yield self-determination to the Cypriotes.

Lambrakis enumerated the terms which, in his opinion, should be met before nuclear bases could be installed in Greece and complete normalcy could be restored in interallied cooperation on the southeastern flank of NATO. He felt that, first, Cyprus's right to self-determination should be recognized and a date set for it to be exercised. Then, the preferential treatment reserved for "spoiled child" Turkey should cease. Finally, equality of rights as well as responsibilities for all NATO members should be granted. Lambrakis' position, given the early 1958 state of affairs, was typical of the political nature of Center evaluations of the pros and cons of nuclear bases. Center analysts considered the granting of nuclear bases as a political concession for which there should be some returns. Most Center leaders felt that the United States should take positive steps to support the Greek cause in Cyprus in return for such concessions.

The position of EDA on nuclear bases installation was slightly to

23. Christos D. Lambrakis, "No Bases Without Equality," *Vema*, 16 March 1958, p. 1; C. D. Lambrakis, "Stability of Direction for National Integrity," *Vema*, 18 March 1958, p. 1.
24. Lambrakis, "No Bases Without Equality" (emphasis supplied).

the left of that expressed by various segments of the Center. Greece, it advocated, should reject the ERE-sponsored installation of nuclear bases, thus sitting out the "dance of death." [25] IRBMs in Europe were intended by the United States to act as magnets which, in case of war, would deflect Soviet retaliatory nuclear missiles away from American targets.[26] In addition, Greece should contribute positively to the creation of a denuclearized zone (zone of peace) in the Balkans, thus removing all threat of war from this very sensitive part of the globe.[27] Eliou, once more spearheading EDA positions, proposed that the Balkan nations, while still remaining in their respective alliances, should be denuclearized under adequate inspection provisions. Coupled with the "Rapacki Plan," which called for a denuclearized north-central Europe, this could create a cooling-off buffer zone in the continent.[28] EDA's leader, John Passalides, attacked the Liberals as well as ERE for not having enough courage to reject unequivocally the installation of nuclear bases in Greece.[29] It is clear that EDA's unquestioning support for the "zone of peace" project, reiterated from time to time by Balkan Communist leaders, was an outright endorsement of Soviet foreign policy in the Balkans.

If any conclusions can be reached on the basis of the early 1958 nuclear bases controversy in Greece, they are the following. The Left, as represented by EDA, to a great extent embraced Soviet-supported foreign policies toward Greece, seeking basically alienation from NATO and diversion toward a friendly-to-all, neutralist course. This policy was to the great advantage of the Soviet Union because Greek disengagement from NATO would render the alliance's southeastern flank helpless, and hopelessly isolate the vitally strategic area of the straits as well as the areas of Eastern Turkey which were contiguous to the Soviet Union.[30]

25. "J. Passalides Responding to *Vema*'s Questionnaire," *Vema*, 1 January 1958, p. 10.

26. E. Eliou, "Against the Nations," *Auge*, 12 January 1958, p. 1.

27. "There Is a Way Out" (Editorial), *Auge*, 1 January 1958, p. 1; "The Devastation" (Editorial), *Auge*, 8 January 1958, p. 1; "Suicidal Policy" (Editorial), *Auge*, 10 January 1958, p. 1.

28. "The Eliou Proposal" (Editorial), *Auge*, 25 January 1958, p. 1.

29. J. Passalides, "The Strength of the People," *Auge*, 19 January 1958, p. 1.

30. For discussion, see supra, pp. 40–41.

The conservative Right, traditionally advancing policies which were axiomatically pro-American and pro-NATO, failed to take a definite stand on nuclear bases other than to assert vaguely that the matter would be handled so as to support Greek interests when the time came. One of the reasons for the conservative policy of noncommitment on the matter of bases, other than dissatisfaction with the allies over Cyprus, could be the fact that they perceived a definitely anti-allied sentiment among the populace and did not take a position for fear of losing votes in the next election.

The Center parties, which also traditionally favored pro-NATO and pro-United States policies, sensing the public's mood, sought to gain popular support by adopting stern positions toward the allies on any subject related to military or political cooperation. A comparison of the Center's position toward installation of NATO bases in Greece between October 1953 and January 1958 illustrates a significant leftward turn, attributable in large part to the strain on the alliance growing out of the Cyprus issue.

Chapter Ten
The Elections of 1958:
The Case and Causes for Neutralism

In February 1958 the ERE government resigned, following the walkout of Ministers Panayotis Papaligouras and George Rallis and fifteen ERE Deputies over a disagreement with Prime Minister Karamanlis regarding the future election law and system. New elections were scheduled for 11 May 1958, in the midst of general dissatisfaction with Greece's Western allies.

The Elections of 1958—Background

The elections of 1958, with regard to foreign policy, focused primarily upon the Cyprus and the nuclear bases issues. The election system called "reinforced proportional" [1] once more discouraged the independent existence of splinter parties and exerted pressures for interparty pre-election cooperation. Efforts were made, therefore, to materialize a pre-election union between EDA and three or four Center/Right personality parties as had happened in 1956. These did not bear fruit. Agreement could not be reached on a common platform in a union which would combine ex-Conservatives, such as Spyros Markezinis, and quasi-Communists, such as Passalides and Eliou.[2] The major disagreement was on NATO. Markezinis insisted that the common platform should include a statement asserting Greece's continued determination to remain in NATO. Passalides wanted, if anything, an anti-NATO statement.

The 1958 elections were contested by the following parties or pre-

1. A modified version of the single-member-district system.
2. *Auge*, 4 April 1958, p. 1; also "Exchanges of Letters between Passalides and Markezinis," *Auge*, 10 April 1958, p. 1.

election confederative movements: (1) ERE, representing the conservative Right; (2) Union of the Populist party, which was comprised of dissatisfied conservative Right elements who felt they could do a better job than the Karamanlis faction; (3) the Liberal party, backbone of the Center, which was headed by the perennial antagonists for number one position, Venizelos and Papandreou; (4) PADE, or Progressive Agrarian Democratic Union, which was a confederation of left and right of Center personality party elements, composed of Progressives (a personality party under Markezinis), EPEK (which had lost most of its previous strength either to the Liberal or to the EDA parties), the Agrarian party (characterized by narrow pursuit of the interests of the Greek farmers), and the Democratic party (which represented the far left elements of the Center movement and which had been founded on a nucleus of elements of the defunct Greek Socialist party); (5) EDA, representing all the crypto-Communists in Greece (since the Communist party was outlawed) and also seeking to lure centrifugal offshoots from the Center parties.

PARTY POSITIONS   The Liberal party platform represented the Center's effort to convince the public that the "Right" and the "Left" were respectively representative of "foreign interests" and that only the Center could pursue an effectively "Greek" foreign policy which would restore the Greek nation to its rightful place in the family of nations.[3] A Greek foreign policy was, in turn, characterized as membership in the free world without the conditions of subservience and vassalage which were plaguing Greece due to the actions and policies of the ERE government. With regard to Cyprus, the Liberal platform stated that the "only acceptable" solution would be self-determination for the Cypriotes, to be exercised within a reasonable time limit.

On the matter of bases, the Liberal party believed that the Left opposed their installation to suit foreign (Soviet) interests, and the Right had, in effect, accepted them to please Western backers. The Center's position was the proper one, namely, that Greece would not be disposed even to discuss the matter of bases unless there was immediate recognition of her role as an equal partner within the

3. "Party Declaration of the Liberals," *Vema*, 2 April 1958, p. 1.

Atlantic Alliance. In this frame of reference, the Liberal party declared that it would nullify any secret commitment on nuclear bases entered into by agreement of the ERE government.

George Papandreou, one of the co-chairmen of the Liberal party, in a major pre-election speech at Ioannina, Epirus, emphasized the flexibility of his party's proposed foreign policy and criticized ERE's "fatalistic" attachment to a Western orientation.[4] Mr. Papandreou presented five major foreign policy guidelines which his party would apply if elected to office. First, the Liberal party would be *uncommitted toward any geographical region* and the sole criterion for its foreign policy would be the Greek national interest.[5] Second, any form of subservience on the part of Greece would be rejected. Third, the interests of Greece required that she be placed in the camp of the free world.[6] The Liberals, however, would insure that Greece remained in this position, enjoying equal rights with the rest of its allies. Fourth, Greece within NATO would enjoy rights as well as responsibilities. One of the basic rights of Greece would be the relentless pursuit of self-determination for the Cypriote people. Fifth, the acceptance of nuclear missile bases in Greece would not constitute one of Greece's responsibilities within NATO. This was an oblique promise to the public that the Center, if elected, would reject nuclear bases.

S. Venizelos, the other cochairman of the Liberal party, in a speech delivered in Thessaloniki reiterated Papandreou's expressions of the Liberal party's foreign policy stand.[7] He added that Greece was mistreated by her allies because the ERE government had consciously adopted a policy of masochistic subservience. For example, Venizelos argued, the ERE government had failed to complain in the face of rapid reduction of American aid to Greece vis-à-vis that to Turkey (which had remained substantially unchanged).

The remainder of the Center movement's oppositon parties banded

4. "Speech by G. Papandreou at Ioannina, Epirus," *Eleftheria*, 26 April 1958, p. 1.
5. This point is indicative of a strong neutralist attraction.
6. This takes the teeth out of point one.
7. "Speech by Venizelos in Thessaloniki," *Vema*, 29 April 1958, p. 1; for a re-expression of these points see also speeches by Papandreou and Venizelos to the Athenians, *Vema*, 10 May 1958, p. 1.

together for election purposes in a confederative body called PADE and propagated a common foreign policy position. They favored, on the one hand, the continuation of Greece's participation in NATO but opposed the installation of nuclear bases as detrimental to the interests and survival of Greece.[8]

The Populist Union, composed of conservative elements outside ERE, also adopted a position opposed to the installation of nuclear bases in Greece unless equality and recognition of Greek rights within NATO were restored.[9] This was another way of saying that concessions to Greece on the Cyprus issue would be required as the price for the installation of nuclear bases.[10]

Generally, the noncommunist parties which comprised the opposition to ERE were solidly agreed on both rejection of nuclear bases in Greece, and disapproval of the subservient role played by the ERE government vis-à-vis the British, United States, and Turkish governments in the matter of Cyprus. Center accusations alleged that the Karamanlis government had attained and retained control thanks to the support of powerful oligarchic local interests as well as foreign support (American and British) in return for adopting a highly conciliatory policy on the Cyprus issue as well as committing Greece to unquestionably harmful policies without consideration for consequences to the Greek nation and people.[11]

The pre-election position of the ERE party was characterized by great caution and a measure of noncommitment especially on the key issue of nuclear bases installation. Konstantinos Karamanlis promulgated his party's approach to Greek foreign relations in major

8. "PADE: Statement to Press on Its Foreign Policy Position," V*ema*, 22 April 1958, p. 3; see also "Speech by Markezinis to Athenians," V*ema*, 7 May 1958, p. 5.

9. Here is a good example of how the Cyprus issue had brought a purely conservative party of the Greek Right to the position of rejecting a NATO-proposed policy.

10. "Populist Union Foreign Policy Position Statement," V*ema*, 22 April 1958, p. 3.

11. These points are stated or implied in the following: "Interview with S. Stephanopoulos [ex-vice president of the Synaghermos government] on the Nature of ERE and Her Leadership," V*ema*, 2 April 1958, p. 1; "Historical Station" (Editorial), *Eleftheria*, 11 May 1958, p. 1; "Pre-election Speech by Tsaldaris to the People of Corinth," *Eleftheria*, 24 April 1958, p. 1.

speeches delivered to large crowds of Athenians and Thessalonians early in May 1958.[12]

He reminded his audiences that ERE had safeguarded and would continue to safeguard Greece's alliances (NATO and the Balkan Pact) which were considered indispensable for her existence. Here Karamanlis was emphasizing his party's determination to remain within the Western alliance system regardless of how strained relations over Cyprus became. The use of the word "indispensable" speaks for itself. Within the framework of the Western alliance, Greece would continue to act independently and in accordance with her national interests. As proof of that, he cited the open conflict against Western allies over the Cyprus question. As another example he mentioned the Greek policy toward the Middle East, which had been expressed in direct contradiction to Western policies in the same area (e.g the Suez crisis). The charge of "subservience" flung at the Greek government was thoroughly unfounded, according to the ERE chairman, unless interallied cooperation were misinterpreted as subservience. The ERE government had accomplished considerable progress on the Cyprus issue, contrary to the Centerites who, when in power, had neglected even to take up the issue, let alone fight for its resolution.

Karamanlis skirted the very important issue of installation of nuclear bases in Greece. He simply stated that such bases had not been offered and, as a result, there was no question of deciding whether to accept them or not. He felt that the new government to be elected would make the decision on the sole criterion of Greek national interest. Karamanlis assured the voters that such an important decision and commitment could not be made, and would not be made, by an ERE government without submitting the matter to Parliament for approval.

The attitude of the Conservative press toward the noncommunist opposition parties (the Center) was one of utter contempt. The Conservatives accused the Center parties of not possessing a distinctive foreign policy and having only one thing in common: the burning

12. "Text of Karamanlis' Speech to Athenians," *Kathimerini*, 9 May 1958, p. 1; see also "Text of Karamanlis' Speech to the People of Thessaloniki," *Kathimerini*, 15 April 1958, p. 1.

desire of their respective leaders to govern Greece.[13] EDA, on the other hand, was accused of being an open instrument of the Communists and the Soviet Union in Greece. A Conservative editorial [14] went as far as to suggest, therefore, that the Communist party be legalized in Greece so that voters would not be fooled by the popular front gyrations of EDA. Thus, communism would once more be reduced to its "realistically small proportions." This suggestion was not heeded; the Communist party of Greece is still illegal at the time of writing.

During the 1958 pre-election period, EDA's major target, as usual, was the conservative ERE. The Conservatives were held responsible for absorbing defeats in the Cyprus struggle, and courting nuclear disaster by welcoming nuclear bases and eagerly subscribing to the Eisenhowever Doctrine. They were also attacked for hurting Greece economically by cutting or curbing trade with East Europe and the Soviet Union.[15] *Auge*, in daily pre-election articles, emphasized the dangers of nuclear bases installation and sought to create an atmosphere of panic among the public by elaborating on the catastrophic consequences of a nuclear war.[16]

EDA promised that, if elected to govern Greece, it would implement a foreign policy program designed to promote peace in the world and at least keep Greece out of a nuclear war.[17] Greek foreign policy would be restored to a status befitting a self-respecting independent nation, without a trace of "national subservience," and with the national interest as the major guideline. Good relations would be cultivated with all nations regardless of their political or social systems.[18] Greece would not be allowed to become a missile base and target for hydrogen disaster. The Cyprus issue would be pursued with the single

13. "The Psychology of the Ballot" (Editorial), *Kathimerini*, 15 May 1958, p. 1.

14. "The Fraud" (Editorial), *Kathimerini*, 7 May 1958, p. 1.

15. E. Eliou, "Two Years of the Rule of Favoritism," *Auge*, 19 February 1958, p. 1.

16. "EDA Announcement," *Auge*, 24 April 1958, p. 1; "The Bases of Death" (Editorial), *Auge*, 16 April 1958, p. 1; J. Passalides, "Message to Greeks," *Auge*, 20 April 1958, p. 1.

17. "The EDA Election Program," *Auge*, 25 April 1958, p. 1.

18. A good and pious wish but difficult to attain realistically in a divided world, where association with the East or the West meant automatic worsening of relations with the other.

aim of attaining self-determination without any conditions.[19] Trade and economic relations would be directed toward all nations on an "equal-to-equal" basis, and the chief criterion for trade policies would be the best marketing of Greek agricultural products.[20] The ERA program emphasized with sorrow that Greece had abandoned independence in foreign and domestic policies and had stooped to dutiful execution of policies in the interest of the United States.

Post-election Parliamentary Debates

The results of the May election[21] gave the victory once more to ERE and Karamanlis. To the great alarm of anticommunists in Greece and throughout the world, however, the vote for EDA jumped well above the expected 10 to 15 per cent and approached 25 per cent, making it the primary opposition party.

The discussion which transpired in Parliament over the new ERE government's foreign policy illustrated a clear-cut rift between the government and the remaining opposition parties. ERE's foreign policy was presented by Karamanlis during the reading of his government's program declarations to the Greek Parliament.[22] Karamanlis restated the Greek devotion to the ideals of peace and liberty which could best be pursued through the medium of the United Nations. He asserted that Greece should remain in NATO in order to protect her national and territorial integrity which had been four times violated in the period of one generation. However, in what appears to have been a warning to Greece's NATO partners, Karamanlis foresaw great strains on the continued viability and cooperative relations of NATO because of the unfriendly actions of certain allies, clearly implying Turkey and Britain.

Prime Minister Karamanlis placed exceptional emphasis in his pro-

19. This position is not only unrealistic but contradictory to the guideline under which good relations with "all" nations would be sought, since the attainment of Greek objectives on Cyprus would not allow for good relations with at least Turkey and Britain.

20. This step, it was understood, would open up more trade with East Europe and the Soviet Union.

21. For complete results, see Dafnis, *The Greek Political Parties: 1821–1961*, p. 190.

22. *Journal of Parliamentary Debates*, 10 June 1958, pp. 10–12.

gram announcements on the importance of continuing friendly relations with Yugoslavia and the Arab world. He also stressed the need to proceed beyond the mere establishment of diplomatic relations with East European nations and achieve friendly relations. This type of friendship could be attained and maintained only through the extension of mutual respect for national independence and mutual noninterference in the internal affairs of one another. The extra emphasis undoubtedly resulted from the existing coolness in relations with NATO and the desire to start paving the way for possible alternatives to membership and association with NATO and the West.

The chief spokesman for the opposition, EDA's John Passalides, frontally attacked the government's proposed foreign program. He stated, in a long speech to Parliament, that Greece should fight British- and Turkish-supported colonialism, discontinue her subservient policy toward NATO which was, in effect, courting with nuclear disaster, and follow the bidding of 60 per cent of the Greek voters (here he included all the votes which were not cast in favor of ERE) by abandoning plans to accept nuclear NATO bases in Greece.[23] Passalides urged the government to adopt a policy of "equal friendship" and reject all policies which directly or indirectly supported colonial interests. He praised the Soviet Union's unilateral moratorium on nuclear testing and advised ERE to join the group of governments that practiced "peaceful coexistence," since the policy of "unilateral Western orientation" had collapsed with the Turkish atrocities against the Greeks in 1955 and the subsequent distasteful stand of the allies following that incident.[24]

Finally, Passalides admonished the Karamanlis government for not taking the matter of Turkish atrocities against Greeks in Cyprus to the Security Council of the United Nations. EDA felt that until satisfaction in the Cyprus issue was obtained, Greece should abandon all contacts with the British and Turkish nations, especially participation in common military conferences, exercises, and the like. This should be coupled with closer relations with the United Arab Republic, whose policies Greece was enjoined to emulate.

23. Ibid., 11 June 1958, pp. 15–19.
24. See also ibid., 12 June 1958, pp. 79–84, speech by Eliou to Parliament, where the major points of Passalides are elaborated further.

George Papandreou, speaking for the Liberals, disapproved of the ERE program and, as a substitute, he again offered the Liberal party's foreign policy program as it had been promulgated during the pre-election period.[25] Other Center parties' leaders sniped critically at the ERE government's foreign policy. Their recommendations, with the exception of not attacking the very core of Greek foreign policy (i.e. continued participation in NATO), were quite similar to those advanced by EDA.[26]

Deputy Allamanis, the head of the Democratic party, although still favoring continued participation in NATO, was opposed to possible acceptance of nuclear bases in Greece, opposed to the subservient role played by Greece on the Cyprus issue, and indignant over the staggering proportions of Greek military expenditures.[27] He urged Greece to imitate Turkey, which not only received greater American aid but also accepted Russian investments, in addition to maintaining a large volume of trade with that country. Allamanis advocated that Russian investments also be sought by Greece in order to supplement losses resulting from extremely high and unproductive military expenditures. To make matters worse, aid to Greece from 1950 to 1957 had been reduced by two thirds while her defensive expenditures had increased 300 per cent. Allamanis recommended, therefore, that Greek military expenditures be cut to the "minimum required sum for Greek security rather than *collective security*." [28]

Deputy Alexandros Baltatzis, the head of the Agrarian party, argued that EDA should not be allowed to monopolize the policy of seeking greater economic cooperation between Greece and Eastern Europe.[29] He mentioned that he agreed with the major points of Deputy Allamanis' criticisms. Deputy John Toumbas, a representative of the

25. Ibid., 11 June 1958, pp. 24 ff. For further Center/Right criticism of ERE's program along the lines of advocating a sterner policy toward NATO allies on the matter of Cyprus, see speeches by P. Kanellopoulos in ibid., pp. 27–30; S. Stephanopoulos in ibid., pp. 30–39; S. Markezinis in ibid., pp. 39–46.
26. This is a very interesting point because the same leaders formed the nucleus of the Center Union party in 1961. It follows that they carried with them foreign policy ideas which are not in harmony with the positions habitually advanced by Papandreou and Venizelos.
27. *Journal of Parliamentary Debates*, 12 June 1958, pp. 51–58.
28. Ibid., p. 58 (emphasis supplied).
29. Ibid., pp. 65–67.

Liberal party, argued that the United States should be asked to exert economic pressures upon the Turks in order to force them to abandon anti-Greek atrocities in Cyprus, that Greece should publicize the Turkish intransigence which was slowly killing the Balkan Pact, and that Greek military personnel in the NATO command at Izmir, Turkey, should be immediately ordered back to Greece.[30] Deputy George Mavros, another Liberal, argued that the government's decision to take the Cyprus issue to the NATO Council was a great folly, since each member nation had veto power, thus deadlocking every possible solution which could be favorable to one or two of the three antagonists.[31] He added that the Cyprus issue would be discussed behind closed doors in NATO, to the disadvantage of Greece, whose main weapon on the Cyprus issue was the moral force of public opinion. NATO, at the least, according to Mavros, needed some major repairs of rifts caused by the Cyprus dispute and was in no position to bring about a satisfactory solution to the thorny problem.

The Disintegrative Effects of the Cyprus Problem

The responses of Foreign Minister Averoff to the criticisms of the Leftist and Center opposition illustrate the damage which the Cyprus issue inflicted upon Greece's loyalties toward NATO. Although the Foreign Minister defended the action of submitting the Cyprus issue to the NATO Council, he admitted that the terms of allied cooperation which were required for Greece's continued participation in NATO were progressively becoming "untenable" due to the actions of certain allies, implying here Britain, Turkey, and, by default, the United States. Averoff stated very clearly in the same speech that Greece "could *not sacrifice* the interests of the Cypriotes for the sake of allied solidarity."[32]

The words of Foreign Minister Averoff soon were to be substan-

---

30. Ibid., pp. 74–75. Ironically enough, the Karamanlis government two days later ordered the withdrawal of Greek military personnel from Izmir. See "Removal of Officers Paralyzes NATO at Izmir," *Vema*, 17 June 1958, p. 1.

31. *Journal of Parliamentary Debates*, 12 June 1958, p. 78.

32. Ibid., 11 June 1958, pp. 24–26 (emphasis supplied). He adopted, therefore, the same position as Liberal Papandreou.

tiated with deeds. On 14 July Greece ordered the withdrawal of her contingent stationed at NATO headquarters in Izmir.[33] This precipitated an atmosphere almost of war hysteria in Athens, and the prospects were portending worse things.[34] The worst, i.e. a Greek-Turkish war, was prevented thanks primarily to the efforts of NATO.

Throughout 1958, the tensions raised by the Cyprus issue brought Greece closer to courting neutralist policies and to ostracizing Britain and especially Turkey. To fill the resultant vacuum, serious efforts were exerted to develop closer relations with Yugoslavia and the United Arab Republic.[35] Another very important side effect of the Cyprus dispute was the atrophy of the all important Balkan Pact. The Greek-Turkish animosities never allowed it to take organizational flesh and blood, but it has not been abrogated by its signatories and can be legally revived whenever the need arises.[36]

In 1958 NATO took a very active part in attempting to heal the major rift within its ranks precipitated by the Cyprus dispute. Secretary-General Spaak made it his primary objective to bring the disputants around the NATO conference table and settle this most embarrassing problem to the unity of the Western world.[37] Although the

33. "Decision of Greek Government to Withdraw Greek Officers from NATO Headquarters at Izmir," *Vema*, 14 June 1958, p. 1.

34. Editorial, *Vema*, 17 June 1958, p. 1.

35. The following articles published in *Vema* illustrate these pro-neutralist tendencies: "Averoff Declares the Possibility of Greek Neutralism," 25 June 1958, p. 6; S. Zotos, "Possible New Greek Orientations," 1 July 1958, p. 1; S. Zotos, "Reaction in U.S.A. to Greece's Inclination toward Neutralism," 17 July 1958, p. 3; "Opposition of Liberal Party to the Government's Silence on Lebanon Issue," 23 July 1958, p. 1; "Greek Position of Neutralism in United Nations Regarding Lebanon," 20 August 1958, p. 1; "Greece Contemplates Abandonment of NATO," 30 September 1958, p. 1, 1 October 1958, p. 1, 2 October 1958, p. 1, and 3 October 1958, p. 1. See also Christos D. Lambrakis, "To Become Respectable," *Vema*, 19 October 1958, p. 1; and "Danger and Utopia," 22 October 1958, p. 1.

36. A. Merenditis, "The Reconstruction of the Greek and Turkish Relationship and the Weakening of the Balkan Pact," *Vema*, 1 March 1959, p. 1; see also L. Karapanagiotis, "Analysis of Yugoslav Position on Balkan Pact," *Vema*, 5 March 1959, p. 1; and "Balkan Pact: Tito's Current Appraisal," *Vema*, 11 March 1958, p. 1.

37. For a good discussion of NATO efforts to settle the Cyprus issue see Mary Margaret Ball, NATO *and the European Union Movement*, p. 142; Carol E. Baumann, *Political Cooperation in* NATO, pp. 63–69. See also Great Britain, Foreign Office, *Discussion on Cyprus in* NATO, *September–October 1958* (London, H. M. Stationery Office, 1958).

issue was not settled through these NATO talks,[38] they were most influential in creating the atmosphere which led to further negotiations between the disputants and eventual compromise.[39] It was not long after the conclusion of NATO talks that Prime Minister Karamanlis and the late Prime Minister Adnan Menderes of Turkey met at Zurich in February 1959 and agreed on a compromise solution which granted independence to Cyprus (with guarantees for the Turkish minority including veto rights over wide areas of legislation) rather than self-determination, which could have led to union with Greece.[40] Britain agreed to these terms shortly afterward, once her military interests were guaranteed.[41] Thus, the Cyprus dispute was "settled," at least in the short run, together with all its unpleasant consequences for the cohesiveness and effectiveness of NATO. The entire range of opposition parties, however, voted against the "betrayal," as they characterized the Zurich and London agreements, of Greek nationalist objectives.[42]

The so-called "settlement" through the Zurich and London treaties in effect planted the seeds which grew into the latest and most dangerous flare-up of the Cyprus problem. The resurrection of the whole Cyprus question—still unresolved at the time of writing—has brought continuous and disruptive pressures in the southeastern sector of NATO. Indeed, with the involvement of the Soviet Union, the problem

38. "Pressures from NATO for Tripartite Discussions," *Vema*, 18 June 1958, p. 1, and 19 June 1958, p. 1. The following in *Vema*: S. Zotos, "NATO and Lack of Greek-Turkish Cooperation," 26 June 1958, p. 1, and 29 June 1958, p. 1; A. Merenditis, "Greece and NATO," 8 July 1958, p. 1; "Not 'Flaming Tide' but Burning Cyprus" (Editorial), 13 July 1958, p. 1. See also in *Vema*, "NATO Efforts to Settle Cyprus Issue": 23 September 1958, p. 1; 24 September 1958, p. 1; 25 September 1958, p. 1; 26 September 1958, p. 1; 27 September 1958, p. 1; 28 September 1958, p. 1; 4 October 1958, p. 1; 5 October 1958, p. 1; 7 October 1958, p. 1; 15 October 1958, p. 1; 23 October 1958, p. 1; 28 October 1958, p. 1. "NATO's Contribution to the Solution of the Cyprus Issue," text of speech by Burgess to Athenian audience, 25 April 1959, p. 1.

39. F. W. Mulley, *The Politics of Western Defense* (New York, Praeger, 1962), p. 231.

40. "Karamanlis–Menderes Agreement on Cyprus in Zurich," *Vema*, 12 February 1959, p. 1; S. Zotos, "What Facts, Influences, and Pressures Led to the Immediate Rapprochement," ibid., 17 February 1959, p. 1.

41. Great Britain, *Conference on Cyprus, London 1959* (London, H. M. Stationery Office, 1959).

42. Center parties and EDA opposed the Zurich agreement. See "Reports on Parliamentary Debates," *Vema*, 26 February 1959, p. 1.

became a potential spark which could detonate a third world war. The reader will find in Chapter 13 a more detailed coverage of the ramifications of the current Cyprus crisis.

The study of the 1958 elections and their aftermath once more illustrates the basic anti-NATO effects which were generated as a result of the Cyprus issue.[43] Conservative and Liberal positions, which had been traditionally pro-NATO, took sharp leftward turns. "Pro-NATO-ism" was now interspersed among numerous neutralist reservations. The Center parties openly argued that without a fair settlement of the Cyprus issue there could be no question of installation of nuclear bases in Greece, or even continued close military cooperation of the NATO partners involved in the Cyprus dispute. The Conservatives, although deeply committed to Greece's permanent need of maintaining close defensive ties with NATO, were so conscious of the popular anti-Western discontent over Cyprus that they did not venture to commit themselves on the question of nuclear bases. The Conservatives also hinted numerous times about the nonviability of an alliance where the stronger provoke, and act unfairly toward, the weaker. They unequivocally stated that the interests of Cyprus clearly overrode the interests of maintaining cohesiveness (at Greek expense) in the Western collective security defense system.[44]

The quasi-Communists of EDA did not move any farther left than they had done in previous elections, unlike the other two political movements. Any stronger leftward orientation would have meant absolute identification of EDA's views with the outlawed Greek Communist party. They urged the acceptance of a neutralist policy, the development of a "peace zone" in the Balkans, and generally counseled in favor of Greece's disengagement from the Western defensive as well as cultural and political environment. The fact that EDA did not adopt an outright pro-Soviet orientation could be explained as a stroke of tactical expediency, seeking to attract the votes of Center or even Conservative elements who had been dissatisfied with the

43. Editorial, *Vema*, 17 June 1958, p. 1; this editorial, for example, clearly illustrates Greece's determination and readiness to fight a war with Turkey rather than succumb to her continuous provocations.

44. This was a reversal from the 1956 conservative position when security considerations overrode the Cypriote objectives. See supra, pp. 104–05.

unpleasant interallied relations over the Cyprus issue, and who wanted Greece to adopt a much more forceful policy toward the West.

The nature and the tone of the major foreign policy issues of the 1958 elections—nuclear bases, staggering military expenditures, loss of prestige, and even independence of Greece over the Cyprus issue— clearly illustrate that the Greek public's acceptance of NATO did not in any way transcend the limits set by purely Greek interests. It can be argued, then, that participation in NATO created no supranational- istic loyalties in the Greek people. Considerations of collective secu- rity were advanced only when they clearly contributed to Greek security and served Greek interests.

As far as the ERE government is concerned, its policies in NATO and Cyprus can best be understood if they are studied as dependent parts of the whole foreign policy of Greece. ERE, being in power and responsible for the entire gamut of Greek policies, had to set priorities of action which, on occasion, resulted in sacrifices of certain Greek interests (such as those in the Cyprus unification case) in order to safeguard more important Greek interests, such as the continuation of the protection of a NATO guarantee against communist aggression, whether external or internal, and continuation of military and eco- nomic aid.

The policy of the ERE government was apparently generated from the premise that Greece stood a better chance of being defended by the allies if they were closely committed with troops and bases on Greek soil. The presence of these troops, it was envisioned, would insure their parent nations' full-fledged involvement in a defensive war, should Greece be subjected to a local attack. ERE's hesitation on nuclear bases stemmed primarily from the general public's fears of possible Greek involvement in nuclear war.

The Center enjoyed the advantage of opposition irresponsibility, permitting it to make promises and also to publicize to the voters necessary compromises forced upon the ruling party by the vicissitudes of international intercourse.

Chapter Eleven
The Elections of 1961:
Return to Normalcy

The Interelection Period: 1958–1961

It is not the intention of this writer to trace and analyze the major events of periods between elections. From the 1958 to the 1961 elections, for example, over three and a half years elapsed. The major characteristic of the interelection period was that, through EDA, Greek Communists acted as the chief spokesmen of the Greek opposition.

In 1959 and 1960 great pressures were exerted on Greece from East Europe (with the exception of Yugoslavia), the Soviet Union, and EDA to enter into negotiations leading to the development of a peace zone in the Balkans and to disengage from an active role within NATO.[1] Pacifism of this type grew to become the chief EDA foreign policy pres-

1. Numerous articles and reports have appeared on this topic. A sample of references from *Vema* follows: "News Conference with Rumanian President Stoica," 5 March 1959, p. 1; "Khrushchev Attacks Greece for Housing American Missile Bases," 27 May 1959, p. 1, and 7 June 1959, p. 1; "Karamanlis' Reply to Khrushchev's Pressures," 29 May 1959, p. 1; "Greece on Denuclearized Balkan Zone," 5 June 1959, p. 1, and 6 June 1959, p. 1; "Averoff on Missile Bases in Greece," 12 June 1959, p. 1; G. A. Exintaris, "The Problem of Missile Bases and the General Soviet Strategy," 13 June 1959, p. 1; "Greek-Yugoslav Talks Regarding Denuclearized Zone," 18 June 1959, p. 1; G. A. Daskarolis, "Denuclearized Balkans," 28 June 1959, p. 7; A. Merenditis, "The Meaning and Consequences for Greece of the Russian Proposals on the Balkans," 16 July 1959, p. 1; G. A. Exintaris, "Greece Must Revise Her Stand toward the Soviet Union and Its Satellites," 3 September 1959, p. 1; G. A. Exintaris, "Balkan Conference Would Be Dangerous," 2 December 1959, p. 1; S. Zotos, "The United States and Balkan Rapprochement," 6 December 1959, p. 3, and 8 December 1959, p. 5; "Peace-Offensive—the Zhivkov Proposals," 29 December 1959, p. 1; S. Venizelos, "Speech to Parliament Arguing for Détente," 11 February 1960, p. 1; G. A. Daskarolis, "The Real Meaning for Greece of the Creation of Denuclearized Balkans," 28 February 1960, p. 3; S. Zotos, "Greece, the New Target of Soviet Pressures," 24 July 1960, p. 1.

sure point upon Greek, noncommunist governments of the early 1960s.

Another significant event of 1960 was the serious effort which was initiated toward achieving unification of the numerous parties comprising the Center movement. Here is a sample of the multitude of parties which revolved around a Center/Liberal position in 1960: the Liberal party headed by Venizelos, the Liberal Democratic party headed by Papandreou, the Progressive party headed by Markezinis, the Populist Social party headed by Stefanos Stephanopoulos, EPEK headed by Papapolites, Progressive Worker Farmer movement headed by Pafsanias Katsotas, the New Political movement headed by George Athanasiades-Novas, the Democratic party headed by Allamanis, the remnants of the Socialist party headed by Tsirimokos, and the Agrarian party headed by Baltatzis. In this assortment of parties, one finds local and foreign policies ranging from conservative Right (ex-Synaghermos elements, such as Markezinis and Stephanopoulos) to socialist Left (Tsirimokos, who had run on the EDA ticket in the 1958 elections). The major domestic political event of 1961 was the consolidation of most of the Center parties into one party under the leadership of George Papandreou. The new party was named the Center Union and, contrary to most expectations, it has managed to remain unified to date, despite numerous inherent centrifugal factors which might fragment it.[2]

The major foreign policy event of 1961 was the decision to associate Greece with the Common Market. On 10 July 1961, the Athens agreement was signed to this effect.[3] To many analysts in Greece the Common Market—as well as the Greek association with it—was

2. "The Formation of the Center Union," Vema, 19 September 1961, p. 1. The current Greek political crisis has dealt an extremely severe blow to the unity of the Center Union party. Following Papandreou's resignation on 15 July 1965 over a disagreement with King Constantine, 37 out of 171 elected deputies of the Center Union party separated their political objectives and support from the remaining 134 members still owing allegiance to George Papandreou. If there are no further defections from the Center Union it may still survive and remain as a strong political entity. Since most of the founding fathers of the Center Union (e.g. Stephanopoulos, Novas, Allamanis, Tsirimokos) have defected, in the event of a reelection and victory of the Center the party will emerge under the undisputed leadership of George Papandreou, and will be more likely to withstand divisive issues in the future.

3. "Complete Text of the Agreement Associating Greece with the Common Market," Vema, 13 July 1961, p. 6.

viewed as a positive step reinforcing the economic foundations of NATO and the gradually growing Atlantic community.[4]

Karamanlis considered October 1961 a good month to test the will of the Greek voters once more. The Conservatives had been in power close to ten years. They felt they had done an outstanding job in creating unprecedented political stability for Greece and were eager to continue along these lines. But this was not the view of the Center politicians who felt that it was high time the Conservatives were dislodged before they became so accustomed to power that they would seek to retain it by irregular means. The Leftists, for their part, believed that any change away from ERE type conservatism would be beneficial to their cause.

Party Positions

The objections of EDA in the sphere of foreign policy during the pre-election period of 1961 revolved around the effects of nuclear war on Greece and the likelihood of Greece being a nuclear target. Slogans of "disengagement," "Balkan peace zone," "neutralism," and advocacy of freedom from the intimidating pressures and influences of the Western allies were in the forefront throughout the pre-election period. The damaging effects which NATO association allegedly brought to Greece were almost daily pointed up in EDA's press organ.[5]

EDA's efforts to form a wide opposition front during this pre-election period failed once more. EDA and EAK[6] only combined their forces to form the Pan-Democratic Agrarian Front of Greece (PAME). Their slogan was "Choose Greek: PAME brings welfare and ERE brings war."[7] Once more the ERE government was branded as an instrument

4. G. Theotokas, "The Common Market and the Future of the Nation," *Vema*, 11 June 1961, p. 3; A. Masouridis, "Our Position in the European Community," *Vema*, 4 August 1961, p. 3; and "The Powers of the Council," 5 August 1961, p. 3.

5. See the following in *Auge* for illustrative examples: "The Shark" (Editorial), 10 September 1961, p. 1; "Declaration of the Executive Committee of EDA," 22 September 1961, p. 1; "Sixth Fleet and Elections" (Editorial), 23 September 1961, p. 1; "EDA: Declaration to the Greek People," 28 September 1961, p. 1; "Protesting NATO Interference in Greek Pre-election Period," 29 September 1961, p. 1, and 30 September 1961, p. 5; "Demilitarized Zone in the Balkans," 6 October 1961, p. 1.

6. EAK = Greek Agrarian Movement.

7. *Auge*, 1 October 1961, p. 1.

of American foreign policy.[8] As the prime illustration of this assertion, the Greek voting record at the United Nations was cited which, in most cases "followed blindly U. S. direction." The Greek delegation, it was argued, either voted against or abstained on the following key issues: entry of Communist China into the United Nations, the Tunisian complaint over the French presence in Bizerte, the United States interventions in Cuba, total and complete disarmament, and the creation of a zone free from nuclear missiles and bases in the Balkans and Central Europe.[9]

The PAME pre-election program contained a clear condemnation of ERE and its entire system of foreign policies. According to PAME, Greece's "foreign and domestic politics served not the national and the people's interests but foreign super-sovereigns and a voracious oligarchy." [10] To safeguard these non-Greek interests, Cyprus was betrayed and the very existence of Greece was endangered with cold war policies such as harboring the warlike offensive bases of the United States. The Greek economy was stifled under the weight of extremely heavy and nonproductive military expenditures. Economic cooperation with East Europe, the Soviet Union, and the Middle East was kept to the bare minimum to serve, once more, Western interests. PAME, as an alternative to the allegedly ruinous ERE policies, advocated an independent Greek policy seeking to attain peace, defend Greek interests, and positively contribute to the adoption of a system of general and complete, inspected, disarmament. Chief among PAME's foreign policy objectives were the attainment of a solution to Greece's basic problem, i.e. to secure Balkan understanding and cooperation and convert the peninsula into a zone of peace without bases, missiles, and atomic weapons; the removal of all foreign bases from Greece and denial of use of Greek soil to any state for operations against any other; and the reestablishment of economic relations with all nations on the basis of Greek economic interests.

Key EDA spokesmen, such as Passalides, Eliou, and Brillakis, campaigned throughout the pre-election period on the basis of the PAME

8. Ibid., 3 October 1961 (Editorial), p. 1.
9. Ibid., 11 October 1961, p. 3.
10. "PAME Pre-election Program," ibid., 13 October 1961, p. 1.

program, amplifying its key provisions to the voters.[11] Passalides specifically accused ERE of following blindly the "offensive" directives of the United States. Significantly enough, he also assailed the newly formed Center Union and its leader, Papandreou, for advocating in effect similar policies as those of ERE.[12] This was unlike previous years when the target of EDA criticism had been restricted to ERE conservatives. Passalides, as well as Brillakis, criticized ERE's refusal to negotiate friendly relations with Balkan nations, its insistence on rejecting Balkan peace zone proposals, and its abandonment of Greece to the domination of "neofascist" West Germany's inflowing capital and influence.

EDA, which had repeatedly accused ERE of inviting foreign intervention in Greece, paradoxically enough often resorted to inviting foreign intervention itself. EDA leaders, as well as *Auge*, often requested international organizations or the foreign press to publicize ERE's terrorist pressures upon voters,[13] a request which could, in effect, invite other foreign pressures and intervention.

Another organization which claimed to be noncommunist, but whose foreign policy position often supplemented that of EDA, was the Greek Committee for International Détente and Peace. This committee, of which more will be said in the next chapter, pleaded with all Greek parties to include détente-promoting objectives in their platforms. It urged a "peaceloving" orientation in foreign policy and the creation of a denuclearized Balkan zone accompanied by disarmament which should be jointly guaranteed by the United States and the Soviet Union.[14] These principles clearly supported EDA's foreign policy platform.

Unlike the 1956 and 1958 elections, inflamed by the Cyprus issue,

11. "Text of Passalides' Speech in Thessaloniki," *Auge*, 17 October 1961, p. 3; "Texts of Speeches by Eliou, Passalides, Argyropoulos, and Kitsikis to the Athenians," *Auge*, 25 October 1961, p. 3; "Texts of Speeches by Passalides and Brillakis in Piraeus," *Auge*, 26 October 1961, p. 3.

12. "Text of Passalides' Speech in Thessaloniki," *Auge*, 17 October 1961, p. 3; see also on this point, "Text of Speech by Brillakis in Piraeus," *Auge*, 26 October 1961, p. 3.

13. "EDA Complains over ERE's Pressures," *Auge*, 15 October 1961, p. 1. (A plea to expose ERE to world public opinion is made in this article.)

14. "Declaration of the Greek Committee for International Détente and Peace," *Auge*, 5 October 1961, p. 1.

foreign policy occupied a back seat compared to domestic issues in the 1961 pre-election debates between ERE and the Center Union party. The foreign policy position of the Center Union was pronounced in a speech delivered by Papandreou in Thessaloniki on 8 October 1961.[15] He acknowledged that "history, geography, and the world of ethical values in which Greece believes" had classified Greece with the free West. However, the West should recognize that Greece had rights as well as responsibilities. These rights were not claimed or exercised adequately by ERE governments. As a prime example of abandonment of Greek rights, the Center considered the so-called solution of the Cyprus issue, which was caustically referred to as an outright defeat.

Regarding general foreign policy orientation, Papandreou coined a famous phrase which is used to the present time—"We are allies with the West and we want to be friends with the East." [16] This, in effect, was at least a promise that the Center, although within NATO, would pursue a moderate and conciliatory (in fact friendly) policy toward East Europe and the Soviet Union, similar to the style set by Scandinavian countries. In order to achieve the best results in foreign policy, he advised the adoption of prudence. One example which he cited as typical of ERE's lack of prudence was a statement made by Karamanlis during an official visit to the United States, recognizing the right of intervention of a large nation into the affairs of a small one. In this instance, Karamanlis had referred to United States intervention in Cuba, thus reviving the dangerous concept of "vital area," which could have very bad repercussions on Greece should it be applied against her. This remarkable example of irresponsibility, according to Papandreou, was the result of Karamanlis' desire to be in the good graces of the late President Kennedy.

The matter of military expenditures was once again a key point of Center criticism. Papandreou asserted that Greece was prepared to spend only in proportion to her ability and also in proportion to what other NATO allies were spending. He complained that Greece was undertaking the burden of military expenditures in much higher proportion than other nations, while ERE had done nothing but express pious

15. "Text of Papandreou's Speech in Thessaloniki," Vema, 10 October 1961, p. 4.

16. Ibid.

wishes to remedy this situation. In addition to enumerating the dangers that could befall Greece on account of her association with the Common Market without adequate preparation, Papandreou stated in another speech that Greece under Center leadership and within the Atlantic Alliance would not be a "passive receiver of directives, but [an] active, creative member." [17] Once again he was hammering at the familiar theme that the ERE government was a "do-nothing," unimaginative follower of Western leadership.

ERE's campaign rested on the record of its "international attainments" while in office from 1956 to 1961. The solution to the Cyprus problem was cited as one of the chief contributions not only to the cause of Cypriote independence, but also to the maintenance of world peace and the solidarity of the Western Alliance.[18] Some of the major points of ERE's foreign policy paralleled the pronouncements of the Center Union. Karamanlis stated that the orientation of Greek foreign policy was "determined" by the nation's geographical location, history, and future objectives. Greece had sought, and would continue to seek, good relations with all peoples, thus defending and fortifying world peace. Greece would remain faithful to her alliances, which afforded her complete security cover. Karamanlis then eulogized the historic and—for the future of Greece decisive—association with the Common Market, and naturally claimed the credit for it. His speech in general did not reveal any new approaches or major turns in what had been the characteristic ERE foreign policy position since 1956.

The elections were held on 29 October amid rumblings in the opposition press that ERE and ERE-controlled governmental machinery were preparing an election coup d'état in order to retain the reins of government once more through illegitimacy and violence. The election results returned ERE to power. The Center Union got a significant segment of the vote, and the Communists were dealt a severe blow in comparison to the proportion of votes they had managed to secure in the 1958 elections.[19]

17. "Text of Papandreou's Speech to Athenians," *Vema*, 27 October 1961, p. 1.
18. "Text of Karamanlis' Speech to Thessalonians," *Kathimerini*, 3 October 1961, p. 1.
19. The results of elections were as follows: in the 300-seat Parliament, ERE got 169 seats (51.3 per cent of the vote), the Center Union 107 seats (34.3 per cent of the vote), and PAME 24 seats (15.1 per cent of the vote).

Parliamentary Debates

Karamanlis swiftly formed a government and presented his program to the newly elected Parliament on 4 December 1961. The Center Union Deputies and the EDA Deputies failed to recognize the legality of the elections and the resultant Karamanlis government. EDA briefly appeared in Parliament on 4 December and a spokesman read a statement on the new government's program, while the Center Union Deputies abstained from parliamentary participation for over one month, refusing to take the oath until January 1962. Karamanlis' foreign policy program included the familiar pronouncements regarding the historical and ideological determinism of Greece's pro-Western orientation and her faith in the United Nations as the best instrument for achieving international justice and peaceful coexistence with adequately inspected general and complete disarmament.[20]

The ERE program clearly indicated once more Greece's permanent orientation toward NATO, the Cyprus issue being settled and no longer requiring the caution that characterized the program of 1958. Greece's NATO participation and its valuable effects were lauded. Karamanlis added that given the long and vulnerable Greek frontiers, which had been repeatedly invaded, Greece had good reason to "always" maintain her position within NATO. He stressed that Greece, seeking to supplement efforts toward securing peace, had attempted to improve relations with Albania, Bulgaria, and especially the Soviet Union. None of these countries, however, had demonstrated through their actions a sincere desire to restore good relations and allow a climate of genuine détente to prevail. The importance of continuing policies of cooperation and friendship with Yugoslavia and Turkey was stressed once more.

Karamanlis then touched upon the very important relationship of economics and economic development to the Greek defense effort within NATO. He argued that "the need for increased investments toward [Greek] economic development, in connection with the *economic burden resulting from . . . defensive* organization, renders inevitable the *dependence* of the Greek economy on sufficient economic reinforcement from foreign nations." [21] He believed that this rein-

20. *Official Minutes of the Meetings of Parliament,* 4 December 1961, p. 8.
21. Ibid., p. 9 (emphasis supplied).

forcement should be of two types: first, loans (on very good terms) from friendly nations designed to be used toward economic development; and second, military aid which should be continued at the "necessary level." To this end, the understanding of the United States was relied upon.

Karamanlis revealed that Greece was seeking to relieve the American burden of supplementing Greek defense costs through the establishment of a special account within NATO to which the strong allies would contribute, and which was designed to help economically weaker allies to maintain the NATO-required levels of defensive capability. The acceptance of this proposal, added Karamanlis, would be the best indicator that NATO was a mutually supporting organization concerned with the national interests of its members as well as their collective interests. With regard to the size of military expenditures, the door was left open for possible increases. Karamanlis indicated that an effort would be made not to increase military costs without reducing the fighting strength of the Greek forces.

Spyros Markezinis and his Progressives,[22] who appeared in Parliament despite their disapproval of the way the elections were conducted and the validity of the results, criticized primarily the lack of flexibility in Greek foreign policy and the lack of exercise of "initiative," especially in the area of achieving better relations with the Soviet Union as well as the Balkan nations.[23] Markezinis also felt that the importance of Common Market association was not brought home clearly by ERE. Yet he warned that Greece should not allow her Western orientation to prevent her from grasping the initiative in independent policies such as exploiting the Russian-Albanian dispute to come to terms with Albania on the outstanding issue of North Epirus.[24]

EDA deputies appeared briefly in Parliament to read a statement charging that the elections were invalid and that ERE had been returned once more to power thanks to the pressures of "local and for-

22. It would be hard to classify the Progressives within either the Conservative or the Center movements. They have vacillated often and have supported both. Markezinis' primary loyalty appears to be to his own ability to rule Greece through policies which would yield maximum advantage for her.
23. S. Markezinis in ibid., 6 December 1961, p. 17.
24. *Official Minutes of the Meetings of Parliament*, 21 January 1962, p. 181.

eign reactionary interests" which had been alarmed by the large EDA vote of 1958. These interests had doomed ERE to Western obedience.[25] EDA interpreted Greek association with the Common Market, of which she did not approve, as an attempt by the West to cut off Greece's contact with East European markets.[26]

ERE's policy in the Balkans, according to EDA, was not conducive to Greek interests but rather followed directives dictated by the occasional American policies in this area. Eliou, a chief spokesman for EDA, deplored ERE's reactionary policy against the establishment of a peace zone in the Balkans and its persistence in fabricating the so-called "Bulgarian danger." He stated characteristically: "Leave the Bulgarians. You know that you are not threatened by them, but those by whom you are threatened you have already established here and they are *your sovereigns*." [27] Here he was undoubtedly referring to the Americans.

Panayotis Kanellopoulos, once more in the ranks of ERE, characterized EDA's criticisms as being basically Soviet-motivated. He accused EDA of systematically negating every single policy or measure adopted by ERE, regardless of its merit.[28] Kanellopoulos implied that the occasional sound criticism was thus robbed of all its usefulness since it was interspersed with systematic, static-like criticism designed to jam or to confuse the effectiveness and purposefulness of Greek foreign policies. Kanellopoulos explained that one of the main reasons why EDA lost votes in 1961, as compared with 1958, was its blanket criticism of Greece's "defensive shield." It was clear to Kanellopoulos that EDA's policies were dictated by the Soviet Union and the outlawed Greek Communist party. Of all Greeks, added Kanellopoulos, only the EDA deputies had refused to be incensed by the constant and provocative threats flung upon Greece by the Soviet Union.[29]

Domestic Issues

Foreign policy was not the top public concern in 1961 as had been the case in previous elections, because the temporary solution of the

25. John Passalides in ibid., 6 December 1961, p. 19; the same point was made in a speech by A. Brillakis in ibid., 9 January 1962, p. 58.
26. E. Eliou in ibid., 9 January 1962, p. 53.
27. Ibid., 19 January 1962, pp. 125, 126 (emphasis supplied).
28. P. Kanellopoulos in ibid., 9 January 1962, p. 56.
29. "Kanellopoulos Criticizes Center Union," *Vema*, 3 July 1962, p. 5.

Cyprus dispute, together with Center/Left accusations that ERE was slowly executing a plan to create one-party domination of Greece, diverted the attention of the voters to primarily local issues. Generally, it can be noted that the solution of the Cyprus issue allowed ERE to return to a solidly pro-Western, pro-NATO position without any reservations, doubts, or complaints. The government's main concern was now to secure enough economic and military aid from the West to maintain Greece's defense requirements, without adverse effects on the planned efforts to achieve rapid economic development. A considerable shift in emphasis was noted, however, in the sense that Western European nations (such as the United Kingdom, France, and West Germany) were projected as possible replacements for the United States in military and economic aid contributions to Greece.

The Center and the Left returned to the Cyprus issue during the 1961 campaign and attempted to keep it alive by emphasizing the "defeatist" solution to which ERE had acquiesced. The Center interpreted the defeat in the Cypriote objectives as due to lack of ability, imagination, and courage of the ERE policy-makers. The Left interpreted the Cyprus solution as a manifestation of the deference of Greek foreign policy to Western pressures and directives which rendered it thoroughly impotent. All three parties or movements recognized the importance of achieving better relations with the Soviet Union and the Balkan nations. The disagreement was over how this betterment could be brought about.

The domestic issues which attracted the public interest away from international affairs in the 1961–63 period were mainly generated by the Center–Conservative antagonism, which reached acute proportions following the 1961 elections. The Center party argued that the elections of 1961 were fraudulent, that ERE was saturating the state apparatus as well as the armed forces and the police with conservative functionaries, and that Greece was marching down the road to a single-party system and dictatorship.[30] The King (Paul I) became a frequent target of George Papandreou's wrath and was accused of favoring ERE, of not intervening to restore political normalcy in Greece by proclaiming new elections, and of establishing himself as the

---

30. "Speech by S. Venizelos in Parliament," *Vema*, 21 January 1962, p. 7; see also "Speech by G. Papandreou in Parliament," *Vema*, 3 March 1962, p. 7.

leader of the Greek political Right.[31] Frequent Center accusations against ERE were aimed at the Conservatives' inability to take timely and effective action on such key problems as: checking emigration, which was assuming alarming proportions; chronically spending less than any other European nation on education while spending more on defense; being unable to reverse the perpetual and vicious cycle of unemployment, or to institute an effective system of progressive taxation which would spare the poor. The Conservatives were held responsible also for neglecting farm problems and for overspending unwisely on luxurious and nonproductive public works.[32] The main critical theme of the Center was that Greece was damaging her world image by appearing more and more as a reactionary police state. ERE's reaction to all this was to dismiss Center criticisms as demagogic and to provide statistical documentation of the steadily growing national and per capita incomes.

Key Foreign Policy Considerations, 1961–62

The primary concern in foreign affairs in the 1961–62 period was with the ever-present conflict between economic development and costly military expenditures. In May 1962, the NATO Council convened in Athens to discuss important organizational issues such as the formation of a multinational nuclear force, problems of political cooperation, and the like. The Greek government sought to impress upon the NATO representatives its need for permanent military and economic aid. NATO was asked to provide yearly aid in the sum of $100,000,000. Following some discussion, it was decided to establish a NATO consortium, of which Greece would be a member, to study the status of the Greek and Turkish economies and eventually assess their needs for aid and technical assistance.

31. "Speech by G. Papandreou in Crete," Vema, 20 March 1962, p. 1. It is interesting to note how George Papandreou in the summer of 1965 reverted to the same type of criticism against King Paul's young heir, King Constantine. Once more, Papandreou felt that the young King had set himself up as the champion of the conservative movement. And he was highly critical of the King's reluctance to resolve the current political crisis in Greece by proclaiming general elections.

32. "Speech by G. Papandreou in Parliament," Vema, 18 May 1962, p. 1; see also "Speech by G. Mavros to the Legislative Committee of Parliament," Vema, 2 August 1962, p. 4.

The Center Union considered that the Greek position was handled quite inadequately in this conference. The Karamanlis government was said to have ruined Greece's chances of receiving NATO aid by unjustifiably bragging about the country's rapid economic regeneration and progress. The consortium was interpreted as an open interference by foreign nations in the internal economic affairs of Greece. Greece was urged, like Britain, Holland, and Denmark, to assess her own economic capabilities and inform NATO that her military expenditures would simply have to be lowered. It would then be up to NATO to support Greece in current levels of defense or absorb another loss in its total defensive capability.[33]

George Papandreou reviewed the Center's criticisms on foreign policy in a speech delivered to the Greek Parliament in May 1962.[34] He summed up Greece's role in NATO as one of fulfilling all her responsibilities but not exercising her rights. Here he advanced the familiar formula that each NATO member should contribute to total defense in proportion to its economic capabilities.[35] Then he produced statistics showing that Greece was spending the most for defense in proportion to its national income, with the exception of the three rich countries (the United States, Britain, and France). Papandreou argued that Karamanlis was responsible for the termination of foreign aid to Greece, which was allegedly the result of his inordinate and presumptuous claims concerning Greece's "phenomenal economic progress."

Papandreou proceeded once more to scold Karamanlis for negotiating the "infamous" Zurich–London agreements on Cyprus, explaining that he had voted for their ratification in Parliament only because he wanted to prevent an acute international crisis involving Greece over the Cyprus question. But Papandreou clearly committed a great error of judgment when he and his party voted in the Greek Parliament for the ratification of the London agreements on Cyprus. His vote was not necessary to bring about ratification. By rejecting them, he would not have prevented their adoption but he would have

33. "Triumph or Failure?" *Vema*, 9 March 1962, p. 1.
34. *Vema*, 18 May 1962, p. 1.
35. This has been the position advocated throughout the 1950s by both Conservatives and Liberals.

left the way clear for future attacks upon the Conservatives for any unpleasant consequences of the treaties, without having to share the guilt. The current crisis in Cyprus is a direct outgrowth of the built-in instability of the London and Zurich treaties; Papandreou cannot make major political capital of this situation because he himself approved the treaties. It should be noted that key Center figures (such as Venizelos, Mavros, Allamanis, Baltatzis, and others) who were not under Papandreou's leadership at the time voted against ratification.[36] Papandreou, in the same speech, attacked ERE for its poor handling of the "Macedonian" issue (that is, allowing the Yugoslavs to revive it) and chastised Karamanlis for failing to safeguard sufficiently the rights of the Greek minority in Egypt.

The Years of Transition

The year 1962 marked the termination of direct American aid to Greece[37] and the beginning of a working association of Greece with the Common Market, as well as continued vacillations between threats and peace offers from the Soviet Union and other East European nations, especially Rumania and Bulgaria.

In 1963, the Greek policy of close association with NATO and the United States remained as firm as ever. Karamanlis and Averoff outlined Greece's position on general NATO issues in a working visit and in opinion exchanges with their opposite numbers in Holland.[38] They placed Greece in favor of the development of a multinational NATO nuclear force, without, however, opposing the desires of individual NATO nations who wished to develop independent national nuclear deterrent forces. This was an obvious attempt on their part to agree with both sides in the Franco-American dispute regarding nuclear control. Greece was declared in favor of a political union of Europe within the Common Market's framework, provided this was done in the vein of further cementing Atlantic strength and unity rather than weakening it. Karamanlis and Averoff declared Greece's neutrality in the Franco-British dispute as well as on the terms of Britain's entry

36. See Vema, 26 February 1959, p. 1, and 27 February 1959, p. 1.
37. "Vice-President Johnson Declares Termination of American Aid," Vema, 30 August 1962, p. 1.
38. G. N. Anastasopoulos, "Karamanlis and Averoff in Hague," Kathimerini, 1 March 1963, p. 1.

in the Common Market, and reiterated their certainty that Greek independence and territorial integrity were firmly guaranteed by the United States and NATO.

The year 1963 found Greece in the midst of a major domestic crisis. George Papandreou, leading the Center Union's forces, pursued his "relentless struggle," as he called it, to the point of questioning the feasibility of continuing the system of constitutional monarchy in Greece.[39] Fears of possible civil strife, coup d'état, or other abnormal solutions to this very dangerous state of affairs became quite prevalent throughout the country. It was in this climate that the events of May–June 1963 [40] brought about the resignation of Karamanlis' government and ended the era of Conservative dominance in Greek politics, which had its origins in the Papagos government of 1952.

39. "Text of Letter from G. Papandreou to King Paul," *Kathimerini*, 28 March 1963, p. 1.
40. For more details on these events see Chapter 13, infra, pp. 166–69.

Chapter Twelve
The Spectrum of Political Views
in the Period of Transition

1963 was the period of transition—the period when conservatism, after twelve years of direct control over Greek affairs, had eroded enough to yield under the relentless criticism of the Center and the Left. It was a period of relative international calm. It was the period of the Kennedy–Khrushchev détente, following the nerve-racking test of the Cuban missile crisis. It follows, then, that in 1963 both extremes eased somewhat their mutual polemics and emphasized issues such as peace, economic development, and social reform. The relaxation in the international situation allowed the majority of Greek politicians and public alike to turn their attention toward national issues, which will be discussed in greater detail in Chapter 13. Foreign policy issues and defense were moved back in the order of importance, and were discussed mainly in relationship to domestic issues such as economic development and national dignity.

The Conservatives: Western Orientation
with a Measure of Dependence

The Conservative position in 1963 was not very different from previous years. Basically the Conservatives could visualize Greece only as a permanent member of NATO, closely associated with the United States and in some measure dependent upon it. A key conservative spokesman characterized the prevailing relationship between Greece and the United States as follows:

it is easy to say that we belong to the Western World and that we will do whatever the United States wishes us to do, and it is equally easy to say that we will conduct an independent policy *vis-à-vis* the Americans. But neither the one is permissible nor the other is possible, neither the one nor the other must be applied.[1]

The same spokesman concluded that a realistic appraisal should place Greece in the middle of the two extremes mentioned above, and he remarked that "whoever argues that there can be real independence, is naïve or a demagogue." [2]

The Conservatives[3] stressed the fact that Greece, at the crossroads of the world, had been historically associated with every major world crisis: the Persian wars, the Byzantine wars, the two world wars, culminating with the Greek civil war which had been a manifestation of the West's resistance against further spread of communism. Greece's involvement was dictated in every instance by her geographical importance, which rendered her a primary target in the paths of occasional invaders. Therefore Greece had no choice but to remain a staunch NATO ally due to geographical, historical, and other circumstances.[4]

In discussing the subject of nuclear armaments, the Conservatives maintained that it would be very useful for as many countries as possible to possess strong atomic arsenals. They qualified their views, however, with the observation that only the United States was capable of mustering a significant nuclear retaliatory force.[5] If one accepted the assumption that there was no defense against total nuclear attack, and that the balance of terror reduced nuclear weapons to a status of idle deterrence, then the reemergence of conventional wars appeared quite possible. The Conservatives, in this respect, felt that the rich

1. Gregory P. Kassimatis, "Rules and Methods of Foreign Policy," *International Relations*, Athens (February 1963), p. 45. This attitude was shared by G. Lyhnos (Chairman of the Parliamentary Committee on Foreign Affairs) who in his article, "The Independence of Great Powers and the International Framework of Greece," *International Relations*, Athens (May 1963), p. 33, stated: "The principle and the meaning of allied entanglements presupposes automatic reduction of the self-sovereignty of all governments." He implied that the smaller the nation, the greater the sovereignty limitation.

2. Kassimatis, p. 47.

3. Evangelos Averoff, "The Collision of the Two Worlds from the Athenian Observation Post," *International Relations*, Athens (February 1963), pp. 5–6.

4. Lyhnos, p. 34. Lyhnos argued that all Greek parties, with the exception of the Communists, were agreed on the correctness of a Western orientation.

5. Averoff, p. 8.

NATO members were not preparing themselves adequately for such conventional wars and alerted them to the danger of being caught inadequately prepared for a conventional response to a limited aggressive probe.

In evaluating NATO, the Conservatives pointed out that individual member nations would have been far behind their defensive objectives without NATO's cohesive coordination.[6] Thus they supported General Norstad's proposals for the establishment of a mobile international NATO force which would be a giant step in the direction of military integration and coordination. Reflecting a typical attitude of NATO states bordering the Warsaw Pact nations, the Conservatives argued that conventional war should be fought at the NATO borders, and that no strategic withdrawals should be relied upon.[7]

It is important, at this point, to record the Conservative Foreign Minister's views on disarmament in the light of the great commotion which has centered around the topic of Balkan denuclearized or "peace" zones, and the exploitation of this issue by leftist elements throughout Greece and abroad. Evangelos Averoff held that disarmament efforts had been used, paradoxically enough, as a major psychological warfare weapon in international relations. He was hopeful, however, that the high costs of modern armaments would force the world powers to consider disarmament more seriously.[8] As to local plans for peace and disarmament, Averoff saw no usefulness in them, since they would be meaningful only as segments of larger plans involving entire continents. Local plans at most were "weapons" in the arsenal of Communist psychological warfare. It could not make much difference, argued Averoff, whether Greece was hit by nuclear missiles launched from a distance of five hundred miles or fifteen hundred miles.

In discussing peaceful coexistence, Averoff cautioned that the underdeveloped neutralist nations should not be allowed to sink into worse economic straits, because the foundations of the Western system as well as world peace would be destroyed. He felt that economic

6. Ibid., p. 10.
7. Ibid., p. 11. This is an especially understandable argument for a small country like Greece, since a strategic withdrawal could mean abandonment of the largest portion of the nation to enemy forces
8. Ibid., p. 9.

aid was not an adequate stimulus for economic development, because losses in exports by single-product exporting countries often canceled out its benefits. Needed were better terms of trade for raw materials which, coupled with technical aid, would bring about much better results than pure economic aid.[9]

Averoff pointed out also some basic weaknesses of the Western world vis-à-vis the Eastern bloc. One was the lack of awareness and propagation of the "ideology of freedom" by the youth of the West. Another paradoxical weakness was that Western systems provided "too much liberty," which was exploited by the Communists to undermine democracy. Averoff felt that a system of "disciplined liberty" would best guarantee the perpetuation of the Western system of government.[10] He intimated finally that Greece would never be intolerant of different (nondemocratic) political systems. As substantiation, he cited Greece's close and constructive relationship with Yugoslavia. Asking nothing more than mutual respect and noninterference in one another's internal affairs, Greece would continue seeking such good relations with the remaining Balkan nations.

The Progressives: A Foreign Policy of Initiatives

Spyros Markezinis' views on Greek foreign policy were quite reminiscent of nineteenth-century personal diplomacy.[11] The leader of the Progressive party, exuding self-confidence, argued that there could be no winners following a general nuclear war. Although war was postponed by the balance of armaments, there was nothing to prevent the spiraling self-perpetuation of these armaments with their concomitant staggering military costs. He felt that "politics" should intervene in the chaotic world of permanent cold warfare to bring about a solution to the many problems, thus averting war. This "political intervention" could be achieved only if "war tactics" were pursued by nations during peacetime, paradoxically, averting a hot war by their employment. Hence, strategic superiority during peacetime ought to be the objective of nations pursuing what Markezinis termed a "forward diplomacy."

9. Ibid., p. 13.
10. Ibid., pp. 15–16.
11. Spyros Markezinis, "Forward Diplomacy," *International Relations*, Athens (November 1962), p. 6.

The meaning of forward diplomacy for the Progressives' leader was synonymous with a diplomacy of "initiatives," an aggressive rather than a defensive diplomacy, a diplomacy which indicts rather than defends, and whose objectives tend to create problems in the areas of the opponent rather than one's own areas. Markezinis felt that the Soviet Union was the best example of a nation following this type of foreign policy.[12] He advocated such a policy for Greece, which although small should not be deterred from playing a decisive role in world politics. He illustrated this thesis with a very characteristic quotation:

> History is, moreover, created not by many but by few able ones. *Pax Atheniensis, Pax Romana* and *Pax Britannica* were the works of a few select men. The survival of the Greeks or the Israelites in history is the application of Darwin's law of the survival of the fittest.[13]

As examples of forward diplomacy, employed by Greece in the past, Markezinis included its policy with respect to the Truman Doctrine, Greek entry in NATO, and the development of a common front with Turkey. In terms of forward policies of the future, Markezinis considered Greek participation in Balkan alliances indispensable. Greece should, within that framework, try to develop a security zone from the Mediterranean to Scandinavia. This was the absolute converse of Communist propaganda that argued for a demilitarized Balkans rather than systems of alliances.

The leader of the Progressives argued that foreign policy in general should not be predictable and bound to tradition. It should be versatile and capable of initiatives and adjustments. He implied here that traditional policies of suspicion and fear toward certain Balkan nations (e.g. Bulgaria and Albania) should be abandoned, and serious efforts to effectuate Balkan détente and friendship should be undertaken.

In comparing Markezinis' policies with those of the ERE some interesting contrasts arise. For example, ERE often spoke of the "traditional classification" of Greece with the free nations of the West. Markezinis, on the other hand, spoke for banning tradition and pre-

12. Markezinis found himself here in the peculiar position of advocating the adoption of U.S.S.R.-like policies.
13. Ibid., p. 9.

dictability in foreign policies and praised Great Britain for being capable of making 180-degree changes in its foreign policy directions.[14] Another obvious difference was Markezinis' willingness to consider talks on Balkan peace and disarmament plans, contrary to ERE, whose policy toward local plans was one of caution and outright refusal to consider them unless they were pieces of larger continental-size schemes. Markezinis' stated position also implied a greater willingness to deviate from NATO-wide policies whenever the "initiatives" he advocated so dictated.

The Center Union: For an Era of Peace and International Cooperation

It is difficult to trace a unified foreign policy position for the members of the Center Union, who were drawn from a broad range of political sources ranging from socialism to conservatism. The analysis below has been based primarily on the writings of the late Sophocles Venizelos,[15] who was widely accepted as the likely foreign minister of a Center government, whenever it came to power. Venizelos' views could be considered typical of a compromise position that would gain the acceptance of the heterogeneous membership of the Center Union. As in the case of all compromises, Venizelos' position contained some inconsistencies. While on one hand he emphasized the importance of Western unity against the Communist threat, on the other hand he underscored the importance of friendship and cooperation with the East and the attainment of a world of cooperation and polycentrism.

Venizelos viewed the world as undergoing a transitional period caused by technological and scientific achievements. In such an environment the chief international problem, especially for underdeveloped countries, was to secure liberty, peace, and prosperity. Science and technology were key factors contributing toward world peace.

14. As an example he cited Britain's apparent (in 1963) abandonment of its traditional oceanic policy and its effort to enter the European Common Market, or the orderly dissolution of the British Empire and its metamorphosis into a commonwealth. See Markezinis, p. 10.

15. S. Venizelos, "Greece amid International Developments," *International Relations*, Athens (February 1963), pp. 34 ff. Venizelos died of a heart attack a year after writing this article, while campaigning for the 16 February 1964 elections which gave the Center Union a solid majority in Parliament.

They contributed in a negative way (through the balance of terror) and in a positive way (through the improvement of methods of production to ameliorate conditions of scarcity). Politics and diplomacy were retarded in comparison to the progress made by science. The pursuit of the dogma advocating domination of one world over the other was the chief obstacle to the attainment of peace, and the chief failure of politics. Suspicion was the only result of this state of affairs.

On the subject of peaceful coexistence, Venizelos held that the two wise leaders, Kennedy and Khrushchev, had made great progress toward the practical application of this concept. It was through their efforts that the world had begun to live in a state of toleration. If humanity were to be guaranteed against nuclear war for a few additional years, toleration certainly would be transformed into cooperation. The Center leader felt that a common "strategy of peace" was becoming unavoidable, as a few years before a common "strategy of war" had been deemed necessary to avert uncontrolled brute force. Ideological, political, and economic contradictions would give way to a spirit of international law.

In the pursuit of this end, the world should cease being divided into the "free" and the "communist," or what have you. The "third world," more numerous than the other two, made up of nations striving to develop economically, deserved primary attention. These underdeveloped nations demanded technical and economic support before democracy in its political form could be brought about. Pressures from a hungry and crowded underdeveloped world could plunge humanity into another worldwide holocaust.

Venizelos felt that international peace would be achieved painfully and gradually. At first, dangers arising from trouble spots should be eliminated through negotiation and compromise. Then, the international balance of armaments should gradually give way to disarmament which, in turn, would free vast material resources to be used for the development of the third world.[16] Venizelos definitely differed from Averoff on the relationship of East to West. While Averoff saw the West defending against the encroachments of the East, Venizelos

16. Ibid., p. 36. It is interesting to note the coincidence of many of Venizelos' views with President Kennedy's inaugural speech of January 1961.

felt that both systems were trying to prevail over one another. The winner of the two worlds, Venizelos was convinced, would be the system concerned with economic welfare, rather than with the dynamic propagation or imposition of its ideology.

Commenting on NATO and Western unity, Venizelos did not see any likely dangers from either ideological or interest frictions within the Western alliance. He believed that the ideological unity of the West was unbreakable, though differences existed and would continue to exist in both camps. The world, despite propaganda assertions to the contrary, could not be monolithic. The very nature of Western ideology promoted the existence of differences of approach. Whatever these differences, Venizelos argued, the common military strategy of the West should not be abandoned. Should that occur, the free world would commence its journey to final destruction.[17] Venizelos believed that Western unity was an absolute necessity in 1963 more than ever. Without that unity, the international balance of power and its war-canceling effects would be upset. He also envisioned that the day would soon arrive when the "United States of Europe" would become a reality and would be closely cooperating with the United States.

The Cretan leader was especially warm to the idea of Greek membership in NATO since Greece had entered the alliance while he was Prime Minister. "Since then," he stated, "the defensive strategy of [Greece had] constituted a segment of the similar NATO strategy." [18] No other way except Greek association with NATO existed, according to the chairman of the Liberals, who believed that any alternative to NATO participation would have accomplished considerably less for Greek national interests. Venizelos discounted Greek neutrality as infeasible. However, he saw great problems for Greece within NATO. Foremost was the need to reduce military expenditures so that productive investments could be increased, thus improving the low Greek standard of living.

17. Interestingly enough, Venizelos became the victim of his own terminology. On one hand, he was trying to speak against divisions in the world; while, on the other, he emphasized the basic difference between the two worlds (i.e. freedom or its absence). By referring to the West as the "Free World," he implied that the East was the "Slave World."

18. Venizelos, p. 38.

Venizelos perceived no immediate dangers to the security of Greece. Bulgaria was not likely to misbehave knowing that a system of collective security was protecting Greek borders. Circumstances favored a climate of pan-Balkan cooperation and understanding. He felt that issues such as the "Macedonian" were outdated and should be deemphasized and forgotten. Rather, common traits and policies breeding cooperation and understanding should be promoted. On the question of possibilities for the creation of a denuclearized Balkans, Venizelos felt that negotiations were useful and should not be abandoned. However, he hastened to add that Greece must act within the scope of her NATO obligations and not endanger her ideological orientation as a result of these negotiations.[19]

Evaluating generally the defensive strength of Greece, Venizelos believed that it ought to depend on the overall strategy of a nation, i.e. on integrated military, political, and economic plans. Greece did not have a coordinated plan for political objectives and economic development which took into consideration the effects of these factors on military preparedness and planning. As an illustration, Sophocles Venizelos pointed out that Eleftherios Venizelos' institution of an interparty common foreign policy had been abandoned by ERE.

There were more similarities than differences in the policies of Averoff and Venizelos. The differences were on matters of emphasis. Although both parties agreed on the necessity of Greek participation in NATO and Western solidarity, Venizelos appeared to be generally more conciliatory toward the Eastern bloc. He was willing to negotiate plans for local disarmament,[20] unlike Averoff, who discarded them as useless Communist psychological ammunition. Venizelos generally minimized the Communist danger from northern Balkan neighbors, in contradiction to Averoff's attitude that previous bitter experience and Greece's geographic importance and vulnerability rendered her a primary target for international communism. The Balkan policy advocated by Venizelos and the Center was closer to that advocated by

19. Ibid., pp. 39–40.
20. This point was shared by another key member of the Center Union Party (member of the Center's Executive Committee) and ex-Greek foreign minister under Papagos, Stefanos Stephanopoulos. See his article, "Does Nuclear Diplomacy Exist?" *International Relations*, Athens (February 1963), p. 23.

Markezinis, although Markezinis' philosophical foundations were quite different from those of Venizelos.[21]

Stefanos Stephanopoulos, a leading figure of the Center Union Party, pointed up another basic difference of approach between the Center and Averoff's ERE. Contrary to Averoff, who stated that the more nations possessing a strong nuclear arsenal the better, Stephanopoulos saw less risk if nuclear weaponry was restricted to the two giant powers, the United States and the Soviet Union. He felt that many dangerous situations could arise if nuclear power were possessed by numerous, perhaps irresponsible, leaders. The price of nonproliferation, he realized, was the abandonment of world leadership to the United States and the Soviet Union, who could easily bypass the rest of their allies if they resorted to direct negotiations. Still, Stephanopoulos saw this as the lesser evil to a world of nuclear power proliferation,[22] approaching what Morton Kaplan has termed the "unit-veto-system."[23]

Variations on the Left

THE PEACE MOVEMENT   One organization whose activities have been increasing and whose influence has been on the rise is the Greek Movement for International Détente and Peace. This organization's growing influence results from the worldwide awareness of the futility of nuclear war as a method of settling international disputes. The Greek peace movement was born in a declaration signed by 77 personalities from the political, intellectual, artistic, business, and labor sections of Greek society on 15 May 1955. Its charter pledged reinforcement with "all appropriate but legal methods" of the work of the United Nations and the activities of organizations for peace and détente all over the world.[24] World peace was understood as "peaceful

21. Markezinis' ideas (see supra, pp. 151–53) indicated that his policy of "initiatives" was not bound by ideological or traditional motivations. Venizelos' exposé, on the other hand, was tinted with the utopian idealism identified with thinkers who hope that men will transcend their evil natures and bring about lasting peace on earth, but who see the need of interim measures for the smooth application of the balance of power system.

22. Stephanopoulos, pp. 21–24.

23. M. A. Kaplan, *System and Process in International Politics* (New York, John Wiley, 1957), pp. 124–25.

24. "Beginning, Objectives and Organization of the Greek Movement for International Détente and Peace," *Roads of Peace* (Athens, Greek Movement for International Peace and Détente, May 1963), p. 7.

coexistence of all nations without discrimination on account of social or economic form of government, with territorial integrity and independence of each nation respected and guaranteed, and with the right of self-determination effectively applied to people still under colonial rule." [25]

The organization's objectives included efforts to bring about quick and final abandonment of nuclear testing; the abolition of armaments under an effective system of inspection; the use of funds freed from armaments to improve the standard of living of the disarming nations and underdeveloped nations in general; the dissolution of military alliances and military bases; the acceptance of the United Nations as the arbiter of international disputes; the prevention of interference in the internal affairs of one nation by another; the improvement of friendly relations among neighboring nations especially, and expansion of trade, economic, and cultural relations and mutual assistance among them.[26] The movement purported to be outside the scope and the influence of any of the Greek political parties. An inspection of its position outlined below indicates, however, a strong coincidence of its views on Greek foreign policy with those of EDA.

The chairman of the Greek Movement for International Détente and Peace, Andreas Zakkas, outlined his movement's position toward Greek participation in NATO in response to a series of questions outlined by the author.[27] Some of his more interesting responses are discussed below, primarily to illustrate this movement's position vis-à-vis that of EDA. Unlike EDA, Zakkas believed that, given certain prerequisite conditions, Greek participation in NATO could be advantageous. These conditions, however, limited seriously the scope of cooperation with NATO allowable to Greece. He considered Greek participation in NATO advantageous only if the following qualifications were accepted: first, that Greek military expenditures were to be for conventional forces only and would remain within the limits of expenditures undertaken before World War II; second, that NATO was to be committed to aid Greece only with conventional forces if she were attacked; or the corollary, Greece would contribute only con-

25. Ibid.
26. Ibid.
27. In Athens, July 1963.

ventional forces if she aided another NATO nation being attacked. Zakkas felt that given these two qualifications, Greece could adequately defend herself without being exposed to the devastating effects of nuclear warfare.

It is clear that, in this instance, Zakkas' position was in disagreement with the consistent EDA condemnation of Greek membership in NATO under any set of circumstances. His position, however, echoed that of EDA when he discussed NATO's influence on Greek politics, manifested through the imposition of a shortsighted effort to fight Communism through reactionary measures and police methods. Many liberal men in Greece, according to Zakkas, rejected, feared, or hesitated to undertake positions which would promote world peace and economic progress because they did not want to fall into disfavor with the NATO supported leadership.

In the area of economic effects of NATO membership, Zakkas, unlike EDA, felt that Greece's participation was initially quite beneficial since it had lightened the burdens of Greek military expenditures. He was in basic agreement with EDA, however, that Greece was, in the longer run, hurt economically due to the constantly increasing NATO-determined military requirements and expenditures, and also because Greek contact with Eastern markets was curtailed.

It should be noted that Zakkas, like EDA, felt that Greece should increase efforts to cultivate a fertile ground for denuclearization and disarmament in the Balkans, the Mediterranean, and Central Europe. He believed that since the tremendous concentration of power in the hands of the United States and the Soviet Union rendered them indisputable world leaders, any measure including denuclearization of the Balkans should be guaranteed by both these powers in order to be effective. The chairman of the peace movement considered that it would be madness for Greece either to participate in a multination NATO nuclear force or to host nuclear bases, since both would result in the nation's virtual annihilation in case of war. The three most important reasons accounting for NATO's very low popularity in Greek public opinion, according to Zakkas, were that NATO participation exposed Greece to nuclear warfare, that military expenditures were too high, and that NATO was to blame for the so-called "solution" of the Cyprus dispute.

Andreas Zakkas was representative of many proponents of world peace who hope to attain it through the voluntary obedience of all nations to world law and international organization. He falls into the category of men who state that if men do good and avoid evil, then all the harassing and dangerous international problems will be ironed out. Zakkas had cooperated with EDA and had been elected deputy under its ticket during the 1958–61 period. He claimed, however, during our interview, to be independent of all political parties in Greece.

THE EDA POSITION   EDA's 1963 position on Greek international affairs was based on the assumption that the ERE government was a faithful organ of the Western alliance and acted in accordance with United States and NATO directives.[28] NATO, led by the United States, was said to be pursuing a policy designed to further colonialist interests and to perpetuate unpopular but obedient regimes, such as the deposed Menderes regime in Turkey and the Karamanlis regime in Greece. [29] In promoting its policies, NATO was employing aggressive measures so as to provoke the Soviet Union into war by brandishing nuclear threats which could, if they materialized, destroy most of the world, including Greece, which was deeply involved in NATO.

The major foreign policy issue for EDA, in fact an issue affecting national survival, was Greece's attitude toward nuclear weapons and the development of denuclearized and demilitarized zones in the Balkans and surrounding geographic areas. EDA uniformly urged the immediate commencement of negotiations leading to the development of a peace zone in the Balkans guaranteed by the United States and the Soviet Union. This, EDA believed, would contribute to the cultivation of a climate of international détente by elimination of trouble spots in the area of the Balkans.[30] The advantages of such a

28. This often-repeated assertion was once more advanced in a short book presenting the leftist position toward Greece in NATO. See M. Kyrkos, *Greece and NATO* (Athens, 1961), p. 28.

29. K. Pyromaglos, "The Denuclearized Mediterranean," *Political Economic Research* (Athens, June 1963), p. 5.

30. For articles urging the adoption of "denuclearized Balkans" proposals and criticisms of the role of ERE in this issue see: Michael Kyrkos, "Conclusions and Judgments from the Last Legislative Battle," *Political Economic Research* (Athens, May 1963), p. 7; St. S. Mercouris, "The Demissilized Balkans," *Political Economic Research* (Athens, 15 December 1962), p. 6; "The Balkans

policy would be the transfer of funds from military objectives to economic development and improvements in the standard of living, as well as the "catching" effects which could lead to worldwide understanding, disarmament, and peace.[31]

The Center party leaders, Papandreou and Venizelos, were criticized by EDA for not condemning ERE outright and even refusing to discuss certain vital issues. EDA believed that the Center leaders rightly condemned the "subservient" role of ERE within NATO; ERE did not pursue Greek rights although it fulfilled Greek responsibilities to the letter.[32] However, the Center's leaders were accused of not criticizing ERE's position on the key issues of a denuclearized Balkans, the installation of nuclear bases or Polaris submarines on Greek land and water, and other NATO-related policies which exposed Greece to the horrible dangers of nuclear devastation.

Another key EDA criticism expounded on the adverse effects of NATO membership on Greek sovereignty. EDA rejected the argument of NATO proponents that Greek membership did not result in loss of independence for Greece but involved only necessary interallied cooperation and integration. There was no consolation either in the reasoning that no nation was "absolutely independent" and that all nations had abandoned a measure of their national sovereignty for the attainment of collective security. This would be fine, EDA maintained, provided that all allied nations gave up the same proportion of sovereignty; however, some gave up more than others, and so created the conditions substantiating charges of subservience. EDA argued that the United States and Britain had not given up any of their sovereign rights. On the other hand "every Greek knew" that in "all cases" dealing with clearly internal affairs (whether political, economic, or social) the "allied factor" had voiced its "opinion" which had been understood and carried out as an "order."[33]

Michael Kyrkos, illustrating EDA sentiments, pointed out certain basic changes in international relations which had increased the advisability of Greece's adopting a neutralist orientation. He felt that the

and the Adriatic Can Be Converted to a Real Peace Zone," *Political Economic Research* (Athens, 30 November 1962), p. 12.

31. Mercouris, "Conclusions," p. 6.
32. Kyrkos, "Conclusions," p. 8.
33. Kyrkos, *Greece and* NATO, p. 28.

early 1950s style of American policy was dead. This policy, under Secretary Dulles, followed the precept of "he who is not with us is against us." Kennedy and Rusk had abandoned that slogan and were willing to tolerate neutralism in order to avoid isolation. The Soviet Union for its part had assumed leadership in technical achievements since the advent of the Sputnik in 1957. It was abundantly clear that the Soviet Union and its leader, Khrushchev, were sincere in their pursuit of world peace. Given these basic "changes" in the international scene, Kyrkos felt that Greece should abandon NATO and follow a policy of neutrality and equal friendship with both camps.[34]

The Military Viewpoint: NATO a Necessity

The military element in Greece does not represent, in theory at least, any given political position. Yet, the opinions of military men on foreign affairs could become exceedingly important should the armed forces come to exercise political power by coup d'état or any other method. This contingency, although undesirable, is not out of the question in a country of the size and socioeconomic level of Greece.[35] On the basis of 1962–63 representative writings, the military appeared generally agreed that Albania and especially Bulgaria had continuing territorial aspirations on Greece. This classified them as definitely potential enemy nations. Bulgaria was viewed with special concern since it had a very strong army and had been spending increasingly larger amounts on defense. The military felt that Greece alone, or Greece and Turkey combined, could not hold out against a Soviet-backed Bulgarian attack without NATO support and assistance.[36]

Military analysts pointed out that, given the nuclear stalemate, limited conventional war was becoming quite possible. They urged the NATO defensive machinery to plan to hold the line at the northern borders of Greece and Turkey, since the loss of these countries would

34. Ibid., pp. 44–48.
35. G. Lowell Field, "Summary of the Theory of Political Development" (Storrs, University of Connecticut, June 1960, unpublished draft).
36. A. Frontistis (ex-Chief of Greek General Staff), "The Defensive Problem in the Greek Area," International Relations, Athens (November 1962), p. 33; T. Tsakalotos (ex-Chief of Greek General Staff), "The Nuclear Problem and Greece," International Relations, Athens (May 1963), p. 99; T. Gregoropoulos (ex-Chief of Greek General Staff), "Current Defensive Problems—Limited Wars and Local Enemy Actions," International Relations, Athens (February 1963), p. 31.

mean the loss of the eastern Mediterranean and would cut off the Western world from North Africa and the Middle East.[37]

General Athanasios Frontistis, ex-Chief of the Greek General Staff, felt that NATO was all-important for Greece, since without it Greek defense would have been in a "virtual state of infancy," unable to keep up with technological modernization in the weapons field.[38] He also argued that Greek financial ability was far from adequate to cover the nation's defensive requirements and had to be augmented by the stronger NATO allies.

General Thrasivoulos Tsakalotos, another ex-Chief of Staff, discussed some of the complaints over NATO's treatment of Greece. He felt that NATO should have supported more strongly the Greek position vis-à-vis Albania and Greece's claim on "Northern Epirus." [39] He believed also that, if relations between Greece and Turkey did not improve, their possible future wartime cooperation would be rendered quite inadequate. On the matter of NATO nuclear leadership, Tsakalotos was opposed to nuclear weapons proliferation for fear of its polycentric effects which could render the leadership of the alliance inoperative and self-canceling. He preferred that the United States continue to retain the decision-making power on the utilization of nuclear weapons.[40]

Some of the key problem areas related to Greece and NATO were discussed in an interview with Colonel Nicolaos Sorokos (Greek Royal Army–NATO affairs).[41] Sorokos believed that Greece's power had been reinforced considerably through NATO membership. Specifically, he felt that in case of a general conflagration the small nation's fate would be linked with the collective fate of NATO and the Western world. The Greek forces would be reinforced by the United States Sixth Fleet, by American tactical air forces, and by nuclear deterrent forces. In case of a local war, he believed that Greece, being strategically vital for NATO, would be safeguarded and supported materially. He expected, however, that some NATO members with neu-

37. Gregoropoulos, pp. 32–33; Frontistis, pp. 33–34.
38. Frontistis, p. 36.
39. Tsakalotos, p. 99.
40. Ibid., pp. 105–06.
41. July 7, 1963. Sorokos' actual views are not necessarily reflected in this account, since he may have been misinterpreted or the author may have surmised where there was no such intention on the part of the interviewee.

tralist tendencies, such as Norway and Denmark, might oppose involvement in a "Greek adventure" (as they would characterize a local Balkan war).

When asked to assess the possible effects resulting from Greek withdrawal from NATO, Sorokos responded that this question should qualify whether getting out of NATO meant also loosening existing relations with the United States and Britain on one hand, or France and West Germany on the other. Here he implied that these two combinations of powers comprised the two major power poles within NATO. Sorokos indicated that if relations with the United States deteriorated, then Greece stood to lose the most militarily. It would appear to follow from this statement that the military group in Greece would tend to support a pro-United States orientation in the event of a possible intra-NATO dispute. On the other hand, Sorokos considered that if Greece preferred a Franco-German orientation, sacrifices in the military sphere could possibly be balanced against benefits in the economic or political spheres. He emphasized, therefore, that NATO policies should be viewed from a combined, political–military–economic vantage point rather than an isolated, functional position. This seemed a remarkably statesmanlike attitude for the military, which has tended in the past to underemphasize political and economic considerations.

Sorokos maintained that if Greece were assumed to be completely divorced from NATO, one of the few advantages resulting would be that its priority in the Soviet Union's target list would be lowered. However, he felt that in case of a general conflagration, even if Greece were outside of NATO, destruction would only be postponed, not averted. Whether within or without NATO, Greece was so strategically located that it would inevitably become a part of the theater of war. As an example, he cited World War II: Greece would have been attacked by the Axis powers even if she had followed a policy of scrupulous noninvolvement.

Sorokos felt that getting out of NATO did not promise savings in military expenditures. Greece outside of NATO would, like Yugoslavia, have to maintain a sizable and costly armed force in order to safeguard its national interests and independence. This would be economically ruinous without American and NATO technical and logistic support. If Greece reduced its military forces to a nominal size, like Austria, then it would be subject to pressures from friends and foes alike and would have to acquiesce to them for lack of ability to back up its international position with military force.

Association with the Common Market

Given this military evaluation of Greece's position in the Western world, a few words should be said about its relationship with the subject of recent Greek association with the European Common Market and the politico-strategic problems besetting the Atlantic alliance. The association with the Common Market has been hailed as one of the most significant political events in modern Greek history. It has turned the sights of Greek diplomacy away from the East, the focus under the concept of *Megali Idea*, and toward the West and modern systems of international cooperation leading to European federalism.[42]

Greece, in signing the Athens agreement of 9 July 1961, associated herself with the Common Market and accepted the principles and political objectives of the Rome Treaty.[43] It appears from current political and military writings that Greece's politico-economic interests are closely associated with Western Europe, while her military interests are better served through American association. It follows from this state of affairs that forthcoming Greek foreign policies will support closer European political cooperation within a larger framework of a closely knit Atlantic military association. An American-European break in the NATO ranks would be catastrophic for Greece, which would be forced to make a thankless choice entailing sacrifices regardless of whether it sided with the United States or with Europe.

42. D. Nicolareizis, "The Foreign Policy of Greece," *International Relations*, Athens (November 1962), pp. 72, 83–84.

43. N. Cambalouris, "The Political Union of Europe and Our Association with the Common Market," *International Relations*, Athens (November 1962), p. 94.

Chapter Thirteen
The Fall of Conservatism

The Beginning of the End

In June 1963, the Karamanlis government resigned over a disagreement with the King regarding the wisdom of carrying out a scheduled state visit by the Greek royal family to Great Britain. Karamanlis opposed the visit, fearing Communist reaction against the King in Britain, where the Communists were vigorously protesting the continued incarceration of "political prisoners" in Greece. The King insisted on going, and the immediate setting for Karamanlis' resignation was thus staged.

Deeper causes for this resignation apparently existed, however. There were rumblings of a deep-seated disagreement brewing between King Paul and Prime Minister Karamanlis. No concrete information as to the substance of this disagreement has become available to date. Furthermore, the "relentless struggle" of the Center Union, coupled with the refusal of Centerites to recognize the legitimacy of the ERE government, motivated Karamanlis to seek another election confrontation and, hopefully, another victory for his party. Karamanlis considered the summer of 1963 a propitious time for new elections. He asked the King to dissolve the Parliament and to proclaim elections within forty-five days with the single-member district system, as required by the law of the land at the time. The King, however, did not cooperate in this proposal. Instead he appointed Panayotis Pipinelis, a member of Karamanlis' resigned cabinet, to form a caretaker government responsible for coordinating a new election system and proclaiming elections as soon as practicable thereafter.[1]

EDA, the Center Union, and the Progressives demanded the simple proportional election system, the replacement of the Pipinelis government with a truly apolitical one, and the cleansing of the state apparatus which, they claimed, had become saturated with key ERE political appointments.[2] These were their minimum conditions for participating in new elections. ERE again voiced its preference for the single-member district system. The Pipinelis government constructed a "reinforced proportional" variation of the 1958 election system which was adopted in Parliament with the votes of ERE deputies only. All other parties abstained from parliamentary deliberations on this issue, insisting on the adoption of the simple proportional system.

The political situation remained thoroughly unsettled, with all parties firmly unyielding on their initial positions until late in September. The Pipinelis government resigned at this time, bowing to relentless Center pressures. The Center, in turn, abandoned its insistence on the adoption of the simple proportional system. A new caretaker government, under the premiership of Supreme Court Justice Stylianos Mavromihalis, was entrusted with the ticklish task of conducting impartial elections. Mavromihalis' government secured the declared confidence of Conservatives as well as the Center. In a highly tense and heated atmosphere, elections were held on 3 November. Foreign policy issues once more were displaced by emotionally charged domestic issues. The choice presented to the voters, according to the Center, was one between democracy of the Center and masked totalitarianism of the Right.

The November elections did not solve the political crisis. The voters gave a very slim victory to the Center Union which secured a plurality

1. This procedure in a sense set a precedent for King Constantine's handling of the most recent Greek political crisis. George Papandreou, upon his resignation on 15 July 1965, recommended that the Parliament be dissolved and new elections held within 45 days. The King instead attempted to have a transitional government formed under one of Papandreou's former lieutenants such as George Athanasiades-Novas, Stefanos Stephanopoulos, and Elias Tsirimokos. None of these attempts have been successful to date and Greece as of early September 1965 remains without a strong representative government.

2. The state apparatus, as used here, includes the armed forces, the police and gendarmerie, the Home Guard units, the courts, educational system, national radio, etc.

of seats in the Parliament, but not a majority. This plurality alone was not adequate to support a self-sustaining Center government.[3] King Paul, in accordance with constitutional procedure, asked George Papandreou, the leader of the Center Union, to form a government. Papandreou formed an all-Center Union government and proceeded to put into effect a number of his pre-election promises, especially those to the rural population.

Karamanlis, at this point highly indignant, decided to withdraw from Greek politics and left for Paris. His party's leadership passed on to his uncle, Panayotis Kanellopoulos, who had been a leading ERE figure. Papandreou, conscious that his government needed a vote of confidence to survive, attempted to attract ERE deputies into the Center Union's ranks but failed. Early in December, the Papandreou government managed a vote of confidence in Parliament only with the addition of twenty-eight EDA votes. Papandreou refused to erect his government on quasi-Communist foundations and resigned, recommending that the King proclaim new elections within forty-five days, with the existing election system.

The King, again following constitutional procedure, asked the minority leader, Kanellopoulos, to form a government. Kanellopoulos attempted to bring together a biparty coalition cabinet but failed because the Center remained firmly united around Papandreou's leadership, and disavowed any cooperation with ERE. The King then dissolved the Greek Parliament once more and asked John Paraskevopoulos, the Deputy Director of the National Bank of Greece, to form a nonpolitical caretaker government to oversee the new elections set for 16 February 1964.

Ironically, the strong views on election systems were exchanged at this time between ERE and the Center. The latter, feeling a victorious dynamism, wanted the reinforced proportional system while ERE, sensing the change in the popular tide, voiced its preference for the simple proportional system. The three major antagonists in the February elections were a coalition of Kanellopoulos' ERE and Markezinis'

3. The Center Union got a little over 42 per cent of the vote and 138 out of 300 seats in Parliament, ERE slightly over 39 per cent of the vote and 132 seats. EDA secured less than 15 per cent of the vote and 28 seats. The Progressive proportion was 5 per cent and 2 seats in Parliament. However, their leader, Markezinis, failed to be reelected as a deputy.

Progressives (purely a marriage of opportunity), the Center Union, and EDA.

The elections of 16 February 1964 vindicated the long, stubborn, "relentless struggle" which the Center Union had waged against ERE. The Center secured an absolute majority with approximately 53 per cent of the popular vote. ERE, running in pre-election cooperation with the Progressives, was limited to 35 per cent, while EDA was reduced further to a meager 12 per cent. The Center Union, with 173 out of a total of 300 deputies, could now easily form a viable government and uninhibitedly advance the program it had been reiterating continuously since its formation in 1960.

The Center in Power

The reader will recall that the disunifying characteristics of the Greek Center movement have been stressed throughout this narrative. The two Papandreou governments, which were formed after the November 1963 and February 1964 elections, passed quite successfully two very serious and vital tests of the Center Union's integrity as a homogeneous party. The Papandreou "50 day government" which emerged from the 3 November 1963 elections did not command a majority of deputies in Parliament. Both ERE and EDA offered to support this government but Papandreou, feeling the pulse of the people and sensing a widespread pro-Center popular tide, preferred resignation and new elections. The first test came when the late King Paul, following constitutional procedures, asked the second most populous party (ERE) to form a cabinet, under the premiership of Panayotis Kanellopoulos, its new leader. Kanellopoulos' efforts to lure enough Center deputies to his side failed. This was a significant indication to the voters that the Center Union had matured into a homogeneous and well-disciplined party. Center deputies were willing to risk a reelection and possible defeat rather than defect to ERE. The results of the February elections proved Papandreou's assessment correct. The Center was overwhelmingly victorious.

The second unity crisis occurred immediately after the February elections. Two of the eight original Center leaders became dissatisfied with the allocation of offices. Elias Tsirimokos (leading the Greek Socialists) was dissatisfied because the presidency of the Parliament was not reoffered to him. Also, Savas Papapolites (head of EPEK) was unhappy because he was only offered the Ministry of Social Welfare when he wanted the Ministry of Labor. These leaders made their dissatisfaction public and were expelled from the Center Union. The dangerous situation was arrested, however, without any further balkanization or defections from the party, and both Papapolites and Tsirimokos were subsequently invited to return to the ranks.

Another unfortunate and unplanned event served, indirectly, to cement the Center's unity. During the pre-election period the Deputy Leader of the Center Union, Sophocles Venizelos, died of a heart attack. Although tragic, the loss of this wise and able statesman enhanced the Center Union's chances for post-election unity. It was a well-known fact that the bonds between Venizelos and Papandreou were shaky indeed. Venizelos' death left Papandreou temporarily the undisputed leader of the Center Union.

Currently (September 1965) the Center Union party is undergoing the latest and possibly a fatal crisis to its future viability as a unified and representative party of the Greek liberal (Center) movement. This crisis started over King Constantine's disagreement with his Prime Minister's attempt to remove certain conservative generals from the ranks of the Greek army and his general apprehension about the growth of Communist activity under the umbrella of the Papandreou regime. The King found an ally in Papandreou's own Minister of Defense, Peter Garoufalias, who around July 1965 began to take steps which were not in agreement with the wishes of the Prime Minister. Papandreou sought to dismiss Garoufalias and take over himself the duties of Defense Minister, but the King opposed that step, in view of allegations that Andreas Papandreou (Deputy Minister of Coordination and son of the Prime Minister) was connected with a clandestine military organization, ASPIDA (Shield).[4] Both the King and Papandreou held obstinately to their stated positions. Papandreou considered the King's refusal to accept his recommendations as lack of confidence and resigned on 15 July 1965, following a stormy 13-minute session with the young monarch.

4. This organization, currently under investigation, is presumably of a leftist, Nasserite variety and it intended to take over Greek affairs by coup d'état at a propitious moment.

The King within two hours asked the Chairman of the Parliament, George Athanasiades-Novas, a leading Center Union figure, to form a new government. There followed a frantic effort to rally Center Union deputies behind the Novas government. This effort failed. So did the two subsequent attempts to form governments under either Stefanos Stephanopoulos or, more recently, Elias Tsirimokos.

This latest political crisis, still unresolved at the time of writing, has managed to divide the Center Union party. Thirty-seven Center deputies, including most of the founding fathers of the Center Union, withdrew support from George Papandreou. Papandreou's strength in Parliament waned from 171 to the present 134 deputies (17 less than a majority) that still are under his control. The result is that no one party or faction has been able to muster a majority of 151 votes in the 300 member Parliament.

Papandreou and the King, like tragic heroes, have stuck stubbornly to their own positions: Papandreou demanding immediate elections (believing the public is behind him) or his return to power; the King, on the other hand, feeling that elections are not desirable at this time and seeking any combination of political forces in the present Parliament that would support a government. The Communists, through EDA, so far have given their unqualified support to the Papandreou forces. The King is opposed to elections at this time because a Papandreou victory would be a heavy blow to his prestige as well as to the very institution of monarchy in Greece.

There were deep-seated conditions which allowed this latest crisis to transpire. Basic among these has been the heterogeneity of the Center Union party and the polycentricity of its nature, which often invited maneuvers among its leading members vying for control or succession to party leadership. In this latest case, months before the crisis erupted an open conflict became apparent between Konstantinos Mitsotakis (Venizelos' heir apparent) and Andreas Papandreou,[5] an up and coming—though late arriving—force in the Center Union

5. The son of Prime Minister George Papandreou, who resigned his position as chairman of the Department of Economics at the University of California at Berkeley, to return to Greece as a high-priced economic consultant. He eventually gave up his American citizenship to enter Greek politics. He was elected a deputy of the Center Union and served twice as Deputy Minister of Coordination. He has often been the target of Conservative and also Center criticism.

movement. A number of other leading Center Union deputies had demonstrated their dissatisfaction with Andreas Papandreou, feeling that he was being unfairly favored and primed for top leadership of the party by his father. Given the intraparty disagreements, it was understandable that an effort was made to assign the premiership to someone else from the Center Union party.

If elections are held soon and if Papandreou, even without the defectors from the Center, wins once more, then the emerging group of deputies will be highly cohesive under the undisputed leadership of the Papandreous. If on the other hand a government is formed that manages to draw away more deputies from the 134 remaining with Papandreou, then the Center Union party will become only a memory. In the meantime, Greece remains without a stable government in the midst of the Cyprus crisis, with indications of economic disturbances, plus rumors and fears of possible military coups and civil disturbances including civil war.

In many public demonstrations throughout August and September 1965 the subject of American influence has been once more revived. This time it is alleged that the United States has interfered against Papandreou, seeking to favor the King, in order to secure more active Greek support in Vietnam, a conciliatory solution in the Cyprus dispute with Turkey, and a curbing of the internal Communist activity in Greece which the Papandreou regime purportedly invited. Appendix F provides two typical examples of the allegations and arguments regarding United States influence in Greece during the 1960s.

THE FOREIGN POLICY PROGRAM OF PAPANDREOU'S "50-DAY GOVERN-MENT"   Papandreou presented his first government's foreign policy program to the Greek Chamber of Deputies on 20 December 1963.[6] Although the Cyprus question was then reaching an explosive phase he refrained from even mentioning it. The elderly Prime Minister plunged instead into the vital matter of defense expenditures. He explained that Greece was obliged to maintain a high ceiling of military forces because Bulgaria, in violation of postwar agreements, was maintaining armed forces far in excess of those authorized by the peace

6. *Official Minutes of the Meetings of Parliament* (Athens, 1963), George Papandreou's speech of 20 December 1963, p. 10.

treaties. He pointed out that the Greek defenses within the scope of NATO had a wide mission which extended beyond Greece's self-protection. Therefore this justified NATO contributions toward the upkeep of the Greek armed forces.

The newly installed Prime Minister placed primary emphasis on reducing the heavy burden of military expenditures. He based his argument on the NATO treaty, which provided that defense efforts of NATO members should be founded on healthy social and economic conditions.[7] Thus he contended that "no . . . country [should] be called upon to bear defensive economic burdens which [were] heavier than those permitted by its economy." Papandreou held that Greece's military expenditures, in proportion to her income, were the highest in the alliance.[8] He blamed this condition on ERE, which had allegedly misled the Greek people and other NATO allies into believing that these expenditures were much lower than their true proportions, by employing inappropriate statistics. Papandreou congratulated his own cabinet for its success in securing additional allied military assistance. He explained in this vein how the Greek representatives at the December 1963 NATO Foreign Ministers Conference, led by Sophocles Venizelos, had forcefully advanced the argument that Greece could not alone execute a program of defense expenditures without substantially hindering domestic programs.

Papandreou left no doubt that Greece would give economic and social domestic programs priority over military programs. The maintenance of wide defensive missions, as required within the scope of NATO, must be financed by supplementary contributions from stronger NATO nations. Greece would continue advancing this position not as "beggary" but as a "right" within the provisions of the NATO treaty. According to Papandreou, such a firm stand of principle resulted in the unanimous NATO Council decision to recognize the special problem of Greek military expenditures. Most NATO members, such as the United States, France, West Germany, Britain, Canada, and Belgium, expressed their willingness to "participate" in Greek defensive ex-

7. This is Papandreou's interpretation of Article 2 of the NATO treaty.
8. The type of income calculation (e.g. national income, per capita income, etc.) was not specified. Subsequent debate revealed that Papandreou's figures were based on the portions of per capita income spent on defense. See infra, p. 175.

penditures to the extent that these could not be covered by the Greek national budget.

The orientation of Greek foreign policy as specified in the December 1963 program was in no major way different from the Center's 1958 and 1961 pre-election platforms.[9] In fact, large portions of the program were worded identically to the 1961 Center foreign policy position. Papandreou reiterated that factors of history and geography placed Greece in the free world, and NATO provided an effective defense against the dangers stemming from local or global wars. He qualified his position, however, by stating that "within the alliance we fulfill all our obligations, but we claim also all our rights. *This is the difference between allies and satellites.*" [10] Papandreou further qualified his pro-NATO stand by stating that while Greece was allied to the West, it wished to be friendly with the East and would seek to develop further economic and cultural relations with the countries of Eastern Europe and the Soviet Union. Papandreou underscored his satisfaction over the fact that Greece had the highest proportion of trade with the Eastern bloc of any Western nation.

The new Prime Minister then proceeded to discuss relations with countries to the north in a manner similar to ERE's foreign policy program declarations of previous years.[11] He characterized relations with Yugoslavia as friendly and pledged his sincere desire to cultivate them further. He expressed the hope that negotiations with Bulgaria would soon come to fruition through agreements to restore friendly relations between the two nations. He reminded his fellow deputies that Greece was formally in a state of war with neighboring Albania, and reiterated the Greek people's agony concerning the fate of their brethren in Northern Epirus (Southern Albania). However, he stated that the Greek government would seek to guarantee the human rights of the Greeks in that area with peaceful means only. In a sense this constituted a subtle reassurance that Greece was not interested in the territorial annexation of Northern Epirus. Papandreou, as Karamanlis had done in previous years, lauded the excellent relations which existed with the Arab world, but voiced concern over the fate of the

9. See supra pp. 120–21 for the liberal party's position on foreign policy; and pp. 137–39 for the Center's 1961 foreign policy position.
10. Emphasis supplied.
11. See supra, p. 140.

Greek community in Egypt which had lost property due to Egyptian practices of nationalization without compensation. He then proudly pronounced that Greece had never been a colonialist nation and pledged his government's firm intent to cement and strengthen relations with the developing nations of the African continent.

The Greek Prime Minister studiously avoided mention of the Cyprus issue during his December 1963 program declarations. As he explained later,[12] he had remained silent so as to preserve a united, pan-Hellenic front on the Cyprus issue. If he had brought up Cyprus he would have been forced to chastise ERE for its many blunders over the past projection and execution of the Greek case. This would have created antagonism and caused disunity during a time of great crisis. Finally, Papandreou cryptically dismissed Greek–Turkish relations as "good" and said that they could be bettered to mutual advantage.

Speaking for ERE, Evangelos Averoff-Tositsas (the ex-foreign minister of the Karamanlis government), asserted that ERE agreed with the foreign policy of the government which consisted "to the letter, of the continuation of the foreign policy of the National Radical Union [ERE]." [13] Averoff, however, sought to set the record straight regarding Papandreou's claim that, thanks to Center pressures alone, NATO had decided to contribute toward Greek military expenditures. He reminded the Greek deputies that this had been achieved thanks to ERE's diplomacy as early as May 1962, during the NATO conference in Athens. The proof was that NATO contributed $23.5 million toward the Greek military expenditures of 1963, close to 20 per cent of the total defense budget for that year.[14] Averoff also explained the difference between ERE and Center Union statistics: while ERE had been reporting military expenditures in proportion to national income, the Center Union was advancing figures in proportion to per capita income.

EDA also exhibited relative continuity in its foreign policy position, as compared with positions taken in previous years. EDA's elderly leader, John Passalides, was quite jubilant over the Conservative defeat. He remarked in an unusually conciliatory note that he noticed

12. See *Minutes*, 30 March 1964, p. 17.
13. *Minutes*, 21 December 1963, p. 6.
14. For detailed statistical information refer to *Minutes*, 2 April 1964, p. 4.

some positive signs in the foreign policies of George Papandreou and Foreign Minister Sophocles Venizelos.[15]

Passalides' deputy, Elias Eliou, presented in greater detail EDA's criticisms of the Center's foreign policy program.[16] He reaffirmed his party's now traditional opposition to participation in military alliances which would involve Greece automatically in strategic wars, although the decision to wage such wars would be made outside of Greece. As an alternative he argued for neutralism and for a Balkan understanding based on territorial integrity and mutual noninterference in Balkan nations' internal affairs. This understanding, guaranteed by both Western and Eastern blocs, would be feasible, beneficial, and longlasting. It would permit reductions in military expenditures, the savings to be applied toward each country's economic improvement. Eliou proposed specifically a 50 per cent reduction in military expenditures. The remainder was to be supplied by NATO, or else the size of armed forces should be reduced accordingly. This was a conciliatory proposal on the part of Eliou because it obliquely accepted the status of Greece within NATO. Eliou further voiced his opposition to the establishment of nuclear bases in Greece and to Greek participation in mixed-crew ships carrying Polaris nuclear missiles.

Finally, he let it be known that he was profoundly sorry that the Center's foreign policy program left two very serious gaps. One was the omission of any mention of a denuclearized zone in the Balkans. The second and more serious omission was the matter of Cyprus. He suggested that the Greek government ought to have taken the matter of the Zurich and London treaties[17] to the United Nations and fought to revise these agreements, which had recognized the right of military intervention by three nations in the sovereign nation of Cyprus. Then, he enjoined the government to settle accounts on the numerous issues dividing Greece and Turkey, especially fisheries and territorial waters.

The Cyprus Controversy in Flames

The elections of 16 February 1964 were conducted in the midst of a very strained atmosphere in Greece, caused by the deterioration

15. *Minutes*, 21 December 1963, p. 1.
16. Ibid., pp. 15–16.
17. See supra pp. 129–31 for a discussion of how these treaties were concluded.

of the situation in Cyprus. Armed conflict between the Greek majority and the Turkish minority of the island erupted early in December 1963. The immediate cause was an attempt by Archbishop Makarios to revise the Cypriote constitution. This constitution was considered unworkable by the Greek Cypriotes, primarily because it allotted veto rights over wide areas of legislation to the Turkish minority. Makarios' revisionary proposals met with unyielding Turkish minority opposition. Fighting then erupted.[18] The British were requested by the Cypriote government[19] to intervene and maintain peace and public order. The Cypriote government also sought to bring the dispute before the United Nations.

NATO, with the exception of France, proposed that a NATO mixed force be moved into Cyprus to prevent further bloodshed, while a political solution would be sought at the conference table. This proposal was agreed to, initially, by both Greece and Turkey, but not by Cyprus' President Makarios. It should be mentioned that Greece at the time (January–February 1964) was administered by the care-taker government of John Paraskevopoulos which had been appointed to conduct the elections of 16 February. However, the foreign policy positions of the caretaker government were set in close consultations with ERE's leader (Kanellopoulos) and the Center's leader (Papandreou).

Makarios' insistence on preventing NATO from entering Cyprus prevailed. Britain finally elected to bring the Cyprus dispute to the U.N. Security Council. The latter, after considerable debate and negotiations, resolved unanimously and with the concurrence of Greece, Turkey, and Cyprus (the Makarios government), to send a United Nations peace force to Cyprus to assist the Cypriote government in maintaining peace and security on the island. Simultaneously an appointed political mediator (the late Zachari Tuomioja, a Finnish diplomat) was asked to work toward an agreement for a formula politically acceptable to all parties in the dispute—a thankless task, to say the least.

18. It is not the objective of this work to conduct a thorough analysis of the Cyprus situation nor to establish facts, such as who was to blame for starting hostilities, igniting the situation, and the like.

19. "Cypriote government," as used in this text, refers to the legal government of Cyprus which is currently manned by Greek Cypriotes only, since the Turkish members have left it as a result of the dispute.

The United Nations Peacekeeping Force has been dispatched to Cyprus and the difficult work of mediation has begun. There are, however, numerous explosive and complicating factors permeating the Cyprus dispute: Turkey has threatened again and again to invade Cyprus to protect the rights of the allegedly threatened Turkish minority. Also, the Turkish government has advanced a policy of partition of the island as the minimum acceptable solution. According to newspaper reports, a Turkish invasion of Cyprus has been averted primarily due to the restraining influence of the United States.[20]

Greece, for its part, has insisted on a policy of noninterference and nonintervention in Cyprus' internal affairs, and has considered the London and Zurich treaties unworkable and in dire need of revision. Greece has proposed the right of Cyprus to independence and self-determination (which could lead to *"Enosis"*)[21] and has unequivocally declared that a Turkish invasion on Cyprus would be countered by the Greek armed forces. The Cypriote government has insisted on its right to revise the Cypriote constitution and the Zurich and London treaties, to render Cyprus independent and governable once and for all.

Makarios has repeatedly assured the Turks of Cyprus and Turkey that he would provide the island's Turkish minority with internationally guaranteed human rights. The Greek Cypriote government has acted primarily to secure the right of national independence and has also supported Cyprus' right of self-determination. The Soviet Union, to complicate matters further, has declared its support of the Cypriote regime, and has warned that the Soviets would not remain indifferent in case of a Turkish invasion. More recently, however, the Soviets have shown great eagerness to improve relations with Turkey and to act as the "honest broker." The possibility of an armed clash between the Greek and Turkish forces remains quite high, threatening to deal a fatal blow to NATO's unity, and possibly to ignite a wider East–West conflict. Apprehension and ill feelings against Turkey have risen in Athens, due to the allegedly bad treatment of Greek-speaking minorities in Turkey, the deportation of Greek nationals living in Istanbul, and persecution of the Greek Orthodox Patriarchate of Constantinople.

20. For an example see *New York Herald Tribune*, 8 August 1964, p. 1.
21. The Greek term for "Union with Greece."

Recent political instability both in Greece and Turkey has diminished the activity of these two countries on the Cyprus problem. In the meantime Cyprus is enjoying a tenuous détente, while Makarios is gradually consolidating his control over the island, and the Turkish Cypriotes are in de facto control of the small enclaves in the island under their occupation.

DEBATES IN PARLIAMENT ON CYPRUS   At this tense and confusing time the second government of Premier George Papandreou took office. The new, Center-dominated Parliament of Greece heard this government's program declarations late in March 1964. Papandreou's foreign policy program echoed the one proposed to the "50-day Parliament" in December 1963.[22] There were, however, some basic additions. A large portion of the foreign program was devoted this time to discussing the ramifications of the Cyprus dispute,[23] while added emphasis was placed on the importance of settling accounts and establishing friendly relations with Bulgaria.[24]

In discussing the Cyprus issue Papandreou recognized that it had caused considerable damage to relations between Greece and Turkey. Contrary to Turkish allegations, Greece was not trying to abrogate the London and Zurich treaties; the course of events had simply rendered them unworkable. As clear proof of this he mentioned the U.N. Security Council's decision to appoint a political mediator for Cyprus, whose very purpose was to construct a revised and workable political accommodation. This was an international recognition that the status quo in Cyprus needed revision. Papandreou then discussed the reaction of Greece in the event of a Turkish invasion of Cyprus. He asked the Turks to display some understanding and to recognize the de facto situation in Cyprus. Nothing could be more painful to Greece than further strain on and possible severance of relations with Turkey. This, however, would be the certain result if the Turks landed

22. See supra, pp. 172–75.
23. For these programmatic declarations see *Minutes*, 30 March 1964, p. 5.
24. An agreement with Bulgaria settling most outstanding issues (such as payments for war reparations, matters of river administration, etc.) was signed in Athens on 9 July 1964. The urgency of restoring good relations with Bulgaria was obviously accelerated by the critical Greek-Turkish dispute over Cyprus. For more details on this topic see Grigorios Dafnis, "The Significance of the Greek-Bulgarian Agreement," *Ethnikos Kyrix* (Greek-American Daily, New York), 19 July 1964, p. 1.

in Cyprus. "In case of attack, defense is a debt of honor," stated Papandreou, when discussing the ramifications of a Turkish invasion. He left no doubt that Greece would respond with arms in the event of a Turkish landing.

The Greek Prime Minister returned to a slogan used in the 1958 elections, when he summed up his government's foreign policy as a "Greek foreign policy." His recommendations for a solution to the Cyprus dispute called for a cessation of all external interference in the young state of Cyprus, and the safeguarding of the rights of the large Greek majority as well as the rights of the small Turkish minority in accordance with the rules of democracy.[25] Given such guidelines, the issue which was threatening Greek-Turkish relations, as well as the integrity of the NATO alliance (and more generally world peace), could be solved.

Speaking for ERE, Panayotis Kanellopoulos endorsed the general scope and direction of the Papandreou government's foreign policy.[26] He sought to prove that, contrary to Center allegations, the London and Zurich treaties were not really bad, unless viewed in retrospect. He reminded the Deputies that Papandreou himself had voted in favor of ratifying these treaties. Thus Kanellopoulos felt that the Center Union's leader was, at best, hypocritical when, based on ex post facto knowledge, he labeled the same treaties a "national crime."

Referring to the anti-NATO and anti-United States slogans which were uttered by many young Greeks during spontaneous street demonstrations, Kanellopoulos sounded a note of alarm.[27] He felt that these youths should have been properly guided and not allowed to fall into Communist-inspired snares. They would constitute Greece's soldiers of tomorrow, and their effectiveness would be questionable in view of their latest anti-Western outbursts. He was certainly opposed to the type of wild demonstrations which had taken place in front of the British and United States Embassies.

Kanellopoulos admitted that the Zurich and London treaties—

25. Under the rules of democracy he included the right to national self-determination and majority rule with constitutional and internationally guaranteed rights for the minority.

26. *Minutes*, 30 March 1964, pp. 7–9.

27. These demonstrations were prompted by what appeared as a clear-cut preference for the Turkish viewpoint on Cyprus by United States and British governments, press, and public.

though acceptable at the time they were negotiated—had proven unworkable, and voiced his hope that they would be revised, "without however disturbing the position of Hellenism in other critical focal points." [28] He stated, finally, that ERE would support the Center Union government in its efforts to defend "Greece's honor and interests" regarding the Greeks of Cyprus, i.e. that ERE would support an armed response to a Turkish invasion of Cyprus.

Evangelos Averoff-Tositsas, following the lead of Kanellopoulos, gave his blessing to the Center's stated foreign policy objectives:[29] "the principles of the program pertaining to foreign policy find us in agreement." He added, however, that relations with Yugoslavia were not as good as they were declared to be, and chided Papandreou for omitting the issue of Northern Epirus[30] from his program. Averoff was quite unequivocal on the possible use of armed force against Turkey. He agreed with the government's firm opposition to any type of Turkish armed invasion against Cyprus and assured the government that it would find ERE in complete and unqualified support, if there were a need for an armed response to a Turkish invasion of Cyprus.

The late Loukis Akritas,[31] the Center's Deputy Minister of Education, provided a few additional insights to what he considered the atrocious handling of the Cyprus situation by the ERE government.[32] He stated clearly (and here he was close to positions advanced by EDA and the left wing of the Center party) that Greece could not oppose the Turkish position effectively within the framework of the NATO alliance, because NATO had assigned a position of primacy to the strategic importance of Turkey vis-à-vis Greece. He accused the

28. He did not elucidate what constituted "critical focal points."

29. *Minutes*, 2 April 1964, pp. 9–13.

30. This points out a subtle difference of foreign policy approach between ERE and the Center Union. The crisis in Greek-Turkish affairs had apparently prompted the Center government to seek an amelioration of relations with Greece's northern neighbors. So reference to Northern Epirus was dropped. If this had occurred to Averoff, then his criticism was the result of his Epirotic ancestry and could be explained by strictly local political reasons. If it had not, it was indicative of the relative, anticommunist inflexibility which was characteristic of ERE.

31. Akritas, a Cypriote by birth, was a member of the Cypriote ethnarchy and had resigned in disagreement with Makarios' decision to accept, even reluctantly, the Zurich and London treaties.

32. *Minutes*, 3 April 1964, pp. 23–25.

ERE government of having been influenced and guided by "foreign factors," which were responsible for securing the reluctant acquiescence of Archbishop Makarios to the infamous Zurich and London agreements. He believed that ERE had "subordinated the Cyprus issue to questionable allied expediency and the interests of the Turkish factor. They [ERE] had groomed themselves into special assistants . . . of Turkish interests in that area [Cyprus]."

As to future actions, Akritas recommended that Athens regain the initiative (which was lost by the ERE government) in handling the Cyprus issue. Revision of the Zurich and London treaties should be vigorously sought, openly and publicly, and only through the United Nations. He advised against any further experimentation with conferences in "insulated chambers," where massive pressures could be exerted upon the Greek negotiators. Akritas then lauded Papandreou for having reestablished the bonds of brotherly cooperation and moral cohesion between Greece and Cyprus. He felt that these bonds had been weakened badly by ERE. Finally, he infused a neutralist note when he theorized that the geopolitical position of Greece could be used to great advantage, as had been done by Nasser and Tito in the case of their strategically located countries. These men, although leaders of small nations, were playing very important roles in world politics; Greece could profitably imitate them.

EDA'S LEFTWARD TURN   Elias Eliou, in a speech to the Parliament, reiterated EDA's habitual foreign policy positions.[33] He interpreted the wishes of the 65 per cent of the Greek voters who opposed ERE as in favor of national independence for Greece, self-determination for Cyprus, reduction of high military expenditures, and reevaluation of foreign pacts which were reducing Greece to a colonial status. He accused the Center government of deflecting its objectives toward the right by adopting half-measures in line with ERE's reactionary direction. He remarked that democracy could not be considered restored in Greece as long as the Communist party remained illegal. He felt that communism could hardly be treated as a crime, considering that it had been accepted by over one billion human beings.

Eliou criticized the Greek policy of association with the Common

33. *Minutes*, 31 March 1964, pp. 1–9.

Market as thoroughly bankrupt. In defense of this assertion he cited figures indicating a worsening of Greece's balance of trade with the Common Market countries subsequent to its association with the Market. Greece's economic salvation should be sought, therefore, through balanced trade agreements with the East. Bilateral trade agreements at least could be regulated in order not to aggravate the Greek balance of payments.

Eliou was certain that the key to Greece's future lay in the disposition of military expenditures. Papandreou's government, he felt, had only effected nominal reductions and had not taken advantage of the situation in the Balkans which permitted reaching an understanding with Greece's neighbors and the creation of a denuclearized and internationally guaranteed peace zone. He advocated, in any event, the decrease of military expenditures by 40 per cent. This would peg them at 3 per cent of the Greek national income, which he considered a fair and economically feasible proportion.

In the field of foreign policy he recommended Greece's disengagement from "aggressive pacts," which were allegedly protecting her against nonexistent dangers. He cited the examples of Sweden, Finland, Austria, and "one hundred other neutralist nations" that protected their independence best through policies of neutralism and nonalignment. However, Eliou reverted to the soft line when he admitted that EDA did not necessarily rule out cooperation with the government, even if Greece were to remain within the Western alliances. All he required, as a minimum concession for EDA's cooperation, was that Greece wield an independent and "Greek" foreign policy which would not bend under NATO pressures.

Eliou, like most other speakers, devoted the lion's share of his treatment of foreign policy matters to the Cyprus issue. He argued that the Turkish position had enjoyed the outright backing of the British and the United States. The motives he attributed to this British-American action were quite vile indeed: he alleged that through continued support of the Turkish position the intercommunity struggle would be protracted in Cyprus, and this would furnish an excellent pretext for "NATO occupation" of the island and continued maintenance of British bases there. These bases were becoming all-important in view of the loss of bases in Libya.

He claimed also that, according to "unimpeachable sources," General Lemnitzer, the Supreme Allied Commander of the NATO Forces in Europe, had sent telegrams to the Greek and Turkish governments proposing that Greece should let Turkey land troops in one area of the island, then land its own in another area; this, in turn, would permit the United States to bring in troops and interpose them between Greeks and Turks to avert a clash.[34] This would have put Cyprus under de facto NATO control, despite Makarios' refusal. Eliou admitted that the Greek government had rejected this alleged telegram, but he was sure that if it had been implemented it would have led to the de facto partition of Cyprus. The chief obstacle to Cyprus' independence, he maintained, was posed by the British bases which occupied "99 square miles" of Cypriote territory in 32 different locations. These bases should be disbanded and British influence removed from the hapless island.

Eliou's next target was the Greek Information Services operating in Britain, Switzerland, Canada, and West Germany. These agencies allegedly had allowed Turkish political propaganda to dominate the television, press, and radio media in these four nations. The situation was better in France and Italy, due, according to Eliou, not to Greek diplomatic efforts but to French and Italian independence from NATO. Eliou generally urged the Greek government to adopt a stern position in the face of Turkish anti-Greek provocations, wherever they occurred.

He informed his fellow deputies that Cyprus was saved from Turkish invasion thanks to Khrushchev's strong warning against any such action. He did not advocate reprisals against Turkish minorities in Greece. He felt that Greece—backed by world public opinion and the U.S.S.R.—had adequate moral and material force to repel the Turks.[35] In summation, he reserved judgment on the Center government's program and stated that EDA was neither condemning it nor endorsing it.

THE PROGRESSIVES CRITICAL   Spyros Markezinis, the leader of the

34. Eliou's assertion was dismissed as completely untrue by P. Garoufalias (the Defense Minister) and George Papandreou. They both denied the existence of such a telegram.

35. He did not mention the U.S.S.R. by name, but he clearly implied that its support, if sought, would be granted.

Progressives,[36] did not support the government's foreign policy program.[37] He felt that there should be harmony between Makarios and Papandreou and that the initiative toward this goal should emanate from the latter. This was not, allegedly, being done. He warned that great dangers would result from a Greek-Turkish breach of relations, and suggested that issues should be settled in direct talks between Papandreou and Inonu. Here Markezinis echoed Turkish, British, and American positions on the subject of a summit meeting between the Greek and Turkish heads of government. Papandreou had resisted any such talks for two reasons: first, he felt that a precondition for a summit meeting should be a declaration that Turkey would not resort to an invasion of Cyprus; second, he believed that Greece and Turkey alone should not have the right to decide the destiny of the sovereign nation of Cyprus.

THE MILITARY VIEWPOINT   Throughout the debates, the subject of military expenditures was given second place only to discussions revolving around the issue of Cyprus. Alexander Frontistis, ex-Chief of Staff of the Greek Armed Forces and newly elected deputy of ERE, presented the military viewpoint in his maiden parliamentary speech.[38] He believed that chief among the factors affecting Greece's defensive posture were the "givens" of foreign policy—Greece's geographic location, the military value of the land and its defensive capabilities, the comparative strengths of friendly and potential enemy forces, the internal situation, and the nation's economic capabilities. Frontistis felt that all of these factors had adverse effects on Greece's defensive problem, but did not clarify the function of each.

Without mentioning Bulgaria by name, Frontistis characterized it as a great danger to Greece, being the strongest Soviet "satellite" and possessing much larger armed forces than Greece. He felt that Bulgaria was always ready to launch a surprise attack on Greece at a moment's notice. He differed in this respect with most deputies, who had mentioned Bulgaria only in a conciliatory tone and who had

36. The Progressives were dealt a very severe blow in the November 1963 elections (when even Markezinis failed to be elected deputy and his party secured two parliamentary seats). In February the Progressives' position improved somewhat, primarily because they entered the elections in cooperation with ERE.
37. *Minutes,* 1 April 1964, pp. 6–7.
38. *Minutes,* 1 April 1964, pp. 15–21.

expressed wishes for speedy establishment of friendly relations between the two nations.

Next to the Bulgarian danger, his main concern was caused by the crack in Greek-Turkish relations. The two nations had been assigned a "common mission" within the NATO alliance and their antagonisms had weakened both nations' defensive postures, since their defenses had been planned interdependently. For the reasons discussed above, Frontistis felt that there should be no further reduction of Greece's defense force structure and, by extension, Greek military expenditures.

During his speech, the ex-Chief of Staff underscored the military dependence of small nations on larger allies, explaining that the cost of upkeep of modern, highly complex armies had become prohibitive for small nations. He reviewed the history of postwar Greek defense expenditures and showed that United States and NATO aid had covered 57 per cent of the costs while the Greek treasury had supplied the remaining 43 per cent.[39] Without this abundant allied aid, the Greek armed forces would have remained weak and stagnant and Greece would have been at the mercy of anyone who wished to take advantage of its weakness. Frontistis reminded his fellow deputies that regardless of their bitterness over the Cyprus issue, they should never cease being grateful to the United States for its massive assistance. Greece should recognize, also, the importance and great usefulness of membership in NATO. Here he was undoubtedly reprimanding deputies like Akritas who placed the Cyprus objectives above Greek defensive objectives.

Frontistis undertook to defend ex-Prime Minister Karamanlis against Papandreou's allegations that he had not done enough to secure allied subsidies for Greek military expenditures. He affirmed Karamanlis' independence and responsibility in this area. For example, Karamanlis had been pressed by all (i.e. the allied military leadership, foreign mediators, top Greek advisors in military and diplomatic affairs, and even his own cabinet members) to accept NATO medium range ballistic missile (MRBM) bases in Greece, as had been done by Turkey and Italy. Karamanlis did not bow under these pressures and persisted in his decision not to accept them.

39. This applies for calendar years up to and including 1962, when the bulk of United States aid to Greece was terminated.

Frontistis also cited Karamanlis' firmness on effecting gradual reductions of Greek military expenditures despite vigorous allied arguments to the contrary.[40] At this point Frontistis reached the very core of his argument. He proclaimed that the numerical ceiling of the Greek armed forces had been cut below the "normal limit," [41] with the excuse that Greece had an excellent mobilization system as well as very high quality personnel. Any additional reductions, he warned, would necessitate the revision of Greece's defensive mission and would allow some of Greece's territory to remain unguarded. Here Frontistis made a pronouncement which got him into trouble with some seasoned politicians.

Is the government prepared to reach that point [i.e. reduce the military forces further]? *Will she find a military leadership that will accept it?* You see I am avoiding to speak about the reaction of the Allies, because the Allies might perhaps prefer the change of the missions, rather than any further weakening of the force backing the present missions." [42]

40. Ibid., p. 18. Frontistis provided during his speech the following tables which were used by the allies in their arguments against any further reductions of Greek military expenditures. These tables are presumably illustrative of the decreasing proportions of budget spent for military purposes:

TABLE 1. PROPORTION OF BUDGET SPENT ON DEFENSE

Year	Percentage	Year	Percentage
1936–40	30.0	1960	19.2
1957	23.9	1961	17.4
1958	20.5	1962	15.0
1959	18.0	1963	14.3

TABLE 2. EVOLUTION OF DEFENSIVE COSTS VS. NATIONAL INCOME

Year	Defense Exp. Index	Nat. Income Index	Year	Defense Exp. Index	Nat. Income Index
1954	100	100	1958	130	147
1955	108	113	1959	138	152
1956	144	132	1960	149	162
1957	131	142	1961	147	183

The allies also argued that while defense expenditures in 1951 were 8.1% of the Greek national income, in 1962 they fell to only 5.1%.

41. As assessed by military and political experts.

42. (Emphasis supplied.) Frontistis did not elucidate what he meant regarding the allied preference to change the mission. Perhaps he was intimating an abandonment of Greek territory in case of attack, compared to the present mission which appears to provide for holding the Greek mainland.

Frontistis was vigorously taken to task on this utterance.[43] His statement was interpreted as a threat of possible military disobedience to civilian control. He repeatedly assured his critics, however, that when he had said that "no military leadership would accept further expenditures reductions," he meant only that military leaders would exercise their constitutional prerogatives by resigning.

Frontistis concluded that there could not be any further reduction in military expenditures (savings resulting from reorganization were considered minimal) without weakening Greece's military strength to an unacceptable level which would necessitate changing the country's mission within NATO. He believed that the mission should not be changed, unless the factors determining Greece's defensive requirements were substantially changed also.[44] For example, if Bulgaria were to reduce her armed forces, or problems with Turkey were to be settled, then with two basic parameters changed Greece could afford to reduce her military force ceiling. Given the status quo, he felt that the only solution would be to maintain current Greek force levels and to impress upon NATO the need for contributing substantially to Greece's defensive requirements. Finally, Frontistis felt that defense expenditures were productive in their own right, since they contributed to a feeling of security and freedom for the Greek population. This in turn permitted a larger amount of investment and prevented hoarding or flights of capital, conditions characteristic of highly insecure nations.

Participation in NATO has represented Greece's basic postwar foreign policy objective—namely, to secure a peacetime military alliance which would guarantee its threatened territorial integrity in view of the great vulnerability of Greece's northern territories of Macedonia and Thrace. The Cyprus issue has been the chief challenge to Greece's affinity to the NATO alliance. This issue represents a deeply sensitive national policy which is testing Greece's ability to act as an independent agent within the NATO alliance. Earlier chapters have discussed how NATO pressures and influences contributed to Greece's negotiated agreements with Turkey and Britain (resulting in the London and Zurich agreements).

43. His most vociferous critics were deputies N. Bakopoulos (of the Center Union) and S. Iliopoulos (of EDA). See *Minutes*, 1 April 1964, pp. 22–23.
44. See supra, p. 185.

It is too early to assess Papandreou's policy, or the policy of any Center government which might follow him, with regard to Cyprus, or to identify the changes in the Greek arena, and more generally the worldwide situation, which have accounted for the Center Union's sternly stated policy on Cyprus. Some general aspects, however, should be considered as contributory: the East–West conflict in Europe is relatively dormant and enjoying the relaxations of a détente; the divisions within the Communist camp have diminished the Western world's feelings of insecurity which were posed by a monolithic, centrally directed Communist bloc; the amount of aid (and therefore relative military and economic dependence) from the United States has been reduced to a mere trickle; the probabilities of an internal reemergence of the Communist threat in Greece appear very low; there are, also, examples of other NATO nations steering independent (of the United States) national policies—chief among them being France.

In this framework, Papandreou summarized the Center's foreign policy as follows: "Our policy is peace and, in case of attack, defense." [45] This policy was designed to prevent Turkey from landing troops on Cyprus, an act which would result in a Greek-Turkish war and major dislocations—to resort to an understatement—within the NATO alliance. Hence, the Greek government's position, fully backed by President Makarios of Cyprus, was and still is to bring about the solution of the dispute within the framework of the United Nations. A solution will be sought on the basis of the principle of self-determination for the Cypriote people. This is likely to lead to union with Greece, which would allay some of the fears in the West that an independent, neutralist Cyprus could become another Cuba in the eastern Mediterranean.

The Cyprus situation is explosive and critical. The big unknown is how the militarily controlled Turkish government will act, in view of events which seem to have handed Turkish foreign policy a series of consecutive reverses in Cyprus. Turkey, presumably, would be satisfied with either the continuation of the status quo (based on the London and Zurich treaty provisions) or a partition of the island between Greece and Turkey. There are indications that Turkey might

45. *Minutes*, 3 April 1964, p. 27.

agree to union of Cyprus with Greece, in exchange for Greek territory elsewhere (e.g. one or two Aegean or Dodecanese islands). This proposal, however, has been unacceptable to Greece: Turkey would be gaining Greek territory in return for giving up only a claim in Cyprus. The possibility of a Turkish landing and the immediate reaction of Greece pose an ever-present danger, and the current[46] political crisis in Greece could possibly invite initiatives in Cyprus on the part of Turkey.

The Center Union's foreign policy, as stated, appears conceptually similar to the ERE stated policies of the 1950s and early 1960s. There is a discernible note of determination and sternness on the Cyprus question which was, perhaps, lacking in ERE policies. It is, however, too early to judge, pending the outcome of the current crisis on the Cypriote island. On the matter of military expenditures the Center Union has not effected substantial reductions, as was promised in pre-election campaigns of previous years. It is too early to judge with finality the Center's policies on this matter either, without allowing some time for the conclusion of staff studies and implementation of programs. Also, the Greek-Turkish crisis which threatens armed action does not allow for relaxation of military strength and vigilance.

With the Center Union's assumption of power after the elections of 16 February 1964, Greece entered into an era of liberalism. This era has been interrupted by the governmental crisis pitting Papandreou against King Constantine. It would be extremely difficult to foresee at this time the direction of Greek politics (domestic or foreign), pending resolution of that crisis.

It is certain, however, that any nationalist government which might succeed Papandreou (unless he is returned to power in popular elections) will continue to consider NATO of utmost importance to Greece's peace, security, and territorial integrity. There were no radical changes in foreign policy as a result of the transition of power from the Conservatives to the Liberals. Should, therefore, the government return to Conservative hands, policies of the type pursued by ERE in the early 1960s may be expected.

46. September 1965.

Chapter Fourteen
Assessment and Prospects

This study has attempted to present and analyze Greek political reaction manifested as a result of the nation's basic foreign policies of active NATO membership and close association with the United States. Because this is a contemporary and continuing subject, the plethora of evidence yet uncovered or unknown can at best allow formation of only tentative conclusions, subject to change as pertinent documents become available. Keeping these limitations in mind, it can be tentatively concluded that the hypotheses which this book set out to test have been substantiated to a large extent.

The time period under study has been the 1950s and early 1960s. But many of the Western allied actions and the corresponding Greek reactions—recounted in the preceding sections of this work—had their roots in the conditions and the aftermath of World War II and the subsequent bloody civil war. Greece emerged from World War II, after four years of occupation, almost totally destroyed. The Communists who had managed to dominate the Greek resistance movement were exercising almost absolute control of the country, following the German withdrawal in October 1944. The years 1944–49 brought great miseries to Greece. In the monumental civil struggle which erupted between the Communists and the Nationalists, the Communists enjoyed unlimited Soviet support through the medium of the Communist Balkan nations.[1] The Nationalists enjoyed initial British support which was replaced in 1947 by massive United States technical, economic, and military assistance.

1. Albania, Yugoslavia (terminated in 1948 after the Tito–Stalin dispute). and Bulgaria.

The late 1940s were marked by acute political instability in Greece. Governments following the elections of 1946 were numerous and short-lived. The strains of the civil war, the massive United States involvement, and governmental instability opened the way for American influence over Greek affairs. During the late 1940s, the main concern of Greeks and Americans alike had been to defeat Communist elements decisively. At that time the United States assumed leadership and exercised measurable control over actions and decision-making of the Greek government. There was no discernible sensitivity among Greek politicians (except Communists) to this great measure of interference, since the very existence of the non-Communist government was at stake. In fact, American aid and guidance were solicited and welcomed.

American Objectives and Influence in Greece

In the early 1950s the main international objective of the United States was to arrest and contain the growth of world communism. This growth was not only territorial but also ideological. If containment were to be achieved, the countries which had to resist Communist infiltration were expected to fulfill at least two prerequisites: political stability and prosperity (coupled with economic growth). The United States sought to bring about the development of these prerequisites in Greece by encouraging and assisting it to join NATO's collective alliance, by contributing large amounts of economic and military aid, and by recommending measures which tended to unify the numerous, splinter, personality parties into well-defined political movements—somewhat after the fashion of the American two-party system. The feeling was that governmental stability was a prerequisite for the stern and unpopular measures required to bring about economic development and for the assumption of effective political and military measures to prevent Communist take-over.

I have termed the years of the early 1950s a period of "influence." During this time, Greece was heavily subsidized by American economic and military aid. Political analysis indicates that the United States, using aid fluctuations as incentives or disincentives, sought to bring about concrete political changes in Greece. The study of the "Peurifoy incident," for example, illustrates one American method of encouraging stability and strong government in Greece. The United States urged the adoption of the single-member district election system in the hope that this system would force splinter parties to unite into large, homogeneous groupings and ideally would lead to the creation of a two-party system in Greece, as in Britain or the United States. In such a situation Conservatives and Liberals would alternate in power while maintaining a relatively constant and continuous foreign policy devoted to active self- or collective defense against communism. It was also hoped that the single-member district system would limit decisively the proportion of seats allotted to the quasi-Communist EDA in the Greek Parliament.

The study of Greek political events in 1952 reveals that the United States achieved most of its objectives regarding Greece. The single-member district election system was used in the 1952 elections. American pressures urging the adoption of this system were backed with threats that aid to Greece would be reduced unless a strong, stable government was voted to power. There is no doubt that the proportional election system would have perpetuated splinter parties and allowed for the formation of highly volatile and often ineffective coalition governments. The 1952 elections brought General Papagos and the Conservatives to power with a crushing majority in Parliament, although their share of the popular vote was slightly less than 50 per cent. The quasi-Communists were totally wiped out of the Parliament, although they received ten per cent of the vote. The Center parties were also greatly weakened.

It appears, then, that the effect of American influence or interference in Greek affairs was a turn toward conservatism. This was not necessarily the result of American preference for conservatism per se. The United States was probably guided in its actions by a twofold objective: first, to elevate a decidedly anticommunist government to power and second, to insure that this government was stable, backed by a large majority in Parliament, and capable of undertaking a serious long-range economic development program, without squandering the large sums of incoming American economic aid.

The American offer was open to both bidders, the Center and the Right. The Conservatives responded with the better bid and won. They managed to unite under a single, strong leader and to put aside personal differences. It took the Center an extra decade before it managed to unite its ranks into a solid, strong party—the Center Union. It took another five years before the critical test of Center unity occurred.

If somehow the Center Union survives the 1965 political crisis that shook its very foundations and remains a strong force in Greek politics, and if ERE retains its unity and cohesiveness, then the foundations for a good two-party system may be laid in Greece. EDA and the Progressives and a few odd personality parties would not manage to secure more than 20 per cent of the popular vote in any election where two well-organized and well-disciplined parties representing the conservatives and the liberals were running.

And this points up the greatest problem in the political mechanics of Greece. Personalities, unfortunately, are still bigger than parties and political philosophies. No orderly and widely accepted procedures exist for party leadership succession or even reorganization of party leadership. Often disagreements among key figures within a party result in expulsions or walkouts, rather than compromise and respect for the majority opinion. Until such time as Greek politicians can develop an orderly political system and learn to play the rules of the game—which in the long run would help everyone's cause—political stability and the two-party system will remain only pious wishes for Greece.

Political Reaction to the United States Presence in Greece

There was a marked compatibility between Greek Conservative policies and American objectives during the years of cold war intensification. This coincidence of objectives could serve as additional explanation why the Conservatives appeared to enjoy the favor of the United States. An analysis of foreign policy positions of the three major movements throughout the 1950s shows that the Conservatives did indeed pursue foreign policies which were most appropriate from the Western (NATO) or American point of view.

The Conservatives were, for example, willing to maintain the level of military expenditures regardless of reductions in aid. Further, they were irrevocably opposed to communism and unwilling to lower their defensive guard during periods of détente, which was understood as tactical expediency on the part of the Communists. Such policies, of course, suited NATO's interests most, since the alliance had been plagued with numerical inferiority in conventional forces compared with Soviet bloc counterparts. The Conservatives, as a group, acknowledged and welcomed American interference in Greece during 1952 which, by inference, can be assumed to have been favorable to their political objectives. Also, they welcomed United States bases in Greece as the best guarantee for external security. Their stated foreign policies gave NATO membership and United States relations priority over most other objectives, including the Cyprus matter. It is entirely understandable that they gained the sympathy and the backing of the United States and the West.

The Center parties, as represented by their politicians and press, reflected considerable resistance to and irritability over real and alleged American attempts to influence the direction, methods, and structure of Greek politics. Although accession to NATO was a Center-executed policy, the Centerites became unpopular with NATO and the United States following their repeated attempts to decrease the size (and the corresponding expenditures) of the Greek armed forces. Their dilemma was one of either cutting Greek military expenditures or facing a situation of continued stagnation in their economic development efforts. Once the Conservatives displaced the Center from power, it split into many personality parties and did not manage to bring forth homogeneous and solid positions either in domestic or foreign policies.

Throughout the period under study, a sizable segment of Center politicians reacted caustically against what it termed unnecessary American meddling and unwanted guidance in purely domestic affairs. But, even on this subject of opposition to United States influence in Greece, the Center was not solidly united. The Center's reaction to the 1953 Greek-American agreement[2] illustrates the heterogeneity of viewpoints among key Center leaders. For example, George Papandreou reacted by outright acceptance of its substance, criticizing only the procedure of its ratification. Loukis Akritas, at the other ex-

2. Agreement to lease Greek bases and other facilities to the United States, under the framework of NATO. For details see supra, pp. 77 ff.

treme, asserted that the agreement was an abandonment of Greek independence.[3] Interspersed between these mutually exclusive reactions were the opinions of Allamanis and Papapolites—who were opposed to some of the terms but not the entire agreement—and Stephanopoulos who, being the Foreign Minister of the conservative Synaghermos at that time, favored not only the concept but also the terms and the ratification procedure. Similar heterogeneous responses to given actions were characteristic of the disunited Center movement throughout the 1950s.

The Communist reaction to the American presence in Greece was unequivocal hostility. The United States was accused of turning Greece into a colony and an outpost of its aggressive policies. American influence, according to EDA, had sought and managed to displace the Center government and install the Conservatives in power, who then pursued policies best serving the interests of the United States in Greece. The objective of EDA throughout the period under study was to disassociate Greece from the United States and NATO, and to achieve policies of nonalignment coupled with restoration of relations with Eastern Europe and resumption of heavier trade with the Soviet bloc. Regardless of its merits or demerits, the EDA-advocated policy coincided with the objectives of the Soviet Union, since the withdrawal of Greece from NATO and her disassociation from the United States would have paralyzed the southeastern flank of the Western alliance, thus exposing the strategic eastern Mediterranean to the Soviets.

It was pointed out above that the United States found the greatest coincidence of interests with the Conservative party, and therefore supported it to maintain itself in power. With the current turn in the tide toward improved relations with the Soviet bloc (excluding the Chinese bloc), the purely anticommunist Conservative policies may become an obstacle to American policies and objectives in the Balkan area.[4] Thus perhaps a shift in support away from the Conservatives and toward the Center may be forthcoming, especially since the United States has been interested in developing a strong two-party

3. For Papandreou's views see supra, p. 82, and for Akritas, see pp. 86–87.
4. These policies, including trade agreements, cultural exchanges, etc., could be designed to promote greater "satellite" independence from Moscow and facilitate potential intracommunist splits.

system in Greece to displace and isolate the Communists. In the interest of these objectives and to frustrate the establishment of single-party supremacy, the Center's turn to enjoy American support may have arrived.

Another way to look at the problem from the American vantage point is this: if one party (e.g. Conservatives) becomes all-powerful it may tend to adopt an independent course of action and not heed American guidelines. On the contrary, with two equally strong parties competing for power, American support may be used as the weighting factor that breaks a tie. Thus support could be given to one or the other of the competing parties in return for certain desirable concessions, the assumption here being that the two-party balance is so close that United States influence alone could tip the scale either way. Future world conditions will undoubtedly influence the direction of United States support in the Greek political spectrum. In times of cold war intensification, the more anticommunist Conservatives are quite likely to enjoy American backing. On the other hand, in times of détente and polycentrism, the more flexible Center—which is also less objectionable to the Communists is likely to attract United States attention and support.

Membership in NATO—Some Effects and Reactions

A large part of this study has concentrated on presenting and analyzing the reaction of Greek politicians of the three major movements to Greece's membership in NATO and some of its most important related issues. Political discussions and statements, whether of the Left, Right, or Center, treated the policies of association with NATO and the United States as interdependent. Greek politicians of all sides considered entry into NATO a by-product of Greek–United States cooperation which had begun with the Truman Doctrine in 1947. The difference was that nationalist politicians (Center and Right) interpreted the United States' actions as benevolent, supporting Greece's bid to enter NATO. The Communists on the other hand, as represented by EDA, branded the United States a colonialist master of Greece, offering no alternative but to join NATO. They then turned around and dismissed NATO as an instrument of "United States aggressive policy." Regardless of their opinions, the three movements did not question the undeniable interdependence of Greek foreign policies vis-à-vis NATO and the United States.

Throughout the early 1950s Greece looked to membership in NATO as an appendage to the general policy of Greek-American relations. One reason for this was that the bulk of military and economic aid was coming from the United States. The United States enjoyed undisputed leadership in the NATO alliance, since the major European powers were too involved in their reconstruction programs to participate in aid programs to underdeveloped NATO allies or to dispute the American preeminence in the alliance.

International developments of the 1960s have changed this picture considerably. France, Germany, and Britain have been gaining an increasing voice over alliance matters. As far as Greece is concerned, these European powers are once more capable of assuming the role of providing military aid to Greece. Greek policy toward NATO can, therefore, no longer afford to ignore these countries and their objectives, which on occasion may differ widely from those of the United States. This will increasingly pose many embarrassing and ticklish choices for Greece in the near and distant future.

How will Greece react, for example, to issues such as the MLF, the French-proposed NATO directorate, or the question of the nuclear deterrent? Will it side with the De Gaulle line, or follow United States preferences? The dilemmas will be compounded when intra-NATO disputes arise between the Continental vs. the North American members of NATO, with Britain on one or the other side. Greek decisions are likely to be abstentions or vacillations since opposing Continental NATO could mean losses in the political and economic sectors and opposing United States/Canadian NATO could mean losses in the military sector.

The initial political reaction in Greece to membership in NATO was one of great eagerness. In fact, such was this eagerness that it appears from the study of parliamentary debates prior to the NATO accession treaty ratification that the government and the opposition had very little knowledge of Greece's expected rights and obligations in NATO. The urgency to secure membership as soon as possible was based on the desire to strengthen the deterrent credibility of the Greek armed forces. It was hoped that this would perpetuate Greek security against external as well as internal Communist take-over and would be a large enough bonus, given the ugly civil war experience, to dwarf most other considerations. Membership in NATO, indeed, fulfilled one of the basic foreign policies of all postwar Greek governments: to gain a peacetime alliance with the great powers of the West which would guarantee militarily the territorial integrity of Greece.

On the whole, it seems that Greek and Turkish politicians underestimated the great value which their membership in NATO added to this alliance. One of the sorest deficiencies of NATO was the lack of sizable conventional troops under direct NATO command. Greece and Turkey, by placing their entire armed establishments under NATO commands, provided a tremendous boost to the deterrent value of NATO's conventional forces. This alone could have permitted Greece and Turkey to map out a combined strategy for participation in NATO under better terms: securing more military and economic aid; attaining a clear-cut definition of the terms of participation prior to accession; and demanding official NATO recognition of the fact that, since the missions of Greek and Turkish forces extended beyond territorial boundaries of these two nations, it was up to NATO to assist in maintaining the requisite readiness of their forces with appropriate aid and funds.

It is difficult to assess at this early time the effects of Greece's membership in NATO. Basic among these effects, however, should be what I would call administrative or logistic dependence. Greek and Turkish armed forces were equipped with American weapons, reorganized and trained according to the American system, and integrated into NATO-wide contingency planning. Granted that both nations were well equipped with these weapons, it was rarely discussed what would happen if the NATO or American supply valve were to be shut off abruptly. No one asked, for example, what the independent endurance of the Greek armed forces would be in terms of maintenance and repair with the spare parts on hand, or the active combat employability of weapons and weapon carriers in terms of ammunition and propellants available. This technical and administrative dependence should by no means be underestimated. It was an added incentive to the continuation of "Greek-Turkish friendship" despite conflicts of interest between them, as well as increasing the political role of NATO as an arbitrator of disputes between these two nations.

Disintegrative Issues

THE MILITARY EXPENDITURES QUESTION   Greek membership in NATO was not free of trials and tribulations. One of the earliest issues brought up in every election was military expenditures. As early as 1952 the Center parties argued that unless foreign aid to Greece was continued, military expenditures would have to be cut to compensate for the losses to the Greek economy. The Center position throughout the 1950s, and up to the present time, has remained constant on this point, arguing for every possible reduction in military expenditures.

The Conservatives, on the other hand, emphasized the necessity of maintaining a given level of military expenditures at all costs. However, they actively sought foreign military assistance, admitting that Greece unassisted would have to stifle her economic development programs in order to provide for the requisite defensive expenditures. The Communists branded the policy of high military expenditures catastrophic for Greek attempts at economic development and industrialization. They insisted that association with the United States and NATO destined Greece to the permanent status of a raw-material-producing nation and discouraged independent industrialization, which might become competitive with Western industries. This was also the general propaganda line advocated by the Soviet Union. The strong feelings of the Greek political world on this subject have, in part, accounted for the large sums of American economic and military aid, and the subsequent formation of a NATO consortium whose purpose was to contribute to Greek military expenditures.

THE REACTION TO NUCLEAR INVOLVEMENT   One of the key disintegrative factors in Greece's relationship with NATO was the matter of installation of nuclear bases on Greek soil. This issue came to a head in 1958. Viewpoints on this subject were heavily influenced by the political effects of the Cyprus dispute. Only military specialists spoke unequivocally in favor of the immediate acceptance of nuclear weapons, which they felt would enhance Greece's deterrent force against any possible Communist territorial incursions. The Conservatives usually bypassed this issue by reserving judgment until nuclear weapons were actually offered. They refused, that is, to take a stand on a hypothetical issue.

The Center representatives generally stood against immediate installation of nuclear weapons, arguing that nuclear weapons could be accepted only in a package deal with concessions on Cyprus, or that they would be installed only if all other NATO nations accepted them. In this case also, a polycentric foreign policy was articulated by the Center, stemming from its inherent disunity. Some Center spokesmen, e.g. Elias Tsirimokos, were unconditionally opposed to installation of nuclear bases in Greece, while many others wanted to treat this issue as a bargaining point to secure a better disposition of the Cyprus dispute. Most Center leaders felt that opening Greece's gates to nuclear weapons would undoubtedly increase the danger that she would be exposed to in the event of an all-out world war.

EDA representatives argued a pro-Soviet line in this controversy also. They felt that the United States was setting up in Europe a gigantic nuclear magnet which would absorb the brunt of the Soviet retaliatory counterstrike in case of future total war. They saw no reason why Greece should volunteer self-sacrifice by occupying a prominent position on this magnet. As an alternative, guaranteeing peace and precluding nuclear holocaust, they projected the Eastern European-sponsored idea of a denuclearized and eventually demilitarized Balkans, guaranteed by both the Eastern and Western blocs. EDA has sought to exploit popular fears and uncertainties regarding the imponderable consequences of a nuclear catastrophe in Greece.

THE CYPRUS ISSUE   The most serious issue which threatened the political association of Greece with the West and NATO, and which characterized the period I have termed "Reaction," was the Cyprus dispute. This issue still persists in very acute form to the present time. The discussion of the 1956–58 and the 1963–64 periods illustrates the significantly leftward changes in the positions of the noncommunist political movements in Greece generated by this dispute. The Cyprus crisis, as a test of NATO solidarity, has been quite revealing.

It seems that the Conservative movement placed the overall importance of Greek-Western relations and resultant territorial guarantees above the gains that might result from a stern and uncompromising Cyprus policy. The Conservatives sought in the 1955–59 period to secure self-determination for Cyprus through the United Nations, but were unsuccessful. At first they could not even manage enough support to enter the item in the U.N. agenda. When the matter finally reached the floor of the General Assembly, Greece realized that most of its NATO partners were not supporting its cause. The United Nations, at best, adopted ambiguous resolutions urging the disputants to reach an equitable solution in accordance with the principles of the United Nations. The Conservatives, who were in control of Greek affairs throughout the Cyprus crisis of the 1950s, were quite disillusioned with the coolness exhibited by their NATO partners. This disillusionment evolved into words and actions, and the leftward trend in Conservative policies was especially marked in statements throughout the 1955–59 period. In the last analysis, however, the interests served by remaining within NATO and enjoying its protection, with the blessing of the United States, outweighed the admittedly sincere Conservative objectives in the Cypriote struggle.

This study has discussed at some length the numerous pressures to which the Conservatives were subjected within NATO. The United States and other key NATO members urged Greece and Turkey to recognize the damaging effects to the entire alliance resulting from the disruption of their friendly relations. The consensus was that Greece, Turkey, and Britain should at all costs reach a mutually agreed solution over Cyprus. Turkey, being a vital member of the alliance, had to somehow be pacified regarding its Cypriote aspirations. The result was, therefore, that after considerable groundwork was laid by NATO, the Zurich and London treaties were signed. These treaties accepted Turkey's consultative status over the disposition of the Cypriote problem. They also contained the seeds of instability which have been the cause of the current and more serious phase of the Cypriote dispute.

Greece's association with NATO and the United States appears to have narrowed the versatility of Greek (Conservative) policies regarding Cyprus. Efforts to gain an equitable solution to the Cypriote impasse were largely channeled through the narrow medium of NATO and direct tripartite negotiations. The Conservatives appraised no gains for Greece on the Cyprus issue by disassociation from NATO, only great damage to the basic Greek policy of effective defense against communism. Consequently, they sought to remain in NATO at all costs while hardening their position as much as possible to achieve their Cypriote objectives.

In the contemporary (1963–65) Cyprus crisis, the Conservatives—acting as the opposition party—have argued a much tougher line vis-à-vis Turkey and the rest of NATO. This is understandable since the best way for an opposition party to attract votes is to speak against NATO and the West whenever the Cyprus crisis reaches a fever pitch. The interests of Greece, Turkey, and Great Britain are indeed incompatible on the subject of Cyprus. The United States has the thankless task of promoting unity and harmony among them. If a choice is to be made, Britain and Turkey understandably tip the balance, with Greece on the lighter side. So the United States is also alienated from Greece as a result of Cyprus polemics. In such circumstances opposition parties, whether conservative or liberal, assume a very critical position toward the West.

The Center parties' polycentricity and heterogeneity of viewpoint was demonstrated in the Center-advocated policies toward Cyprus in the 1955–59 period. Papandreou's position, for example, was close to the Conservative government's position; i.e. to stay in NATO and fight for Cyprus' self-determination. George Kartalis,[5] on the other hand, pointed out that NATO participation was dooming Greece to failure in pursuit of Cyprus objectives. These objectives being paramount, Kartalis advocated a return to a more flexible and independent policy and even suggested withdrawal from NATO. Other Center leaders vacillated between these two positions. The Center-advocated policies on Cyprus were again disunified.

After the formation of the Center Union in September 1961, the Center movement developed one voice, particularly in the field of international policies. Thus during the current Cyprus crisis, the Center has exhibited a very firm Cyprus policy, shunning efforts to have the issue rediscussed and solved either within NATO or through direct negotiations with Turkey and Britain. The Greek (Center) policy currently seeks to guarantee the recognition of Cyprus as an inde-

5. Minister of Coordination during the Plasteras government of 1951–52.

pendent nation, free to apply the principle of self-determination. The United Nations, and especially the General Assembly, is seen as the proper forum to discuss and secure these objectives.

The Center's position vis-à-vis Turkey, the United States, Britain, and NATO is clearcut: Cyprus is no longer to be compromised in the interests of NATO solidarity. With improving relations between Greece and her northern neighbors, and the relative impotence of local Greek Communism, the Center can afford to deemphasize somewhat the priority of Greek association with the West over Cyprus objectives or other national objectives which may be in conflict with those of other NATO members. Joint membership in NATO has not prevented the Center government from declaring unequivocally that a Turkish attempt to invade Cyprus (and impose a military solution) would mean war between Greece and Turkey.

EDA sought to prove through the Cyprus issue that it had been correct all along in advocating a nonaligned policy for Greece. This party argued that Greece through NATO had been forced to align herself with "enemies" such as Britain and Turkey, thus hampering the pursuit of unimpeded, independent policies which would have secured national self-determination for Cyprus.

Neither EDA nor any other critics of NATO and of Conservative policies provided the answer to a very basic question: assuming Greece's withdrawal from NATO—and the initiation of a nonaligned policy—how would Britain and Turkey have been induced to give up their objectives in Cyprus? Other than a sympathetic and ineffective nod of compassion from world public opinion, what else would Greece stand to gain by NATO disassociation? Questions such as these must have been paramount in the minds of Conservative policy-makers of the 1955–59 period.

One of the most substantial side effects of the Cyprus issue has been the destruction of the basic policy of Greek-Turkish friendship. The dispute between these two countries has naturally weakened their combined bargaining position within NATO. A solution of the Cyprus problem and other outstanding differences between Greece and Turkey will undoubtedly bring them into close and friendly relations very rapidly. The main incentive for this is their interdependent defensive planning within the framework of NATO.

What were, then, some of the basic lessons which have already been learned from the serious and continuing Cyprus dispute? It can be argued that although NATO association was treated as a top priority foreign policy in Greece, it was not ever considered beyond revision. For example, Greek political opinion from 1955 through 1959 harbored serious neutralist trends. It follows that NATO participation was questioned whenever it conflicted with more vital Greek interests. The Greek public's response is illustrative of the fact that no supranationalist loyalties developed in Greece as a result of NATO membership. Although the importance of NATO to Greek security was recognized, the public revolted against the alliance as soon as some of its key members demonstrated extreme anti-Greek attitudes over the Cyprus issue.

The current phase of the Cypriote crisis illustrates that membership in the NATO alliance does not preclude the development of serious crises between its members—in this case Greece and Turkey. Both nations are adamant on their policies and have been balancing at the razor's edge between strained peace and armed conflict. On the other hand, the argument could be turned around. One could claim that it is thanks to membership in NATO and the pacifying pressures emitting from this organization (as well as the U. N.) that Greece and Turkey have been kept from each other's throats.

Assessment of Greek Parties' Foreign Policies

The Conservative foreign policy could best be described as strictly pro-Western and anticommunist. There were some basic reasons justifying the Conservative affinity for the West and its fear of communism. Communism had seriously threatened the existence of Greece as a democratic state. After World War II a large domestic Communist nucleus developed in Greece, which also was exposed along its lengthy, vulnerable borders to three dedicated Communist states, all having territorial aspirations. Historically, Greece had learned the lesson that the nation was not only vulnerable from the north, it was thoroughly defenseless from the south against anyone who controlled the Mediterranean Sea. The United States and NATO had absolute control of the Mediterranean, so there was no question of choice. If Greece, for the sake of argument, belonged to the Eastern bloc, there would be no defense against the preponderant Western forces controlling the huge "sea-lake." Of course there was the alternative of remaining neutral, but this did not correspond with the basic objective of the small and vulnerable nation: to secure a peacetime alliance with one or two of the great powers which would protect Greece from neighboring revisionist and irredentist states such as Bulgaria.

If Greece's territorial claims were directed toward members of one bloc, then it would make sense for her to join the other. But Greece had claims against both blocs (e.g. Northern Epirus from the East and Cyprus from the West). Since communism was ideologically repugnant to the Conservatives, since defense against the North was possible within the scope of a powerful alliance such as NATO, since the Mediterranean was controlled by the West which was ideologically compatible with Greece, and since there was no defense against anyone controlling the Mediterranean, it only made sense for Greece to enter and remain in NATO. Greece within that alliance would enjoy an international territorial guarantee and greater economic and military aid, and would be freed from fear and uncertainty to embark on the huge task of reconstruction and development.

The Conservatives considered Western orientation and NATO membership as axiomatic, resulting from ideological as well as pragmatic factors. As members of NATO, they followed an actively anticommunist policy and maintained military vigilance. Even during periods of greatest strain, the necessity of remaining in NATO was not questioned by the Conservatives, although they did admit that a pro-Western policy was not absolutely beyond revision.

Regarding NATO-related policies, the Conservatives tried to disappoint no one. They were in favor of a mixed crew NATO fleet (MLF), but also in favor of independent national nuclear deterrents. They recognized that only the United States had the power to maintain an effective and credible nuclear deterrent. They were quite concerned with NATO's relative weakness in conventional forces and often worried that a tactical withdrawal of NATO forces would abandon northern Greece to the Communists in the event of a local war.

Finally, the Conservatives were opposed to any notions of local disarmament or local "peace zone" plans. Disarmament was considered good only if comprehensive in scope and at least continent-wide. One practical reason for this position was that Greece in case of disengagement would not only lose the benefit of NATO's tactical and strategic umbrella, but also vast amounts of technical, material, military, and economic aid that have been of vital importance to the very physical survival of the Greek nation.

The Center parties, like the Conservatives, strongly supported Greece's participation in NATO and a Western orientation. However, in times of strain and crisis, the Center was willing to consider seriously limitation of association with, or even disassociation from, NATO. The Center was, generally, less willing to keep military expenditures high. Also, in theory at least, it tended to be more amenable to possible settlement of disputes with Eastern European nations and achievement of cooperation. Complaints originated often from Center spokesmen to the effect that Greece did not have equal status within NATO, that she should be given a greater voice within the organization, and that her sovereignty should be respected.

On the whole, Center policies were quite similar to those of the Conservatives, varying only in emphasis, if at all. Center politicians, for example, made more frequent overtures to attaining peaceful relations with the Balkans and deemphasized the danger from the north. They were not opposed to discussing local peace zone or disarmament plans, although they admitted that such plans were futile. The Center, at least in its stated position, gave greater priority to matters of economic development and national issues such as Cyprus than to NATO and Greek-American relations. The Center frequently accused the Conservatives of being too subservient to the Americans and the West and promised that, if installed in power, it would execute a truly "Greek" foreign policy. Like the Conservatives, it emphasized the absolute need for rapid development of the underdeveloped countries.

Any differences between Center and Conservative policies could be explained, in part, by the fact that the Center enjoyed the advantage of opposition parties everywhere: not having to back its words with deeds. The similarity of Center foreign policies to those of the Conservatives was made apparent by the relative continuity of foreign policy after the transition from a Conservative to a Center government in 1963. It is true that the Center has adopted a hard policy toward NATO regarding Cyprus. But it should be remembered also that the world setting was quite different in 1963–64 than in the 1952–55 period or even the 1956–59 period.

The Center parties suffered throughout the 1950s from internal divisive troubles. Their inability to unite under the direction of a strong leader and their constant in-house bickering harmed their chances of attracting the Greek public's vote or taking advantage of the single-member district system which was a definite structural incentive for splinter party unification. The party positions of the Center ranged from conservative to liberal to socialist and agrarian. Naturally these differences were expressed in foreign policy statements as well. It can be concluded, then, that diverse policies represented by such Center leaders as Papandreou, Allamanis, Papapolites, Stephanopoulos, and Tsirimokos, who are now grouped in the "homogeneous" Center Union party, can in the future render the foreign policy positions of this party subject to potential contradictions, thus causing intraparty political crisis.[6]

The leftist EDA position could, at best, be described as a moderated Communist position, but seeking to recruit a wider audience than a purely Communist one. NATO was condemned by EDA's mass media, which tried to create the public impression that NATO and American association brought nothing but economic miseries, exploitation, and dangers for Greece. EDA's official positions were not, however, always in outright condemnation of NATO as such. Although accession to NATO had been initially rejected by EDA, once Greece was admitted, it concentrated on attempting to limit Greek participation to the greatest extent possible. Hence it advocated policies for Greece similar to those pursued by Norway: refusal to host foreign conventional or nuclear bases on Greek soil; efforts to enter into treaties of friendship and nonaggression with East Europeans and also achieve economic cooperation with them; and reduction of standing armies to an absolute minimum necessary for defense, applying the money saved to productive economic endeavors.[7] EDA's first preference was always

6. The 1965 Greek political crisis has alienated Papandreou from most of his Center Union lieutenants—such as Stephanopoulos, Novas, Tsirimokos, Allamanis. Foreign policy, however, was not the cause for the split, but rather intraparty competition for the succession to party leadership when the elder Papandreou retires.

7. This was EDA's interpretation of Norwegian-like policies.

for Greece to withdraw from NATO and pursue a foreign policy of non-alignment as followed by Nasser, Nehru, and Tito. At no time did the author find EDA statements which advocated the induction of Greece into the Eastern bloc and the conclusion of a military alliance with the Warsaw Pact nations.

EDA representatives were vehemently opposed to the United States presence in Greece. They felt that Greece had been reduced to a veritable colony (or, at best, had suffered serious losses in sovereignty). They charged that association with the United States prevented normalization of relations with the North, because bad relations were needed as a pretext to perpetuate the aggressive and warlike NATO/American policies.[8] Other frequent charges made included Greece's economic dependence on the West, which prevented industrialization; the losses from politically motivated trade boycotts against the Soviet bloc; and above all the fatal nuclear danger that Greece was exposed to by being part of the NATO alliance. EDA has pleaded unceasingly for the legalization of the Greek Communist party, without any success to date.

This study has, on occasion, presented the military viewpoint, not because the author wishes to imply that the military has any official political role in Greece, but because it represents an identifiable viewpoint which is expressed through the mass media and which influences the public. And, the military in Greece could be a potential political movement in the eventuality of a coup d'état and subsequent military take-over. The military evaluation of NATO has, as could be expected, stressed the tactical/strategic aspects of this alliance and has agreed in principle with the Conservative movement's evaluation. For example, military analysts have maintained a hard line toward Greece's Communist northern neighbors, have welcomed the addition of American and NATO nuclear bases, and have considered local demilitarized zones in the Balkans infeasible.

Greek military specialists have classified the hypothetical role of combatant Greece in NATO in terms of either a local war in the Balkans or a general world war. Little consideration has been given to technical

8. EDA has been especially wrong in this respect. Relations with Yugoslavia have been good to excellent since 1949, with brief relapses of mutual suspicion. Diplomatic relations with Bulgaria have been reestablished, and the technical state of war remains only with Albania.

variations in types of wars, other than local (limited) or general (total). The Greek military establishment embraces, in most instances, the theory of escalation and expects a local conflict in the Balkans (between Communists and non-Communists) to develop into a full-scale, nuclear war. Given the "balance of terror," there is confidence in the war-deterring capabilities of the NATO forces and a belief that Greece is all but guaranteed against a local attack by Communist nations.

It appears that the Greek military has not been overly concerned with doubts about the credibility of the American deterrent. Nor has there been demonstrated a great desire on the part of the military or political sector to seek and gain partial or total control over the utilization of nuclear weapons deployed in Greece. American weapons in Greece have been considered as effective for tactical or strategic defense as if they were manned and controlled by the Greek armed forces.

This book has by no means exhausted the subject of Greece's participation in NATO. Military and strategic considerations have been discussed, for example, only as to their relationships with Greek parties' political positions. There has been only tangential concern with Greek positions on NATO-wide problems such as nuclear control, methods of political and economic integration, the credibility of the American deterrent, bloc capability analyses, problems of disengagement or disarmament, reunification of Germany, multilateral force control, administrative and logistic dependence, and scores of others.

Another basic topic which has received limited coverage here has been Greece's participation in the United Nations. Although the United Nations has been of central concern in the formation of postwar Greek foreign policies, it has been discussed here only in relation to the main theme of American and NATO influences in Greece and corresponding reactions. Membership in NATO appears to have had some limiting effects on Greece's behavior (e.g. voting patterns) and activity in the United Nations. On the issue of Cyprus, for example, Greece was pressured often to settle the dispute directly with its NATO partners, or through the NATO secretariat's good offices, rather than washing the alliance's dirty linen in front of the world forum.

It would be very fruitful to investigate and analyze Greece's United Nations voting pattern vis-à-vis the United States and other member nations. Greece's actions in the United Nations and the extent to which these actions have been influenced by the United States and NATO could constitute a full separate study, but are beyond the scope of the present book.

Despite the ideological affinity between Greece and the rest of the Atlantic community, analysis supports the view that Greek association with NATO and the United States has been primarily affected by considerations of national interest, as well as geopolitical and strategic imperatives. Post-World War II Greece has not been afforded the luxurious alternative of effectively pursuing a policy of nonalignment. Since it successfully resisted an attempted Communist take-over and since the Communist threat remained alive—even if at times dormant —in a world of highly bipolar tendencies, Greece, in the last analysis, had to choose what might otherwise have been imposed upon her: Western orientation.

Greece's participation in NATO and association with the West have had significant, yet not overpowering, influences upon the nation, i.e. Greece was not reduced to a NATO or American "satellite." The post-World War II era of national interdependence has left its mark on all of Europe. Greek participation in NATO and the resultant influences represent specific manifestations. Some of the conditions described here could serve as useful references or bases for comparison when analyzing similar current relationships between nations. For example, the United States position in Vietnam today compares, to some extent, with the 1947–49 period of the Greek civil war. If the West wins the war against communism in Vietnam, problems of reconstruction and political stability will undoubtedly be paramount in that country also. Although history does not repeat itself, universals of human behavior often manifest themselves in similar fashion regardless of changes in setting or time.

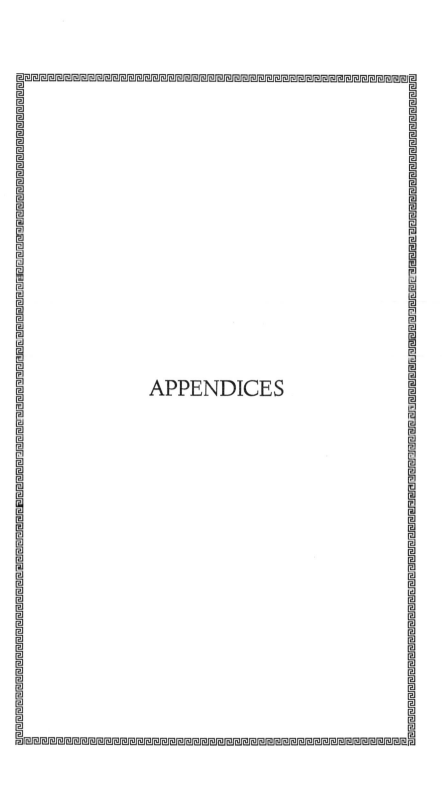

APPENDICES

Appendix A

QUESTIONNAIRE*

Instructions: Every question has two or more possible answers. Circle one or more answers which coincide with your personal opinion. Feel free to respond more fully if you believe that the responses to a given question deny you the proper range of choice.

1. Do you consider Greek participation in NATO beneficial to Greece's interests?
   a. Yes
   b. No

2. The following was the effect of Greek participation in NATO upon Greece's sovereign rights:
   a. They were reinforced
   b. No effect
   c. They were limited

3. From an economic viewpoint, the results of Greek participation in NATO were:
   a. Favorable to the country's economy
   b. Harmful to Greece's economy

4. Do you consider that Greece's participation in NATO precipitated direct or indirect influences upon the internal political affairs of Greece?
   a. Yes
   b. No

5. If your response to question (4) was affirmative, do you believe that the political influences reinforced:
   a. The liberal (Center) parties
   b. The conservative parties
   c. The Left, pro-communist parties

6. Greek participation in NATO in connection with the "Cyprus issue" had the following effects upon Greek policies on Cyprus:
   a. The Greek position was reinforced
   b. The Greek position was subjected to foreign pressures urging it toward moderate and conciliatory practices

* Translated from the Greek.

    c. The Greek position was determined by NATO and the United States

7. What is your opinion regarding the installation of NATO bases on Greek soil?

    a. Useful to the defensive objectives of the country

    b. Harmful to the defensive objectives of the country

    c. Reinforce the possibility of nuclear attack on Greece

    d. Diminish the possibility of nuclear attack on Greece

    e. Contribute to the likelihood of material allied assistance to Greece in case of a local Balkan conflagration involving her

8. In your opinion, what is the position of Greek public opinion concerning Greek participation in NATO?

    a. Enthusiastic

    b. Negative

    c. Cautious

    d. Fluctuating through a, b, and c

    e. Hostile

    f. Dissatisfied, especially because of Cyprus

    g. Indifferent

    h. Positive, because of the protection afforded to Greece

    i. Dissatisfied on account of the large size of military expenditures

9. Are you in favor of the proposal urging the participation of Greek armed forces in a multinational NATO nuclear force?

    a. Yes

    b. No

10. Do you believe that Greek association with the Common Market had any effects upon the closeness of Greek-American relations?

    a. Yes

    b. No

    c. Yes; namely, effects orienting Greece closer to Western Europe and loosening her American orientation

11. In the event of a Western European–American dispute, what should the position of Greece be?

    a. Neutral

    b. Pro-American

    c. Pro-European

    d. Conciliatory

12. What is your position concerning the creation of a denuclearized peace zone in the Balkans?

    a. Positive

    b. Negative

    c. Positive, if first Balkan nations' disputes are resolved

13. Is the Greek position toward disarmament in any way different from that of NATO?

    a. Yes
    b. No
14. What has been the effect of NATO upon the Greek armed forces
from an organizational viewpoint?
    a. Cooperation and independence
    b. Cooperation and limited independence
    c. Loss of independence
15. Was the flexibility of Greek foreign policy diminished due to
Greek participation in NATO?
    a. Yes
    b. No
16. What should be the foreign policy orientation of Greece?
    a. Western (NATO)
    b. Eastern (Warsaw Pact)
    c. Neutralist (such as the UAR)
17. Has the position of your political movement concerning NATO
fluctuated considerably in the last ten years?
    a. Yes
    b. No

Appendix B[1]

NORTH ATLANTIC TREATY (April 4, 1949),[2] as Amended by the PROTOCOL ON THE ACCESSION OF GREECE AND TURKEY (October 17, 1951).[3]

The Parties[4] to this Treaty reaffirm their faith in the purposes and principles of the Charter of the United Nations and their desire to live in peace with all peoples and all governments.

They are determined to safeguard the freedom, common heritage, and civilization of their peoples, founded on the principles of democracy, individual liberty, and the rule of law.

They seek to promote a stability and well-being in the North Atlantic area.

They are resolved to unite their efforts for collective defense and for the preservation of peace and security.

They therefore agree to this North Atlantic Treaty:

Article 1. The Parties undertake, as set forth in the Charter of the United Nations, to settle any international disputes in which they may be involved by peaceful means in such a manner that international peace and security, and justice, are not endangered, and to refrain in their international relations from the threat or use of force in any manner inconsistent with the purposes of the United Nations.

Article 2. The Parties will contribute toward the further development of peaceful and friendly international relations by strengthening their free institutions, by bringing about a better understanding of the principles upon which these institutions are founded, and by promoting conditions of stability and well-being. They will seek to eliminate conflict in their

1. From *International Regional Organizations, Constitutional Foundations,* ed. with introductory notes by Ruth G. Lawson (New York, Praeger, 1962).
2. TIAS (U. S. Treaties and Other International Agreements), 1964, United States Statutes at Large (81st Cong., 1st sess., 1949), 63, Part II, 2242.
3. TIAS 2390, United States Treaties and Other International Agreements, 3, Part I, 43.
4. The original signatories were Canada, Belgium, Denmark, France, Iceland, Italy, Luxembourg, the Netherlands, Norway, Portugal, the United States and the United Kingdom.

international economic policies and will encourage economic collaboration between any or all of them.

Article 3. In order more effectively to achieve the objectives of this Treaty, the Parties, separately and jointly, by means of continuous and effective self-help and mutual aid, will maintain and develop their individual and collective capacity to resist armed attack.

Article 4. The Parties will consult together whenever, in the opinion of any of them, the territorial integrity, political independence, or security of any of the Parties is threatened.

Article 5. The Parties agree that an armed attack against one or more of them in Europe or North America shall be considered an attack against them all; and consequently they agree that, if such an armed attack occurs, each of them, in exercise of the right of individual or collective self-defense recognized by Article 51 of the Charter of the United Nations, will assist the Party or Parties so attacked by taking forthwith, individually and in concert with the other Parties, such action as it deems necessary, including the use of armed force, to restore and maintain the security of the North Atlantic area.

Any such armed attack and all measures taken as a result thereof shall immediately be reported to the Security Council. Such measures shall be terminated when the Security Council has taken the measures necessary to restore and maintain international peace and security.

Article 6.[5] For the purpose of Article 5, an armed attack on one or more of the Parties is deemed to include an armed attack:

(i) on the territory of any of the Parties in Europe or North America, on the Algerian Departments of France, on the territory of Turkey, or on the islands under the jurisdiction of any of the Parties in the North Atlantic area north of the Tropic of Cancer;

(ii) on the forces, vessels, or aircraft of any of the Parties, when in or over these territories or any other area in Europe in which occupation forces of any of the Parties were stationed on the date when the Treaty entered into force or the Mediterranean Sea or the North Atlantic area north of the Tropic of Cancer.

Article 7. This Treaty does not affect, and shall not be interpreted as affecting, in any way the rights and obligations under the Charter of the Parties which are members of the United Nations, or the primary responsibility of the Security Council for maintenance of international peace and security.

5. As amended by Article 2 of the Protocol on the Accession of Greece and Turkey. This Protocol otherwise delineates the procedure for accession, which in the case of both states took place on 18 February 1952.

Article 8. Each Party declares that none of the international engagements now in force between it and any other of the Parties or any third state is in conflict with the provisions of this Treaty, and undertakes not to enter into any international engagement in conflict with this Treaty.

Article 9. The Parties hereby establish a council, on which each of them shall be represented, to consider matters concerning the implementation of this Treaty. The council shall be so organized as to be able to meet promptly at any time. The council shall set up such subsidiary bodies as may be necessary; in particular it shall establish immediately a defense committee which shall recommend measures for the implementation of Articles 3 and 5.

Article 10. The Parties may, by unanimous agreement, invite any other European state in a position to further the principles of this Treaty and to contribute to the security of the North Atlantic area to accede to this Treaty. Any state so invited may become a party to the Treaty by depositing its instrument of accession with the Government of the United States of America. The Government of the United States of America will inform each of the Parties of the deposit of each such instrument of accession.

Article 11. This Treaty shall be ratified and its provisions carried out by the Parties in accordance with their respective constitutional processes. The instruments of ratification shall be deposited as soon as possible with the Government of the United States of America, which will notify all the other signatories of each deposit. The Treaty shall enter into force between the states which have ratified it as soon as the ratifications of the majority of the signatories, including the ratifications of Belgium, Canada, France, Luxembourg, the Netherlands, the United Kingdom, and the United States, have been deposited and shall come into effect with respect to other states on the date of the deposit of their ratifications.

Article 12. After the Treaty has been in force for ten years, or at any time thereafter, the Parties shall, if any of them so requests, consult together for the purpose of reviewing the Treaty, having regard for the factors then affecting peace and security in the North Atlantic area, including the development of universal as well as regional arrangements under the Charter of the United Nations for the maintenance of international peace and security.

Article 13. After the Treaty has been in force for twenty years, any Party may cease to be a party one year after its notice of denunciation has been given to the Government of the United States of America, which will inform the Governments of the other Parties of the deposit of each notice of denunciation.

Article 14. This Treaty, of which the English and French texts are equally authentic, shall be deposited in the archives of the Government of the United States of America. Duly certified copies thereof will be transmitted by that Government to the Governments of the other signatories.

In witness whereof, the undersigned plenipotentiaries have signed this Treaty.

Done at Washington, the fourth day of April, 1949.

Appendix C

AGREEMENT
BETWEEN
THE UNITED STATES OF AMERICA
AND THE KINGDOM OF GREECE
CONCERNING MILITARY
FACILITIES

The United States of America and the Kingdom of Greece being parties of the North Atlantic Treaty, which was signed at Washington on April 4, 1949[1] and having regard to their respective responsibilities under the aforesaid Treaty to provide for the security and defense of the North Atlantic Treaty Area, and under Article 3 thereof to develop their collective capacity to resist armed attack, have entered into the following Agreement:

ARTICLE I

1. The Government of Greece hereby authorizes the Government of the United States of America, subject to the terms and conditions set forth in this Agreement and to technical arrangements between appropriate authorities of the two Governments, to utilize such roads, railways and areas, and to construct, develop, use and operate such military and supporting facilities in Greece as appropriate authorities of the two Governments shall from time to time agree to be necessary for the implementation of, or in furtherance of, approved NATO plans. The construction, development, use and operation of such facilities shall be consistent with recommendations, standards and directives from the North Atlantic Treaty Organization (NATO) where applicable.

2. For the purpose of this Agreement and in accordance with technical arrangements to be agreed between the appropriate authorities of the two Governments, the Government of the United States of America may bring in, station and house in Greece United States personnel. United States Armed Forces and equipment under their control may enter, exit,

1. Treaties and Other International Acts, Series 1964, 63 Stat., Pt. 2, p. 2241.

circulate within and overfly Greece and its territorial waters subject to any technical arrangements that may be agreed upon by the appropriate authorities of the two Governments. These operations shall be free from all charges, duties and taxes.

3. The priorities, rates of consumption and charges established for the United States Armed Forces for such services as electric power, sewerage, water supply, communication systems, and freight and personnel transportation by rail, will be no less favorable than those established for the Greek Armed Forces.

ARTICLE II

1. Equipment, materials and supplies imported by or on behalf of the Government of the United States of America in connection with the construction, development, operation or maintenance of agreed installations and facilities and the official support of the United States Forces, civilian components, and their dependents shall be exempt from all duties, taxes, custom restrictions and inspections.

2. All removable facilities erected or constructed by or on behalf of the Government of the United States of America at its sole expense and all equipment, materials and supplies brought into Greece or purchased in Greece by or on behalf of the Government of the United States of America in connection with the construction, development, operation and maintenance of agreed installations and facilities will remain the property of the Government of the United States of America and may be removed from Greece. No such removal or disposition will be undertaken which will prejudice the mission of the NATO.

3. The United States of America will be compensated by the Greek Government for the residual value, if any, of the facilities acquired, developed and constructed at United States expense under the present Agreement and not removed or otherwise disposed of in accordance with paragraph 2 of this Article, including those facilities developed or constructed jointly by United States and Greek funds, when such facilities or any part thereof are no longer needed by the military forces of the United States. The amount and manner of compensation shall be in accordance with agreements to be made between the appropriate authorities of the contracting parties. Negotiations as to the method for treating the residual value of these facilities will be without prejudice to agreements within the NATO.

ARTICLE III

For the implementation of this Agreement the provisions of Article I, paragraphs 3a and 3b of Legislative Decree 694 of May 7, 1948, and the Memorandum of Understanding between the Government of the United

States and the Government of Greece dated February 4, 1953,[2] shall be applied in accordance with terms mutually agreed.

2. The United States Armed Forces in Greece under this Agreement may also establish and continue to use or operate United States military post offices.

ARTICLE IV

The present Agreement will come into force from the date on which it is signed, and will remain in effect during the period of the validity of the North Atlantic Treaty.

DONE at Athens in duplicate, in the English and Greek languages, the two texts having equal authenticity, this 12th day of October, 1953.

<table>
<tr><td align="center">FOR THE
UNITED STATES OF AMERICA[3]</td><td align="center">FOR THE
KINGDOM OF GREECE [4]</td></tr>
</table>

RELIEF FROM TAXATION ON DEFENSE EXPENDITURES

Agreement between the United States of America and Greece

Effected by exchange of Notes
dated at Athens, February 4, 1953

Entered into force February 4, 1953

The American Embassy to the Greek Ministry of Foreign Affairs
    Embassy of The
United States of America

No. 252

The Embassy of the United States of America presents its compliments to the Royal Ministry of Foreign Affairs, and has the honor to refer to the Embassy's note No. 160, dated November 3, 1952,[5] and to subsequent discussions between representatives of the Greek Government and the Government of the United States regarding the privileges, immunities and exemptions from taxes or other levies and charges which shall be accorded by the Government of Greece in the interest of facilitating and expediting the implementation of the common defense program and any and all foreign aid programs of the United States.

2. Treaties and Other International Acts, Series 2775, 4 United States Treaties 166.
3. Cavendish W. Cannon
4. Stephanopoulos
5. Not printed.

There is transmitted herewith a Memorandum of Understanding dated February 4, 1953, incorporating the agreements reached in the course of the aforementioned discussions.

It is respectfully requested that the Ministry confirm that the Memorandum of February 4 transmitted with this note is acceptable to the Government of Greece.

The Embassy avails itself of this opportunity to renew to the Royal Ministry of Foreign Affairs the assurances of its highest consideration.

Enclosure:
Memorandum of Understanding
Athens, February 4, 1953

To the
Royal Ministry of Foreign Affairs,
Athens.

MEMORANDUM OF UNDERSTANDING BETWEEN THE GOVERNMENT OF GREECE AND THE GOVERNMENT OF THE UNITED STATES RE IMPLEMENTATION OF THE COMMON DEFENSE PROGRAM AND ANY AND ALL FOREIGN AID PROGRAMS OF THE UNITED STATES

PRIVILEGES, IMMUNITIES AND EXEMPTIONS FROM TAXES OR OTHER LEVIES AND CHARGES

The Government of the United States, by virtue of common defense agreements, is presently engaged in a variety of expenditures for the common defense effort, including construction and/or procurement in Europe of military supplies, materials and equipment, facilities, and so-called common-use items required by the United States and by countries participating in the North Atlantic Treaty Organization. Such programs may be implemented by agreements to which the United States Government is a party entered into directly with the governments of member countries or with manufacturers and/or suppliers in the member countries, or by agreements to which the United States Government is not a party but which are financed in whole or in part by the United States Government. The United States Government is also bringing into member countries materials, equipment, supplies, and goods required for such common defense.

Consequently, in the interest of facilitating and expediting implementation of the common defense program and any and all foreign aid programs of the United States, the Government of Greece agrees that property to which the United States has acquired title or a lien shall be accorded extraterritoriality (immunity from the jurisdiction of the Greek civil and criminal courts), and that any expenditures of the United States Government for equipment, materials, facilities, or services connected with such common defense program and such foreign aid programs of the United States Government will be exempt from taxes, dues, or fees which might affect such expenditures. This exemption will be afforded to the United States Government pursuant to mutually satisfactory arrangements and procedures developed in consultation between the two Governments and implemented by decisions of the Minister of Finance.

In addition, the Government of Greece will extend to the United States, its property, and the contracts, sub-contracts, and activities entered into, undertaken, or financed in whole or in part by the United States in Greece in connection with the common defense or any foreign aid programs, the same privileges and immunities and exemptions from taxes or other levies and charges as have heretofore been granted to the American Mission for Aid to Greece by the provisions of Legislative Decree 694/1948 [6] re settlement of matters regarding the American program for aid to Greece.

J E P

Athens, February 4, 1953

The Greek Ministry of Foreign Affairs to the American Embassy

Ministère Royal
des Affaires Etrangères
No. 408

NOTE VERBALE

The Royal Ministry for Foreign Affairs presents its compliments to the Embassy of the United States of America and has the honour to acknowledge receipt of its note 252 and of a Memorandum of Understanding between the Government of Greece and the Government of the United States dated February 4, 1953, concerning the implementation of the Common Defense Program and any and all foreign aid programs of the United States.

The Ministry for Foreign Affairs confirms that the provisions contained in the Memorandum quoted above are acceptable to the Government of Greece.

The Royal Ministry avails itself of this opportunity to renew to the

6. Not printed.

Embassy of the United States the assurances of its highest consideration.—

Athens, February 4, 1953

(SEAL)

To the
Embassy of the United States of America
Athens

LEGISLATIVE DECREE NO. 694 OF 7 MAY 1948, "ON THE REGULATIONS OF
MATTERS CONCERNING THE AMERICAN AID PROGRAM IN GREECE," ARTICLE
3, PARAGRAPHS (a) AND (b).[7]

Article 3. The members of the Mission, together with their families, who
are of non-Greek citizenship or are not residing permanently in Greece,
will enjoy the following privileges and immunities:
(a) Extraterritoriality (immunity from the jurisdiction of the Greek
criminal and civil courts) for the persons named above, for acts or omis-
sions during the conduct of their official duties as well as in their private
capacity.
(b) Immunity from all direct or indirect taxes, customs duties, fees,
claims, deductions, or contributions generally in favor of the government,
the municipalities and communities, of the legal persons in public law,
and in general all third parties which might be burdening in any way the
above personnel and members of their families.

7. This translation is the author's and is strictly unofficial.

Appendix D

GREECE

Defense: Status of United States Forces

Agreement signed at Athens September 7, 1956
Entered into force September 7, 1956

AGREEMENT BETWEEN
THE UNITED STATES OF AMERICA AND THE
KINGDOM OF GREECE
CONCERNING THE STATUS OF
UNITED STATES FORCES IN GREECE

The United States of America and the Kingdom of Greece having entered into a Military Facilities Agreement on October 12, 1953, and having become parties to the "Agreement Between the Parties to the North Atlantic Treaty Regarding the Status of Their Forces," dated June 19, 1951, agree upon the following regarding the status of United States forces in Greece.

ARTICLE I

1. Paragraph 1, Article III of the Agreement between the Governments of the United States of America and the Kingdom of Greece concerning Military Facilities, dated October 12, 1953, is abrogated except insofar as it refers to the Memorandum of Understanding dated February 4, 1953, which shall continue in effect.

2. "Agreement between the Parties of the North Atlantic Treaty Regarding the Status of Their Forces," dated June 19, 1951, shall govern the status of the forces of the United States in Greece as well as members of these forces, members of the civilian component, and their dependents, who are in Greece and who are serving in that country in furtherance of objectives of the North Atlantic Treaty Organization, or who are temporarily present in Greece.

ARTICLE II

1. The Greek authorities, recognizing that it is the primary responsibility of the United States authorities to maintain good order and discipline

where persons subject to United States military law are concerned, will upon the request of the United States authorities, waive their primary right to exercise jurisdiction under Article VII, paragraph 3(c) of that Agreement, except when they determine that it is of particular importance that jurisdiction be exercised by the Greek authorities.

2. In those cases, where, in accordance with the foregoing paragraph, there is waiver of jurisdiction by the Greek authorities, the competent United States authorities shall inform the Greek Government of the disposition of each such case.

ARTICLE III

1. In such cases where the Government of Greece may exercise criminal jurisdiction as provided for in Article II above, the United States authorities shall take custody of the accused pending completion of trial proceedings. Custody of the accused will be maintained in Greece. During the trial and pretrial proceedings the accused shall be entitled to have a representative of the United States Government present. The trial shall be public unless otherwise agreed.

ARTICLE IV

1. In civil matters, including damages arising from automobile accidents, Greek courts will exercise jurisdiction as provided in Article VIII of NATO Status of Forces Agreement.

ARTICLE V

This agreement will come into force from the date on which it is signed.

DONE at Athens in duplicate, in the English and Greek languages, the two texts having equal authenticity, this 7th day of September, 1956.

FOR THE
UNITED STATES OF AMERICA
RAY L. THURSTON

FOR THE
KINGDOM OF GREECE
AVEROFF TOSITSAS

Appendix E

ELECTION RESULTS AND PARTY LINE-UPS (1952–1964)

Elections of 16 November 1952
Registered Voters: 2,123,150
Number Voting: 1,600,172
Valid Ballots: 1,591,807
Election System: Single-member-district

Breakdown of Parties and Vote

	No. of votes	% of total vote	No. of seats out of 300
CONSERVATIVES			
Greek Rally (Synaghermos)	783,541	49.22	247
Populist[a]	16,767	1.05	—
CENTER			
Association of EPEK & Liberals	544,834	34.22	51
Agrarian Party	10,431	.66	—
LEFT			
Unified Democratic Left (EDA)	152,011	9.55	—
INDEPENDENT	84,223	5.30	2

a. Came into pre-election association with the Center parties, EPEK and Liberals.

Elections of 19 February 1956 [a]
Registered Voters: 4,507,907
Number Voting: 3,379,445
Valid Ballots: 3,364,361
Election System: Modified single-member-district system (provided for proportional representation of first two parties in large districts)

Breakdown of Parties and Vote

	No. of votes	% of total vote	No. of seats out of 300
CONSERVATIVES			
National Radical Union[b] (ERE)	1,594,112	47.38	165
Populist Social [c]	29,375	0.88	—
Progressive[c]	74,545	2.22	—

CENTER–LEFT COALITION			
Democratic Union[d]	1,620,007	48.15	132
INDEPENDENT	46,322	1.37	3

a. Women voted for the first time in parliamentary elections.
b. Replaced Synaghermos.
c. Both parties comprised of ex-Synaghermos members that did not join ERE.
d. A coalition of the following parties: Liberal, Liberal Democratic Union, EPEK, Agrarian, Populist, Democratic, and EDA.

Elections of 11 May 1958
Registered Voters: 5,119,148
Number Voting: 3,863,982
Valid Ballots: 3,847,785
Election System: Reinforced proportional

Breakdown of Parties and Vote

	No. of votes	% of total vote	No. of seats out of 300
CONSERVATIVES			
National Radical Union (ERE)	1,583,885	41.16	171
Union of Populist Party[a]	113,358	2.94	4
CENTER			
Liberal	795,445	20.67	36
Progressive Agrarian Democratic Union[b] (PADE)	408,787	10.62	10
LEFT			
Unified Democratic Left (EDA)	939,902	24.42	79
INDEPENDENT	6,408	0.19	—

a. Coalition of Populist and Populist Social parties.
b. Coalition of Progressive, Democratic, Agrarian, and EPEK parties.

Elections of 29 October 1961
Registered Voters: 5,478,157
Number Voting: 4,333,411
Valid Ballots: 4,313,235
Election System: Reinforced proportional

Breakdown of Parties and Vote

	No. of votes	% of total vote	No. of seats out of 300
CONSERVATIVES			
National Radical Union (ERE)	2,186,607	49.6	174
CENTER			
Center Union[a] (EK)	1,515,284	34.3	103
LEFT			
PAME [b]	670,373	15.1	23
INDEPENDENT	40,859	.9	—

a. The merger of the following splinter parties: Liberal, Liberal Democratic, Progressive, Populist Social, EPEK, Progressive Worker Farmer Movement, New Political Movement, Democratic, Socialist, Agrarian.

b. Coalition of EDA and EAK (Greek Agrarian Movement).

Elections of 3 November 1963
Valid Ballots: 4,579,146
Election System: Variation of reinforced proportional

Breakdown of Parties and Vote

	No. of votes	% of total vote	No. of seats out of 300
CONSERVATIVES			
National Radical Union (ERE)	1,786,008	39.01	132
Progressives	171,278	3.74	2
CENTER			
Center Union (EK)	1,931,289	42.18	138
LEFT			
Unified Democratic Left (EDA)	666,233	14.54	28
INDEPENDENT	24,338	.53	—

Elections of 16 February 1964
Number Voting: 4,533,784
Valid Ballots: 4,504,818
Election System: Variation of reinforced proportional

Breakdown of Parties and Vote

	No. of votes	% of total vote	No. of seats out of 300
CONSERVATIVES			
National Radical Union (ERE) with Progressives	1,576,550	35.0	105
CENTER			
Center Union (EK)	2,377,647	52.78	173
LEFT			
Unified Democratic Left (EDA)	540,687	12.0	22
INDEPENDENT	9,934	.22	—

Appendix F

The first of two items in this Appendix is a letter written by Margaret (Maggie) Papandreou (the wife of Andreas Papandreou), about a week before George Papandreou's resignation, to Drew Pearson and the wives of President Johnson and Vice President Humphrey. It is not of course an official document, but it reflects some of the typical allegations circulating in Greece in the summer of 1965 regarding United States influence. The second item is an editorial published in *Ethnikos Kyrix* (a conservative daily which has recently shown signs of dissatisfaction with ERE and the leading newspapers supporting it). The editorial, once more, is illustrative of the flavor of non-Communist writing regarding the subject of American influence, and it makes its dissatisfaction with CIA activities in Greece quite plain. (The translation is the author's.)

REPORT ON GREEK POLITICAL SITUATION
JULY 8, 1965

I write with a sense of great urgency, anxiety, and concern. Greece is on the edge of a dramatic clash between democracy and monarchy, between progressive, democratic forces and reactionary, dictatorial forces. It is an old issue in Greece, which never having been successfully resolved, raises its ugly head periodically.

The story briefly goes as follows: When my father-in-law formed his government, he put into the Ministry of Defense a man (Garoufalias) satisfactory to the King, a pro-royalist, the monopolist "beer king" of Greece. The man was also an old friend of the Prime Minister. The P.M. did this knowingly and not necessarily as a gesture to the King—although it seemed that way—feeling he could control Garoufalias, and under him make the essential changes in the army to give it a more democratic character. (The theory: The King would be more amenable to changes with a man of his confidence in the Ministry.) He started with the theme, and has remained with it: "The army belongs to the nation, not to parties or persons."

Because for years the Royal Family has looked at the army as its own (and the true protector of the monarchy) changes were delicate matters, and the young King asserted himself frequently in matters pertaining to the Army. In the first major change of generals, shortly after the (P.M.'s) election, the P.M. permitted a General to remain who had been a symbol of the ERE regime, and a pro-royalist to boot. This was the carrot handed to the King so other changes could be made. It became, however, a festering sore in the democratic camp. The Army was soon aware that the General, under such constant pressure and demand for his removal by the democratic elements, would be asked to leave.

It was at this time, around February or March, that the Army staff "discovered" a para-military organization of young officers, captain rank, called "Shield" which was apparently organized some years back under Karamanlis as a democratic-minded, liberal force—perhaps, who knows, of the revolutionary Nasserite variety—and brought it to the attention of the Minister of Defense and P.M. The King *demanded* that the officers involved be brought to special court, and the P.M. took the necessary steps, but decided at this time to also prosecute the officers involved in a plan called the "Pericles Plan" which had functioned in the elections of 1961 under Karamanlis to achieve an electoral coup. (The Army that year, which votes separately, voted 90% for ERE. The villagers were terrorized by para-military organizations in a systematic fashion and voted as they were ordered.) This Government found in the files of the Secret Service here the detailed outlining of the plan, left unwittingly no doubt, by an ousted ERE official with the signatures of various officers, including the above-mentioned General.

The King was furious. Apparently an organization within the Army working for him on a scheme to frustrate the will of the people is acceptable (Pericles). Other para-military organizations must be penalized severely (Shield).

This was the beginning of the major trouble. Minor troubles had existed prior to this, and some people argue that the P.M. should have taken a firmer stand then. He was actually trying primarily to protect the tenuous balance of power, showing some gestures of good will to the palace at one moment, being obstinate vis-à-vis the palace at others.

Greece is something called a "crowned democracy." It has a very democratic constitution, similar to the British parliamentary one, and gives the King powers that were meant to be formal, symbolic, ritualistic, ceremonial, etc. His signature on each decree making a deputy a minister, for example, is pro forma, and not supposed to be held as a tool of power. He has the right—which *is* a source of power—to name a Prime Minister when the ruling P.M. loses a vote of confidence in Parliament. The new P.M. is given 45 days to form a government, after which, if he fails, elections must be held.

To get back to the facts. The King's anger at the P.M.'s announcement that he would also prosecute the Pericles para-military group, was unbounded, and perhaps was the beginning of a scheme to overthrow the

P.M. in Greece. Garoufalias began taking some initiatives of his own, without the approval of the President of the government. When the President, for example, said that four officers of the organization Shield, known as "Aspida," would be taken to court—those whose signatures were found on an oath—the King said "10" and Garoufalias charged "10." When the P.M. sent the Minister of Defense a list of officers acceptable to him to sit on the court-martial, Garoufalias got orders from the King and announced the members, without consultation with the P.M.

These are small examples of basic infidelity to the P.M. and loyalty to the King. In essence the situation was always thus but less openly executed.

The fantastically incredible thing was that suddenly the organization "Aspida" was linked with the name of the son of the P.M.—Andreas! Stories started leaking out that officers under inquiry had written depositions asserting that Andreas Papandreou was their true leader. A real conspiracy was purported to be underway and was being handled by people skilled in the task, forces that had operated professionally for years of rightist regimes. The thinking was "get Andreas." If he is tarnished, proved guilty, and falls, the Prime Minister falls.

It became clear that under our noses the professionals had prepared a trap. Garoufalias' disobedience to orders of the P.M. left only one action to be taken. Request for his resignation. This the P.M. did one week ago. He refused to resign, said he would have to be fired. He let it be known that he was staying on the job at the "request of the King." The Prime Minister had informed the King that he himself had decided to take over the Ministry, a prerogative which he has in his government. This was strictly a political decision. The King's refusal to accept this meant that he had "lost confidence in the P.M." The same Prime Minister, by the way, who had captured 53% of the popular vote in February 1964, and whose popularity is higher today by all public opinion reports.

In the meantime, we await the birth of a royal child on the island of Corfu, and the King has asked that the discussion with the Prime Minister be delayed until that moment. Then the P.M. will go to congratulate the King—and to confront him. The issue is clear—either Greece has and continues to have a "crowned democracy" with all the constitutional limitations (he has no right to interfere in the make-up of the Government) or Greece has a monarchy. The P.M. does not raise the question of the monarchy, yes or no—but the manner in which the King functions in this country. In the 20th century, in Europe, is it conceivable that a monarchy can function as in medieval times? Where is the King getting his advice, and where his strength?

If the King refuses to withdraw his objections to the dismissal of Garoufalias, the Prime Minister will be obliged to resign. This will throw the country into chaos, and possibly civil war. Furthermore, the Communists are ready to seize this opportunity to take to the streets and try to gain power. Under my father-in-law's democratic, liberal regime, the Communists were dispersed. Now they have a cause, and the youth is attracted to the cause, being violently anti-royal, and as in all countries, progressive, idealistic, and inherently to the Left. Bosch of the Dominican Republic said it most prophetically: "When the youth of Latin America become indignant at the injustice committed against honest democratic leaders, they react by shifting towards Communism. If the accusation comes from the most hated circles of the Hemisphere [in this case the circle of the palace] the youth respond to it by taking a position against the accusers at precisely the opposite extreme. And so, day after day, the most audacious young people in Latin America, led by those from the upper and middle strata of the middle class, have been swelling the Communist ranks in all our countries."

My bringing in Bosch is not incidental. There is a similarity in the case, which makes it all the more ominous. The argument is not that my father-in-law is communist (50 years of political history testify definitively to this—in fact, he is credited with preventing a communist take-over in Greece in 1944) but that he has allowed Communists to infiltrate his government—and particularly, guess who—ANDREAS!

I quote again from Draper's article in the *New Leader*, May 25, 1965:

"The campaign of defamation went on: if he was not called a Communist or a 'Communist agent,' he was accused of permitting or encouraging 'Communist infiltration' of the government. The UCN leader, Dr. Veriato Fiallo, raised a storm declaring publicly that Communists were occupying 'key posts' in the government."

I quote further: "The political line adopted by Bosch upon his return in 1961 was simple: complete independence and no entangling alliances." Papandreou made an even more pro-Western statement declaring his position on foreign policy: "We are allies with the West, and want friendly relations with the East. Our foreign policy will be a *Greek* foreign policy with no outside influence."

Again, "on the other hand, a popular landslide had put Bosch in power. For the first time in Dominican history, the 'masses' had become an active political force, and they were massively behind Bosch."

George Papandreou came in with a popular landslide (53%), and the people do feel themselves as a political force.

What are likely to be the consequences of a refusal by the King to back down and accept the removal of Garoufalias? The P.M. will be obliged to resign. But his resignation will touch off a series of strikes, riots and marches. Many of these will be truly democratic forces, but the Communists will be waiting to take advantage of the situation (their newspaper this morning said the people must get ready). If a new government can be formed immediately, it will have the responsibility of taking action against this disturbance of the peace—but how? Since it will necessarily have to be a collaboration government with the party of the Right, and those members of the Center who "desert" the Prime Minister, it will take repressive measures and squelch the one hope Greece had in over 15 years for a "true" democracy. It will in any case be an unstable government which cannot last. *But,* if no government can be formed, or the new government finds itself inadequate to the task, a military take-over will occur.

For years now, under the Karamanlis regime, and through this one, the Americans have associated themselves here with the Right, and particularly with the military. There are three groups of Americans in Greece: the Embassy, the CIA, and the Mission. The latter two, but particularly the CIA have the upper hand here in terms of American policy. Ambassador Briggs has reported on this situation in a Senate hearing, and declared that there is often no communication or collaboration between the CIA group and the Embassy. Furthermore, Greece in the State Department is under the Near East section, not the European; and the Near East is more generally the bailiwick of the CIA.

Ambassador Labouisse and the present acting Ambassador, Chargé d'Affaires Anschuetz, seem to have taken a positive attitude toward Papandreou's Union of Center government; the CIA, together with the military mission, a negative attitude. The fear, and the talk, is that they lend support to the hard line of the Palace.

The question one raises is are we again going to make the mistake of lining up with the minority, reactionary forces of a country, and find another Dominican Republic in our hands?

I have written this detailed account because I know your sentiments on such issues. I beg you to use whatever influence you have, *BEFORE* a disaster occurs. A wire to anyone you have a connection with in Washington to the effect that America must support the popular will of the people in Greece, and must line up with those forces that express our own ideals is essential. Anything else you can do, any friends you can get to send similar telegrams may help to awaken American leaders to the danger here.

I will keep you informed.

As ever,
Maggie

P.S. The economic growth rate each of the last two years under Papandreou has been approximately 8%, there is a free press (although a defamatory one), police no longer use oppressive measures, education through the University has been made free for the Greek student, the farmers have received substantial benefits.

THE AMERICAN CIA

As a result of a letter which was prepared by an unofficial source and which dealt with Greek affairs and was addressed to important Americans, so that they would be apprised of these affairs, a letter which obviously was publicized by the American CIA, our friends the Americans will permit us to speak with sincerity about our friendly and allied relations with them. In principle we condemn the method of informing our friends and allies through non-responsible relatives of Greek politicians. What was said in the letter of the wife of an ex-minister could best be transmitted, where necessary, through the diplomatic channel which was available to the previous [Papandreou] government. But regardless of all this, the matter is—and this is already well known by Greek public opinion—that there are three American agencies in Greece each of which, it seems, is functioning independently of the others. These are: the American Embassy, the American Aid Mission, and the American CIA. As it appears, and it is said by American diplomats, there is not even the slightest amount of cooperation among them.

The American Aid Mission now has limited authority because, simply, aid has ceased to be given. Previously, however, the Americans of the Mission governed our economy; they had become a state within a state, they ordered our ministers, and many losses were caused for the Greek economy when the money of the American taxpayers should have had better luck. The American Embassy, on the other hand, admittedly steered a course which was strictly diplomatic and prudent. So it never collided with the commonly shared feelings of the Greek people and did not attempt interferences which would offend the people's sovereign rights. The American CIA, however, has unobtrusively played in recent years—due to its mission perhaps—a peculiar if not suspect role. There are many speculations on this subject, some names are named, there are whispers about various "sums of money." All this talk, of course, is neither official nor verified. However, something is the matter. It is moreover a fact that the officials of this American agency, possibly acting in good faith, were dragged into the recent political crisis by various circles, and in the distant past also had some involvement in the development of Greek political affairs.

The interference of foreigners in Greek affairs is, however, totally unacceptable. The American CIA has no business in Greece. Our friends the Americans may cooperate with Greek military authorities in the strictly military sector, but they cannot involve themselves in the elevation and fall of our governments. During the time of the Karamanlis government, interferences were attempted sometimes to favor him and sometimes to oppose him. And one reason that Constantine Karamanlis abandoned the government and Greek politics was that he knew, among other things, that these foreign agencies desired his fall. It seems that the American CIA tries to maintain "factions" within groups ranging from the Palace to the various political parties and from there up to various economic and press organizations. Since we are true friends of the Americans and we believe in the American leadership of the struggle for the liberty of the Western world, it is proper that the American presence should be felt here only through the American Embassy and through the Greek Ministry of Foreign Affairs. On the military side cooperation should manifest itself through the staffs of our armed forces and the American Military Mission and only within the scope of the defensive effort for the protection of the free world, to which Greece belongs. *So let us have things straight.* . . .

Index

Acheson, Dean, hears complaints on "invasion," 56

Aegean Sea, Slavs to be kept out of, 19

Agrarian Party: on nuclear bases as abdication of sovereignty, 114; in 1958 elections, 120; see in Appendix E, 230–32

Akritas, Loukis: Progressive-Left spokesman, 86–87; Center spokesman, 181; disagreement with Makarios, 181 n.

Albania: to cede northern Epirus, 19; guerrillas operate from, 24; NATO no bar to rapprochement, 41; danger from, 89; negotiation urged, 107, 141, 152; discouraged, 108; Center policy and report on, 174; present relations, 209 n.

Allamanis, Stelios (Dem.): on loss of initiative in U.S. pact, 81, 83; on nuclear bases, 114; joins Center, 134

Arab world, ERE, EDA seek friendly relations with, 126, 129, 174–75

ASPIDA, plans coup, 170

Athanasiades-Novas, George: joins Center, 134; unable to form government, 171

Auge (Left newspaper), documentation from, 3

Averoff-Tositsas, Evangelos (ERE): charges playing on nuclear fear, 112–13; defends Cyprus and NATO policies, 128; neutral in Common Market dispute, 146; on election issues, 1952, 150–51; claims credit for NATO help, 175; supports Center, 181

Axis, occupation by, 14

Baklatzis, Emanuel, speaks for EPEK, 82

Balkan alliance: proposed participation, 16; party positions on, 1952 elections: indispensable (Prog.), 152; must not jeopardize NATO (Center), 156; efforts to be pushed (EDA, GMIDP), 159

Balkan countries: ERE on "balkanization," 4, 112, Rapacki Plan for, 117; U.S.S.R. influence through, 191; war expected, 210

Balkan Pact (Greece, Yugoslavia, Turkey): reinforces NATO, 84–85, 93; invites defections from U.S.S.R., 93; weakened by Cyprus issue, 93–94; Turkey killing, 128

Balkan "peace zones," EDA slogan, 135, 150, 176

Baltatzis, Alexandros (Agrarian), agreement with Democrats, 1958, 127

Bases, nuclear: political, not military discussion of, 111; necessity of, 111–12; 1958 debate in Parliament, 111–17; Center on equal-partner relationship, 112–14, 120–21; new government to negotiate, 113; EDA on loss of sovereignty, 114; Cyprus issue and, 117–18; ERE hesitant on, 118, 123, labels false security, 132, 149; GMIDP calls futile, 157; proliferation opposed, 163; strain on NATO relation-